THE LOST HEGEMON:

WHOM THE GODS WOULD DESTROY

THE LOST HEGEMON:

WHOM THE GODS WOULD DESTROY

F. WILLIAM ENGDAHL

mine.Books
Wiesbaden

Library of Congress cataloging in Publication Data applied for.

ISBN: 978-3-9817237-0-0

Published by: mine.Books,
Bunsenstrasse 6G, 65203 Wiesbaden, Germany
www.williamengdahl.com

Cover design: Antje Abisch

The American flag on cover is a remnant found after the September 11, 2001 attacks on the World Trade Towers

I dedicate this work to Antje, whose extraordinary and loving insights into the deeper themes of human abuse in the name of religion defined this work; to Sibel and Buket, who guided me so skillfully through the complexities of *Hizmet*; and to all children raped in the name of wars of religion everywhere, that they may use their experience of murder of the soul to help break the generations-long cycle of hate and killing.

Contents

THE ISLAMIC STATE AND THE LOST HEGEMON

As I sit down to write these words, Western Europe is being overwhelmed with a cultural and social challenge unprecedented in her history. A brutal four-year long war in Syria has spread around the world. An organization calling itself ISIS or the Islamic State erupted violently onto the world stage in 2014 to claim the right to create what they termed The Global Caliphate. The conditions of war and terror in Syria had created more than two million refugees on the move for safety, more than one million of them coming to Europe seeking asylum during the final months of 2015 alone.

On September 30, 2015 the Russian Federation accepted a call from Syrian President Bashar al-Assad to help defeat ISIS in Syria. That call came despite bombing from the United States, allegedly against ISIS strongholds, for more than one year, a bombing that appeared only to have expanded the control of ISIS.

The direct Russian involvement in military action far from her shores signaled a new era in global politics following the collapse of the Soviet Union a quarter century before. The world seemed to be ineluctably moving towards a new world war, this one with religion at its core. Ultimately, Islamic terror was being instrumentalized as a weapon of war, one being aimed to defeat Russia, China and pre-empt emergence of a rival to the sole hegemony of the United States.

On November 13, 2015 grotesque suicide bomber attacks across Paris signaled a new phase in the attack on civilization. Yet few asked who or what was actually behind the IS and its reign of terror. To answer that it would be necessary to go back to the early post-World War II period and the birth of a new American intelligence agency.

For more than six decades, a faction in the US intelligence community used, and even trained, various Islamic political groups for their goal to extend an American hegemony in the world. The relationship between the CIA and certain specific groups of political Islamists began in the 1950s in postwar Munich and reached a new dimension in the 1980s, when the CIA, together with Saudi Arabian intelligence, brought a wealthy Saudi Islamist named Osama bin Laden to Pakistan to recruit Islamic Jihadists for a terrorist war against the Soviet Red Army in Afghanistan.

The success of the CIA's Operation Cyclone, to arm and train Afghani and other Mujahideen Islamic combatants, led Washington to deploy the same tactic after the collapse of the Warsaw Pact and the Soviet Union in the early 1990s. Veterans of the Afghan Mujahideen war, many of them Saudi and other Arab nationals recruited by bin Laden's organization, Al Qaeda, were brought on CIA private air transports into Azerbaijan, where British and US oil companies had their eye on the petroleum riches of the Caspian Sea. The CIA brought them into Yugoslavia to fan the flames of war there, from Bosnia-Herzegovina to Kosovo. They smuggled them into Chechnya and Dagestan to sabotage Russian oil pipeline routes.

As evident success grew with each attempt, some in Washington became heady with their strategy. They were convinced they had discovered the ideal instrument for making terror anywhere in the world to advance their agenda of global hegemony now that the Soviet Union had collapsed, while blaming it on crazed "stirred up Muslims," as Zbigniew Brzezinski once termed them.

The CIA and Pentagon finally had their new "enemy image" to replace the old Soviet communism when they blamed the events of September 11, 2001 in New York and Washington on Osama in Laden and his Al Qaeda network, whether true or not. Washington promptly declared a War on Terror and, under that banner, spread US military bases and its hegemony across the globe to places inconceivable just a decade before. Fear gripped an uncertain American population. They joined in the new war.

US military forces had their excuse to invade oil-rich Iraq in 2003. There they proceeded to unleash an unholy military terror that pitted Sunni Muslim Iraqis against Shi'ite Muslim Iraqis. Out of the bloody US occupation new recruits for Al Qaeda in Iraq grew dramatically. At the same time, the CIA worked across the Turkic world, from Uzbekistan to Xinjiang in western China, the site of China's major oil and gas activities. They trained new recruits to a Turkish Jihad, using the illusion of restoring an Ottoman empire to unleash terror and chaos across mineral-rich Central Asia to ultimately open it for penetration by Western multinationals in the power vacuum left with the collapse of the Soviet Union.

By December 2010 Washington was ready to unleash their most ambitious form of spreading radical political Islam. In Tunisia, using the event of the self-immolation of the young Tunisian, Mohamed Bouazizi, the CIA, US State Department, George Soros' Open Society foundation, Freedom House, NED, and other CIA-linked NGOs unleashed a wave of Arab world Color Revolutions. It was CIA- and US State Department-backed regime change using Twitter, Facebook, and deploying youthful activists Washington had trained months before.[1]

Once millions of naïve, hopeful students and workers had poured into Tahrir Square in Cairo, in Tunis, and across the Islamic North Africa and Middle East, Washington and the CIA backed their "asset," the Muslim Brotherhood, to establish new regimes they believed that they could control.

The oil-rich Islamic world was becoming too independent of British and American banks and oil companies. Egypt's Hosni Mubarak, Tunisia's Ben Ali, and Libya's Ghaddafi were combining to create an interest-free union of Islamic banks that potentially threatened the domination of Wall Street and the City of London. Moreover, China was moving in to the region for the first time, investing billions in Sudan, Iraq, Libya and beyond, in order to secure its oil supplies.

However with the launch of their so-called Arab Spring, a nightmare began to unfold for Washington and her allies in NATO and Tel Aviv. Tectonic fault lines surfaced which were not anticipated. The Muslim Brotherhood dictatorship that the CIA backed under Mohammed Morsi in Egypt was toppled by a military coup backed by the Egyptian people and financed by a nervous the Saudi monarchy. Libya descended into tribal warfare and its oil flows dwindled to near extinction as civil war raged.

However, the planners in Washington—the Pentagon, Langley CIA headquarters, the State Department and the Obama White House—had no Plan B. Unleashing CIA-financed and CIA-trained Jihadists and their terror in the name of Allah was Plan A. It was their only plan.

ISIS?

With a wave of shocking successes, an Islamic terror organization with the imposing name of Islamic State of Iraq and Syria (ISIS)—otherwise known variously as Islamic State of Iraq and Levant (ISIL), al-Qaeda in Iraq, Islamic State (IS), or, in Arabic, Da'ash—scored shocking military victories in the summer of 2014. Well-armed with the most modern weapons and vehicles, they overtook the strategic city of Mosul and key oil centers in Iraq, including Kirkuk, then swept over the border into Syria as far as the border to Turkey.

The organization ISIS became a household word when YouTube videos—later forensically proven to have been faked using professional actors—of the alleged beheading of an American journalist, James Foley, created a groundswell for a US-led NATO military action in Iraq and Syria.[2]

ISIS, later calling itself IS, had been created as a joint project by the CIA and Israeli Mossad to combine psychotic mercenaries posing as Islamic Jihadists, gathered from around the world—Chechnya, Iraq, Afghanistan, Saudi Arabia, even China's Turkic Xinjiang Province—in what the CIA called Operation Hornet's Nest. When some Israeli journalist experts pointed out that the letters "I-S-I-S" stood for the English name of Mossad—Israeli Secret Intelligence Service—the Jihadis quickly proclaimed over YouTube a new name: Islamic State, or IS in what appeared to be a clumsy coverup attempt.[3]

ISIS' self-appointed head, Abu Bakr al-Baghdadi, self-proclaimed "direct descendant" of the Prophet Mohammed, announced he was the (again, self-proclaimed) Caliph of all Muslims worldwide. It was a claim disputed by Islamic scholars and religious leaders worldwide.

Al Baghdadi, whose name meant simply, "the one from Baghdad," and who declared he had directly descended from Mohammed, and his Caliphate were pure CIA and Mossad fabrication, with money from Qatar and other Sunni states including Erdogan's Turkey, designed to terrify a gullible American public into going to war again in the Middle East.

A "trusted source" close to the Saudi multi-billionaire and former Lebanese Prime Minister Saad Hariri said, on condition of anonymity, that the final green light for the war on Iraq and Syria with ISIS was given behind closed doors at the Atlantic Council's Energy Summit in Istanbul, Turkey, November 22–23, 2013. The Atlantic Council was one of the most influential US think tanks with regard to US and NATO foreign policy and geopolitics.

The same source stated that the key coordinator of ISIS, or Da'ash, military actions was US Ambassador to Turkey Francis Riccardione. "As far as I know, nothing moves without Ambassador Riccardione," the Hariri intimate declared.[4]

The origins of ISIS could be traced directly back to the Afghan Mujahideen project of the CIA in the 1980s, where CIA-trained assets and a Saudi named Osama bin Laden, along with his Jordanian associate, Abu Musab al-Zarqawi, waged the largest CIA covert operation in history to drive the Soviet Army out of Afghanistan and humiliate Russia.

After 1989, al-Zarqawi moved into Iraq, where he was commissioned by his CIA handlers to found Al-Qaeda in Iraq—the direct predecessor of ISIS—first against Saddam Hussein's secular Baath Party rule, then, after 2003, as a Sunni terror force waging attacks on US occupation troops, as well as against Shi'ites, to justify a permanent US military occupation of Iraq. In that, they failed, when the Shi'ite government of Nouri al-Maliki ordered Washington to remove US troops from Iraq.

As a consequence, out of the Al Qaeda in Iraq, the Pentagon and CIA created a new, far larger Jihadist killing machine. Its purpose was to create the preconditions needed to bring US military troops back into Iraq, into Syria, Lebanon and beyond, and to remove Russia's ally Assad in Damascus.

The key fighters of ISIS were trained by CIA and US Special Forces Command at a secret camp in Jordan in 2012, according to informed Jordanian and other sources. US, Turkish, and Jordanian intelligence were running a training base for the Syrian rebels in the Jordanian town of Safawi in the country's northern desert region, conveniently near the borders to both Syria and Iraq. Saudi Arabia and Qatar, the two Gulf monarchies most involved in funding the war against Syria's Assad, financed the Jordan ISIS training.[5] Other reports claimed that a part of ISIS was also trained in secret camps in Libya as well as in NATO bases in Turkey near to the Syrian border.

A geopolitical contest between the US against Russia and increasingly against China was the ultimate objective of leading neoconservatives in the CIA, Pentagon, and State Department. On November 7, 2015 US Defense Secretary Ash Carter delivered a major speech in which he singled out China and Russia. He stated, "Moscow's nuclear saber-rattling raises questions about Russia's leaders' commitment to strategic stability…We do not seek to make Russia an enemy. But make no mistake; the United States will defend our interests, and our allies, the principled international order…" He added, "In the face of Russia's provocations and China's rise, we must embrace innovative approaches to protect the United States and strengthen that international order." [6] Clearly radical Islamic terrorism was one such "innovative approach."

In the early 1990s, during the dissolution of the Soviet Union, the CIA transported hundreds of Mujahideen who were Saudi and other veterans of the 1980's Afghanistan secret war against the Soviet Red Army. They were smuggled into Chechnya to disrupt the struggling new Russian Federation. They aimed particularly to sabotage the Russian oil pipeline running directly from Baku on the Caspian Sea into Russia. James Baker III and his friends in Anglo-American Big Oil had other plans. It was called the BTC pipeline, owned by a British-US oil consortium, running through Tbilisi into NATO-member Turkey, free of Russian territory.

In 2014 after a bloody, failed attempt over three years to unseat Bashar al-Assad, the ISIS terrorist assaults in Syria and Iraq conveniently gave the US neoconservative war hawks the pretext for their proxy war against Russia, Iran, and China's strategic Middle East ally Bashar al-Assad in Syria. The paranoid and obscenely rich Sunni rulers of Saudi Arabia and Qatar—aided by deluded Turkish President Erdogan with his delusions of restoring Turkey to its lost Ottoman glory—did the dirty work for Washington and Tel Aviv in Syria.

On one level, the IS war was about oil, gas, and pipelines to control the vast oil riches of the region, as well as to deny Russia the South Stream gas route to a Europe independent of Ukraine. On a deeper level, the IS war was part of a larger global strategy to defeat the only effective resistance to the creation of a new 21st century universal fascism, a return to the dark times of the Middle Ages but on a world scale, "one world" that would be controlled by very rich Western families whose agenda was total control over the world and reduction of global population through eugenics, wars and terrorism.

The Washington war against Syria and the US-created war in Ukraine were two fronts in what, in reality, was one war. It was a war against Russia and, at the same time, a war against China. Those two Eurasian powers, the key nations of the BRICS and of the Eurasian Shanghai Cooperation Organization, represented the center of gravity for the only effective counterweight to a new global fascist barbarism, a barbarism the Pentagon called Full Spectrum Dominance and the American oligarch David Rockefeller called his New World Order.

Roots of Arab rage

To comprehend the psychopathic, murderous rage of the Jihadists and mercenaries of IS, it was necessary to search into their historical roots. The search led back to the First World War, to Sykes-Picot, and to the historical roots of Arab rage. It led back to Egypt in the 1920s and the creation of a Sunni-based Islamic death cult known as the Sunni Muslim Brotherhood under Hasan al-Banna. It led to the evolution of that Muslim Brotherhood and their profane alliances to various non-Muslim intelligence services, from the British MI6 to Heinrich Himmler and the Nazi SS to, finally, the CIA beginning in the 1950s.

By the early days of 2015, it was becoming more and more clear that as a Washington war in Ukraine faltered, as a Washington war in Syria became an unspeakable debacle, and as their creation of a new Islamic Ottoman Empire in Turkey around Fethullah Gülen's *Cemaat* organization faced existential threat in a confrontation with former ally, Turkish President Erdogan, the Washington tactic of using political fundamentalist Islam to secure a revitalized American global hegemony was failing everywhere.

The American oligarchs who controlled Washington through their influential think tanks and ownership of mainstream media—names like Gates, Rockefeller, Soros, and Bush, the families who owned the American military–industrial complex—were becoming desperate. In their growing desperation, they threatened a new world war, using their old nemesis Russia as pretext. Literally, as the words of the ancient proverb attributed to Euripides expressed it, "Those whom the gods wish to destroy they first make mad." By the early weeks of 2015 the Sole Superpower, the global Hegemon, the American Oligarchs were not only lost, but also going mad. The world was slipping from their grasp.

—F. William Engdahl, Frankfurt am Main, November 2015

Endnotes

1   Freedom House, Egyptian Activists Stress Democracy Human Rights in Talks with US Secretary of State, Freedom House website, May 28, 2009, https://freedomhouse.org/article/egyptian-activists-stress-democracy-human-rights-talks-us-secretary-state#.VQk-5uHXmec.

2   Bill Gardner, Foley murder video "may have been staged," August 25, 2014, The Telegraph, http://www.telegraph.co.uk/journalists/bill-gardner/11054488/Foley-murder-video-may-have-been-staged.html. See also, James F. Tracy, Steven Sotloff Video Was Released by Intelligence Group linked to Homeland Security and Washington Think Tanks, Global Research.ca, September 04, 2014, http://www.globalresearch.ca/steven-sotloff-video-produced-by-intelligence-group-linked-to-homeland-security-and-washington-think-tanks/5399200.

3   Nafeez Ahmed, How the West Created the Islamic State, Counterpunch, September 12–14, 2014, http://www.counterpunch.org/2014/09/12/how-the-west-created-the-islamic-state/.

4   Christof Lehmann, US Embassy in Ankara Headquarter for ISIS War on Iraq Hariri Insider, nsnbc, June 22, 2014, http://nsnbc.me/2014/06/22/u-s-embassy-in-ankara-headquarter-for-isis-war-on-iraq-hariri-insider/.

5   21Wire, Team America: ISIS is "McCain's Army," November 21, 2014, http://21stcenturywire.com/2014/11/21/team-america-isis-is-mccains-army/; RBN, Blowback US trained ISIS at secret Jordan base, June 18, 2014 in News by RBN, http://republicbroadcasting.org/blowback-u-s-trained-isis-at-secret-jordan-base/; DEBKAfile Exclusive Report, Syrian rebel Yarmouk Brigades ditch US and Israel allies defect to ISIS, December 17, 2014, http://www.debka.com/article/24301/Syrian-rebel-Yarmouk-Brigades-ditch-US-and-Israel-allies-defect-to-ISIS; Henry Kamens, The US and ISIL Nexus, New Eastern Outlook, October 28, 2014, http://www.veteranstoday.com/2014/10/28/neo-the-us-and-isil-nexus/.

6   Ashton Carter, Secretary of Defense, Remarks on "Strategic and Operational Innovation at a Time of Transition and Turbulence" at the Reagan National Defense Forum, November 7, 2015, http://www.defense.gov/News/Speeches/Speech-View/Article/628146/remarks-on-strategic-and-operational-innovation-at-a-time-of-transition-and-tur.

BROTHERHOOD OF DEATH—ORGANIZING THE "NEW CRUSADE"

On September 16, 2001, five days after the shocking attacks on the World Trade Center and the Pentagon, US President George W. Bush announced at a White House press conference, "This is a new kind of—a new kind of evil. . . And the American people are beginning to understand. This crusade, this war on terrorism is going to take a while. . . It is time for us to win the first war of the 21st century decisively."[1]

Later, at the suggestion of various advisers, Bush dropped the reference to his War on Terror as a "new crusade." Nonetheless, the War on Terror that George W. Bush announced after September 11 was the beginning of what—as of this writing more than twelve years later—became, in every sense of the historical term, a new "holy crusade." It was to become a series of endless wars and conflicts, of mass killings, and brutality spreading from the mountains of Afghanistan through the valleys of Pakistan, into China and Russia, on to Yemen, Syria, Somalia, Jordan, Tunisia, Egypt, and Libya, and across the Islamic world.

Throughout recorded history one of the striking features of most religions was their sanctioning of the killing of other groups in the name of each with their own self-proclaimed "superior God." President George W. Bush's call to wage a new crusade in defense of American freedom, America's national security, was masked as a crusade in defense of America's "God-given Innocence." The mobilization around the idea of a divine mission was so effective that it had been used by emperors, kings, prime ministers, and presidents to mobilize masses to wage wars since before Emperor Constantine. Constantine the Great, the first Christian Roman Emperor, used it to build a world empire three hundred years after the birth of Jesus Christ.

Christ's Glory with bloodstained swords

In 1146, Saint Bernard of Clairvaux wrote a letter to the Knights Templar, the most powerful and wealthiest military order during the era of the medieval Christian Crusades against "infidel" Islam. Bernard declared to the Templars, "The Christian who slays the unbeliever in the Holy War is sure of his reward, the more sure if he himself is slain. The Christian glories in the death of the pagan, because Christ is thereby glorified" *(De Laude Novae Militiae, III—De Militibus Christi)*. Those words of death as glory were echoed or repeated in another context by leaders of the fanatical Muslim Brotherhood, of Osama bin Laden's al Qaeda, and of countless other Holy War sects.

The charismatic French abbot, Bernard of Clairvaux, mobilized tens of thousands of poor, largely illiterate peasants from southern Germany and from France. His battle cry was, "Hasten to appease the anger of heaven. . . The din of arms, the danger, the labors, the fatigues of war, are the penances that God now imposes upon you. Hasten then to expiate your sins by victories over the Infidels, and let the deliverance of the Holy places be the reward of your repentance. . . Cursed be he who does not stain his sword with blood." [2]

For Bernard of Clairvaux and the Christian Crusader Knights, all infidels, even non-Muslims, were creatures of Satan whose murders were justified as acts of atonement for the Holy Crusaders' sins. The papal indulgence—forgiveness of all sins and eternal life—were promised to all soldiers of the Christian Cross who should die confessing their sins. The Crusades were marketed to the ignorant populations as wars to "seek after the Good" for the would-be redeemed Christians.

The Church, in the person of Saint Bernard of Clairvaux, had deployed one of the most powerful psychological weapons of destruction yet discovered—wars in defense of innocence and to secure redemption in an afterlife. Dying by the sword in the name of Christianity was declared an atonement for the Christian crusader soldier's Original Sin, one that was said by the Christian Church to trace back to the Garden of Eden.

An Old, Ugly Story

George Bush's new War on Terror was but a repeat of an old, ugly story. It once more fanned the flames of hatreds and animosities that went back at least to the 11th and 12th centuries, some thousand years before September 11, 2001.

Like the new War on Terror crusade, the Holy Crusades of the Middle Ages had been wars of slaughter of innocents, of looting, wars of unspeakable destruction nominally organized by western Christendom to recover the holy land of Palestine from the Muslims and sanctioned by the Roman popes. However, the Crusades had little or nothing, at the highest levels, to do with religion. Rather they were about power, the power to destroy.

As George W. Bush's War on Terror, in true fact his Clash of Civilizations, fomenting a war between Christian and Muslim and wars within Islam, was to unleash the deepest hatreds and desire for revenge between the West and East—between Western Christendom and Eastern Islam—the template for which had been cast in those Holy Crusades.

Hordes of illiterate peasants were recruited by European kings and noblemen, militarily guided by the Templar Knights, by recluse hermit priests and others, to slaughter perhaps as many as nine million Muslims, Orthodox Christians, and Jews—"Infidels." In the slaughter several million Roman Catholic Christians perished in the blood-stained orgy of redemption called the Holy Crusade as well.

The papal armies looted their way from Europe to the Holy Lands of the Middle East. They raped and pillaged, in some documented cases even committing acts of cannibalism, with an utter lack of respect for human life. The crusaders knew that no matter how extreme their evil deeds, the pope in Rome had guaranteed them a papal indulgence for their deeds. Those Holy Wars called the Crusades lasted the better part of two centuries.[3]

In 1095, Pope Urban II proclaimed what became the First Crusade, a Holy War to recapture the sacred Jerusalem and the Holy Sites deemed sacred from the time of Christ. The armies of the pope were led then by an "unwashed priest," Peter the Hermit, whose "army" was mainly illiterate French and German peasants drawn to the fight by the Pope's promise of indulgences, a license to commit any sin they liked with the guarantee of papal forgiveness. They had few inhibitions.

On their way across Europe to the holy land, they massacred, tortured, and plundered the property of any Jew they could find. They stole and raped and destroyed. For towns of villages who tried to defend their homes against these "Holy hordes," Peter's answer was war. In one such battle, in the area of what later became Yugoslavia, Crusaders slaughtered more than four thousand local residents who dared to defend their homes. In all, a total of three hundred thousand Christians died during the march of the psychopathic Peter the Hermit.

When a later Crusade finally captured Jerusalem in 1099, the Crusaders carried out such a slaughter of the Muslims and Jews living there that one eyewitness recorded the victorious Christian soldiers were

> killing and cutting them down as far as Solomon's Temple, where there was such a massacre that our men were wading ankle deep in blood . . . Then the crusaders rushed around the whole city, seizing gold and silver, horses and mules, and looting the housing that were full of costly things. Then, rejoicing and weeping from excess of happiness, they all came to worship and give thanks at the sepulchre of our saviour Jesus. Next morning, they went cautiously up the temple roof and attacked the Saracens [Muslims—F.W.E.], both men and women [who had taken refuge there], cutting off their heads with drawn swords. . . Our leaders then gave orders that all the Saracen corpses should be thrown outside the city because of the stench, for almost the whole city was full of dead bodies . . . such a slaughter of pagans had never been seen or heard of.[4]

During the Crusade of 1147, a French abbot, Bernard of Clairvaux, close to the Pope in Rome and the patron of the newly formed Templar Knights, fired up the crusaders in a killing frenzy almost verbatim of what the Muslim Brotherhood founder, Egypt's Hasan al-Banna, would demand of his followers in the 1920s and later with his "Death is Art" Jihad cult.

Bernard told his soldiers of Christ that the infidels, or pagans as he called them, deserved a merciless war: "It is better to massacre them so that their sword is no longer suspended over the heads of the just." For Bernard, to kill an infidel constituted a holy act: "The Christian glorifies in the death of a pagan because thereby Christ himself is glorified."[5]

The aim of the Crusades was no less than the conquest of the Holy Land and the defeat of Islam as the Crusaders and their financiers in Venice and elsewhere quested for a World Empire. Enthusiasm for Christ was a motivating driver for the soldiers, joined, of course, by other motives such as ambition, avarice, hope of earthly, and, above all, heavenly reward.

George W. Bush's invocation of a new "Holy Crusade" in a War on Terror, and the response of radical Jihadists within Islam with their calls for Global Caliphate, marked a revival of ugly hatreds that went far back.

"Holy War versus Jihad"?

More than eight and a half centuries after St. Bernard's invocation to shed blood for the glory of Christian redemption, an American president called on his fellow Americans to wage a new crusade, to shed their blood, against Islam in the name of "defending American democracy, her Christian values." The formula was little changed from that of Bernard of Clairvaux.

President George W. Bush, a proclaimed born-again evangelical Christian, appealed to the tens of millions of Americans who, during the 1970s, 1980s, and into the 1990s, had embraced a black and white simplicity of a vengeful version of Christianity dubbed Christian Fundamentalism.

In a meeting in 2003, President Bush told a group of senior Palestinian political leaders at Sharm el-Sheikh that he was on a mission from God when he launched the invasions of Afghanistan and Iraq. In the words of Nabil Shaath, Palestinian Foreign Minister who was present, "President Bush said to all of us: 'I am driven with a mission from God.' God would tell me, 'George go and fight these terrorists in Afghanistan.' And I did. And then God would tell me 'George, go and end the tyranny in Iraq.' And I did."[6]

The fundamentalist evangelical Christians, as they were known, concentrated their forces in a takeover during the 1980s of the Republican Party, Bush's own party. They were trained to be militant, to hate, and to make war on infidel Muslims, whether they were the Taliban in Afghanistan or Sunni or Shi'ite Muslims in Iraq.

By the time George W. Bush became US President in 2001, fundamentalist Christian Evangelicals had become the fastest-growing religious group in America, with churches costing tens of millions of dollars each and membership numbering over 90 million believers. Their organizations had consciously infiltrated the various branches of the US Armed Forces, of the US Congress, and of the Executive Branch of government, much as the Muslim Brotherhood had done in Turkey, Egypt, Syria, Qatar, Pakistan, Afghanistan, and numerous other Islamic countries.

The turning of a highly vocal and well-organized minority of Christian churches and smaller sects into militant born-again fundamentalists was a radicalization which very well suited the effort of a US military-industrial complex and the US government's intelligence community in their drive to create an imperial military force willing to sacrifice itself for global holy wars "in the name of Christ," wars to be waged by those who believed that they were, thereby, seeking after the Good.

The fundamentalist churches had traditionally been strongest in the poorer US southern states, the so-called Bible Belt, an idiom for the largely rural region where the ultraconservative Southern Baptist Convention denomination was strongest. Many other church denominations or congregations, such as the Churches of Christ and the Assemblies of God, were represented, as well as Pentecostalists.

The Bible Belt was a huge swath stretching across Virginia, Alabama, the Carolinas, Georgia, Mississippi, Louisiana, Texas, and Oklahoma. Conveniently, for Pentagon war planners and for neoconservative think tanks steering the War State after 2001, these were the very same regions where the overwhelming majority of recruits for the US Armed Forces' all-volunteer army came from. Right-wing absolutist Christian sects and ultranationalist militarism went hand in hand in late-20th-century America.

"My God Was bigger than his"

The infamous case of US Lieutenant General William G. Boykin, the United States Deputy Under Secretary of Defense for Intelligence under Don Rumsfeld, was indicative of the new culture of US religious absolutism mixed with military conquest in the name of Christ—a very peculiar version of the Biblical Christ of love and forgiveness.

General Boykin was a member of the elite Delta Force special unit, where he led the disastrous April 1980 Iranian hostage rescue attempt. During the 1990s, Boykin served at the Central Intelligence Agency as Deputy Director of Special Activities and was promoted to the rank of Brigadier General. He was later made Deputy Director for Operations, Readiness, and Mobilization and assigned to the Army Staff in the Pentagon. In June 2003, he was appointed Deputy Under Secretary of Defense for Intelligence, where he played a key role in fabricating the fraudulent intelligence alleging proof that Saddam Hussein possessed weapons of mass destruction, the basis on which Congress voted to give the President authority to declare war on Iraq in 2003.

Boykin, a radical born again Christian from North Carolina's rural Bible Belt land, told CNN, after he had led the disastrous Mogadishu mission in the early 1990s against Muslim forces under Osman Atto, that the Muslim warlord had given an interview on CNN. Boykin related the remarks of Osman Otto: "He laughed at us, and he said, 'They'll never get me because Allah will protect me. Allah will protect me.'" "Well, you know what?" Boykin told CNN, "I knew that my God was bigger than his. I knew that my God was a real God and his was an idol."[7]

In June 2003, General Boykin declared to a journalist, "The enemy is a spiritual enemy. He's called the principality of darkness. The enemy is a guy called Satan." He later stated in words that almost verbatim echoed the words, in another context, of the founder of the Muslim Brotherhood, Hassan Al-Banna: "We will never walk away from Israel... Many of us are worried about heaven. Heaven is your reward. You are here as soldiers to take on the enemy." [8]

Then, Boykin added, "But those who hope in the Lord will renew their strength. They will soar on wings like eagles; they will run and not grow weary, they will walk and not be faint. . . . If there is no God, there is no hope. Don't let the media, the liberals, sway you in your faith. Pray for America, and we will be victorious."[9]

His words bordered on violation of the US Constitutional concept of separation of church and state, but Boykin was openly defended by Defense Secretary Rumsfeld, by President George W. Bush, and by the Chairman of the US Joint Chiefs of Staff.[10] It was an indication of how pervasive and useful the influence of the born-again Christian Right within the higher ranks of the US military had become.

One analyst of the phenomenon of American Christian right politics noted that the true believers demanded "an American foreign policy based on militant nationalism as an almost holy virtue. They believe that the United States has been specially dedicated to Jesus Christ for His purposes. To question or resist militant nationalism is to be unpatriotic, and to be unpatriotic is to be un-Christian in the eyes of the religious right."[11]

Gog and Magog

When George W. Bush declared a War on Terror after September 11, 2001, few doubted that he meant a War on Islam, what Samuel Huntington had earlier referred to as a Clash of Civilizations.[12]

In a private meeting with French President Jacques Chirac in 2003 on the eve of the US invasion of Iraq, Bush told the French President a story about how the Biblical creatures Gog and Magog were at work in the Middle East and how they must be defeated. He added that in Genesis and Ezekiel, Gog and Magog were forces of the Apocalypse who were prophesied to come out of the north and destroy Israel unless stopped. The Book of Revelation took up the Old Testament prophesy: "And when the thousand years are expired, Satan shall be loosed out of his prison, And shall go out to deceive the nations which are in the four quarters of the earth, Gog, and Magog, to gather them together to battle . . . and fire came down from God out of heaven, and devoured them." [13]

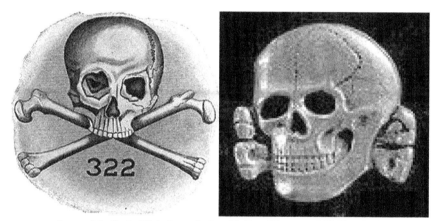

Logos of the Bushes' Yale Secret Society Skull and Bones and SS Totenkopf.

Bush believed the time had now come for that battle, telling Chirac, "This confrontation is willed by God, who wants to use this conflict to erase his people's enemies before a New Age begins." [14]

What George W. Bush did not tell Chirac was that he, like his father, George H. W. Bush, had been inducted into an occult secret society at the elite Yale University, where they had studied. Known as Skull and Bones Club, its actual name was The Brotherhood of Death, much like the Nazi SS *Totenkopf* or the Muslim Brotherhood, as will become clear later in this book.

Each inductee in Skull and Bones was given a code name on joining and performing what were described as satanic rites of passage. George Herbert Walker Bush, George W. Bush's father, had the code name Magog.[15]

War to Foster Terror

George W. Bush told Chirac only half of the story. America's War on Islam, thinly disguised as its War on Terror, had been planned from the start to create a fundamentalist, radical, political Islam reaction that would sweep across the Muslim peoples of Eurasia and beyond.

In Tunisia on December 18, 2010, what was to become the greatest wave of mass protests for regime change across the entirety of the Islamic world began. The Tunisian protests forced President Zine El Abidine Ben Ali to flee with family and hordes of jewels to Saudi Arabia. Soon, demonstrators streamed into the streets of Cairo in neighboring Egypt, guided by Facebook, Twitter, and other social media messaging. With a fury that spread like a wildfire, protests broke out in Yemen, Libya, Bahrain, Kuwait, Jordan, Iraq, Morocco, and the far away Xinjiang Province in China. They spread to Chechnya and Dagestan in Russia and to Myanmar, Indonesia, and Pakistan, demanding everything from reform to regime change to total revolution.

When citizen protests failed to gain the desired results, NATO was forced to reveal its hidden role and impose a no-fly zone in Libya, complete with massive civilian bombings to oust Muammar Qaddafi from power.

Yet rather than usher in a springtime across the Arab world of genuine democracy, as millions had hoped and demonstrated for, the mass protests soon gave way to seizure of power by a well-organized secret society across the Islamic world known as the Muslim Brotherhood. The fight for democracy by young students and others was rapidly being transformed into a seizure of power by a highly-organized spectrum of Islamic groups whose Sharia agenda was every bit as totalitarian or fascist as that of Mussolini's Italy or Hitler's Germany.

In 2007, in an interview with the Indian newspaper *The Hindu*, Ramsey Clark, a former US Attorney General and civil rights lawyer, stated,

> The war on terrorism is really a war on Islam. Most of the politicians are putting it as Islamic terrorists but what they really mean is the threat of Islam. So the idea of the war on Islam is the idea of extermination of a proportion never seen in history at any time. . . . The U.S. government's need for an enemy, its search for new enemies is really a way of uniting the country, covering its real motives and appealing for patriotism that is

called the last refuge of the scoundrel. Patriotism is not the real motive. The real motive is domination and exploitation, and to get away with it you have to have a rallying ground, an enemy. That is where the military comes in.[16]

As that US War on Terror evolved over more than a decade after September 11, 2001, it became more and more evident that its main goal was not merely to control the oil of the Middle East, but it was ultimately to contain the threat of a rising Eurasian economic challenge to America's declining power, a challenge which combined the economic colossus of an emerging China with the nuclear deterrence of Russia.

The Pentagon and factions of the US intelligence community determined to increasingly cultivate political Islam as a weapon to weaken the emergence of an independent, self-sufficient China, a resource-rich Russia, and potentially much of the European states, especially Germany. With America's global role in existential danger, Washington used its influence over various Islamic Jihadist groups to try to drive new wars and unrest globally "in defense of America's innocence." After September 2001, America's elites had decided to launch a new great crusade, in effect, an American Jihad in a determined bid to hold that global hegemony.

—F. William Engdahl, Frankfurt am Main, April 2015

Endnotes

1   George W. Bush, *Remarks by the President Upon Arrival*, Washington DC, 16 September, 2001, accessed in http://georgewbush-whitehouse.archives.gov/news/releases/2001/09/20010916-2.html.

2   James Meeker Ludlow, The Age of the Crusades. Christian Literature Co. (1896) pp. 164–167.

3   David Almighty, *The Root Causes of Religious Atrocities*, January 18, 2006, accessed in http://davidalmightyiii.blogspot.de/2006/01/root-causes-of-religious-atrocities.html.

4   Gesta Francorum, cited in, *The Crusades*, accessed in http://davidalmightyiii.blogspot.de/2006/01/root-causes-of-religious-atrocities.html.

5   Ibid.

6   Ewen MacAskill, George Bush: 'God told me to end the tyranny in Iraq,' The Guardian, October 7, 2005, http://www.theguardian.com/world/2005/oct/07/iraq.usa.

7   CNN, *General explains statements criticized by Muslims*, CNN News, October 18, 2003, http://edition.cnn.com/2003/US/10/17/boykin.apology/index.html.

8   Ibid.

9   Richard Cooper, *General Casts War in Religious Terms*, The Los Angeles Times, October 16, 2003.

10   AP, *Rumsfeld defends general who commented on war and Satan*, www.CNN.com, October 17, 2003.

11   Michael Webb, *On the rise of the radical religious right and the breakdown of democracy in the United States*, 2003, accessed in http://www.sklatch.net/thoughtlets/pall.html.

12   Samuel P. Huntington, *The Clash of Civilizations and the Remaking of World Order*, 1996.

13   Revelation 20:7-9, Holy Bible, King James Version.

14   Clive Hamilton, *Bush's Shocking Biblical Prophecy Emerges: God Wants to "Erase" Mid-East Enemies "Before a New Age Begins,"* http://www.alternet.org/story/140221/bush%27s_shocking_biblical_prophecy_emerges%3A_god_wants_to_%22erase%22_mid-east_enemies_%22before_a_new_age_begins%22. See also, Alexandra Robbins, *George W., Knight of Eulogia*, The Atlantic Monthly, May, 2000. And, Marcus Dam, *Consumerism and materialism deadlier than armed occupation*, The Hindu, December 17, 2007, accessed in http://www.thehindu.com/2007/12/17/stories/2007121754781100.htm.

15   Alexandra Robbins, Op cit.

16   Marcus Dam, Op cit.

CHAPTER ONE

JIHAD COMES TO GERMANY

"You must move in the arteries of the system without anyone noticing your existence until you reach all the power centers. . . until the conditions are ripe, they (the followers) must continue like this. If they do something prematurely, the world will crush our heads, and Muslims will suffer everywhere. . . . You must wait until such time as you have gotten all the state power. . . . Until that time, any step taken would be too early—like breaking an egg without waiting the full 40 days for it to hatch. It would be like killing the chick inside."

—Turkish Imam Fetullah Gülen, CIA-linked head of the
worldwide Gülen Movement that controls schools around
the World, including 126 Charter Schools across the USA

Salafists go for the Young Boys

Only a few years earlier, a public debate about applying Islamic Sharia law in Germany was inconceivable. Even the word was unknown but to a handful of scholars. Other Arabic words, such as fatwa, burka, Salafist, Sunni, Shi'ite, Alawite, and, above all, Jihad, were completely foreign to the ordinary German.

That state of affairs regarding the inner world of Islam and its many currents was to change drastically after September 11, 2001, with the decision by the United States Government to launch what it called their "War on Terrorism."

Despite the vehement denials by then President George W. Bush, it was clear to most Americans that the "terrorists" in Washington's War on

Terror were "Islamic terrorists" and not any old Baader-Meinhof or Red Army Faction variety of organization.

A dramatic series of offensive US military and psychological actions in the wake of the September 11 destruction of three World Trade Center towers and the assault on the Pentagon created a global incubator to spawn Islamic hate groups claiming the true interpretation of the Koran as their guide.

Almost unnoticed, at least by most of the authorities, fundamentalist Islam or Salafist Jihadism as some termed the current, began to spread also in Germany, the country with the image as the most prosperous and stable of European countries. It took root among discontented and often unemployed youth, many of whose parents or grandparents had been recruited from the remote peasant regions of Anatolia in Turkey to work in Germany in menial jobs as "Guest Workers" (*Gastarbeiter)* or from Islamic regions of Africa for cheap labor in the German steel and other heavy industries.[1]

By the end of the first decade of the new century, radical Islam was becoming alarmingly well known in Germany.

On June 14, 2012 in the largest raid on Muslim extremist organizations in the history of the Federal Republic, the German Federal Ministry of the Interior issued a ban against the Islamic Salafist association *Millatu Ibrahim* and initiated criminal investigations against DawaFFM and DWR—*Die Wahre Religion* (The True Religion).[2]

Leading members of *Millatu Ibrahim* had been arrested a month earlier that May in a demonstration in Bonn, where members had stabbed several police after one of their leaders, Denis Mamadou Cuspert, had appeared on *YouTube* to call for Jihad against the German Chancellor and German ministers for waging a war against the Islam of the Muslim Brotherhood in Egypt.

Cuspert, born to a broken home of German-Ghana parents, was a former "Gangsta Rapper" under the artistic name Deso Dogg. He had converted to Islam and become a preacher under various names, including Abu Talha al-Almani. As Abu Talha al-Almani, Cuspert had posted various Islamic Jihad songs calling for violent Jihad action against the Federal Republic and praising Osama bin Laden.[3]

Cuspert managed to flee to Egypt and then, reportedly, reappeared in Syria fighting with the Al-Qaeda-linked al-Nusra Front, claiming in videos he wanted to die as a martyr.[4]

The nightmare scenario dreaded by German security police was emerging—a revolving door of fundamentalist, fanatical Salafist Jihadists going from Germany to war zones, such as Syria or Egypt, then, ultimately, returning to Europe as combat-seasoned veterans of Jihad.

The ban on the *Millatu Ibrahim* organization was enforced in Berlin, Bavaria, Hesse, Hamburg, Lower Saxony, North Rhine/Westphalia, and Schleswig-Holstein. It was based on the fact that *Millatu Ibrahim* was an association "directed against the constitutional order and the concept of international understanding." *Millatu Ibrahim* taught followers to reject German law and follow Islamic Shariah law and were taught that "the unbelievers are the enemy," that is all who did not profess belief in their brand of fanatical Islam. [5]

On March 13, 2013, there was a second round of German police raids against radical Salafist organizations in Nordrhein-Westphalia and Hessen.[6] The background to the rise of radical Islam in Germany went far deeper and was far more ominous than most Germans realized.

Munich: Jihad Base for Europe

In Munich, the Muslim Brotherhood, a secret Jihadist organization we will revisit in detail throughout this book, established what they saw as a "beachhead" to spread Jihad Islam across the West from Europe on to North America. They gained control of the Islamic Center of Munich (*Islamisches Zentrum München*) on Wallnerstrasse, a small back street of Munich in Catholic Bavaria. The obscure mosque was listed in some Islamic books as one of the four most important mosques in the world, right alongside the Great Mosque of Mecca and the Blue Mosque of Istanbul.[7]

The Islamic Center of Munich, up until the 1990s, was the heart of Muslim Brotherhood activities in Europe and beyond.

The Munich mosque, built initially with German government aid and used during the Cold War as a base for the CIA to deploy anticommunist Muslims against the Soviet Union, was taken over in the 1970s by the Muslim Brotherhood.

The Munich mosque became a refuge for international leaders of the secret Muslim Brotherhood until at least the first decade of the 21st century. As a center controlled by the Muslim Brotherhood, the Munich Islamic Center went on to cofound the influential Central Council of Muslims in Germany (*Zentralrat der Muslime in Deutschland*, or ZMD).[8]

Salafist Jihadism

After the raids of 2012 and 2013 Salafism in Germany became almost a household word. It was virtually interchangeable with the word "Muslim" for many who did not look more closely at vital differences between the numerous Islamic groups and currents. In reality, it represented a tiny minority of Muslims but one whose resonance went far beyond their numbers.

The *Bundesamt für Verfassungsschutz* (BfV), the German equivalent of the US FBI, estimated at the time of the raids that there were some 29 Islamist groups active in Germany with around 35,000 members who wanted to establish a "Koran-state" in Germany based on Islamic Sharia law. They estimated that there were among them about 4,000 Salafist Jihadists in Germany. Those were said to be the fastest growing Islamic group in Germany out of an officially estimated total Muslim population of 4.3 million. They numbered roughly one tenth of one percent of all Muslims in Germany. Unofficially some estimated the German total Muslim population could have been over 7 million, if illegal or unregistered Muslim immigrants were included, making the Salafists even a smaller minority but a highly aggressive and dangerous one. [9]

Salafism, a political brand of what was sometimes called Islamic Fundamentalism, had its origins in the arch-conservative Wahhabite Sunni Islam prevalent in Saudi Arabia. For decades, it had been passive if austere. It was not politically aggressive.

That was to change, however. According to Gilles Kepel, an Islamic Salafist researcher who had followed Salafism over decades, a radically new current he described as Salafist Jihadism emerged during the 1990s. There, Jihad in the form of violence and terrorism was justified to realize the political objectives of imposing Sharia strict law and, ultimately, of forging a global Islamic Great Caliphate, a global world government run by Islamist strict laws.[10]

The Salafists' origins went back to a secret, outlawed movement that arose in Egypt during the 1920s called the Muslim Brotherhood. Salafists' rejection of all things non-Muslim—including "mainstream European society"—and their advocacy of violent Jihad created a volatile cocktail as some German authorities had begun to realize.

Koran in Every German Home. . .

In October 2011, just weeks before the major police raids on Salafist organizations across Germany, Ibrahim Abou Nagie, a 47-year-old Palestinian Salafist Imam or teacher from Cologne, announced a campaign to give away for free twenty-five million copies of the Koran in the German language across Germany, Switzerland, and Austria, a distinctly different tactic than open violence and stabbings of police. Nagie was head of a group with the modestly unassuming name, *Die Wahre Religion* (The True Religion).

Nagie was considered by the *Bundes Verfassungsschutz* as one of the most dangerous Islamic Jihadists in the Federal Republic, contrary to his mild and friendly external appearance and soft-spoken voice.[11] His message was simple: either one had to embrace "true Islam" Salafist-style or be condemned to Hell. He preached that democracy was a political creation that should be rejected in favor of Sharia law.

Ibrahim Abou Nagie, Salafist Imam in Cologne, was considered by the Bundes Verfassungsschutz as one of the most dangerous Islamic Jihadists in the Federal Republic.

He claimed that his Koran action was aimed at giving the "unsaved" Germans a chance to see the true religion. His action was organized in every major German city with over 100 book tables in the public shopping streets. At the same time in his videos and writings, the same Nagie preached that it was legitimate to use violence against so-called *Kuffar*, the non-believers. [12]

Nagie's Koran action was joined by other Salafist Jihadist organizations in Germany, including the Hessen-based DawaFfm. Abdellatif Rouali, leader of DawaFfm, was under official investigation by the Frankfurt Public Prosecutor's Office for recruiting young Muslims to go abroad to be trained in special camps to fight Jihad wars in various foreign countries. He was arrested in February 2011. On the surface, his organization appeared to be doing good work in taking restless, unemployed, often violent young Muslim youth off the German streets. DawaFfm sponsored football games for young Muslims and seminars on Islam. The seminars however featured some of the most radical and charismatic of Germany's Salafist Jihadist Imams.[13]

Abdellatif Rouali, Ibrahim Abou Nagie, Pierre Vogel, and Mohamad Mahmoud, alias Usama al-Gharib, all were at the heart of one of the fastest-growing religious movements in Germany—Salafist Jihadism. Usama al-Gharib, considered one of the most dangerous Salafists in Germany, had recently moved his headquarters from Solingen to Erbach in the Hessen Odenwald not far from the Frankfurt international finance center.

By the account of the German authorities and information recovered from the police raids in 2012 and 2013, a picture emerged of an extremely well-oiled Jihad recruiting machine which targeted weak youth, including non-Muslim youth, gave them an apparently potent identity, and transformed them into fanatic true believers in a fundamentalist Islam.

With the Patience of a Spider. . .

What Nagie and other Salafi Jihadist preachers were spreading on the streets and immigrant ghettoes of Germany was far from unique to Germany. But while they were drawing the attention of German police and prosecutors, stabbing police, engaging in violent clashes with various non-believers, or giving away German-language Korans, a different brand of Islamism was spreading its influence across Germany. To the outside world, they pro-jected a cultivated image of democracy, tolerance, and religious freedom. The reality was quite the opposite.

Under the mottos "build schools not mosques," and "our Jihad is educa-tion," a reclusive Turkish-born Imam named Fethullah Gülen was spreading his international Islamic fundamentalism in Germany, too. His method was such that even the German public, who were engaged in fostering a dialogue between native Germans and Islamic Turkish in Germany, knew little about the Gülen organization and its true nature.

His movement quietly and effectively worked through special schools and local reading centers for Koran study. Gülen's Movement or *Cemaat* in Turkish, established countless "Light Houses" (Lichthäuser), which his followers carefully called "normal student living collectives." They were, in fact, collective (male only) living centers, like military barracks, where strict discipline, absolute obedience, enforced Koran readings, five-time daily prayers, and constant studying of the writings of Gülen were demanded.[14]

Gülen's followers built special schools, private High Schools called Gymnasiums, such as the $20 million Cologne Dialog-Gymnasium in Köln-Buchheim. In all, the secretive Gülen Movement had an estimated hundred or more education centers across Germany, twelve in Berlin alone. They deliberately recruited gifted students, often children of Turkish background in Germany, as cadre for the future building of influence.[15]

Gülen had been extremely careful to create a public image of "moderate" Islam, of an ecumenical current in Islam seeking interreligious dialogue. The Gülen organization in Germany, as of 2012, had founded fifteen "Dialogue Associations," such as the Berlin Forum for Intercultural Dialogue (*Forum für Interkulturellen Dialog or* FID). The associations organized conferences, inviting various rabbis, priests, and Imams. Often select guests would be invited to Gülen's original home base in Istanbul, where his influence in the ruling AK Party of Erdogan was, at that time, enormous.[16]

Fethullah Gülen's people were masters at going to the top. The chairman of the German Association of Turkish-German Academics (Türkisch-Deutscher-Akademischer Bund e.V.), Alp Saraç, was a member of the Gülen Movement.[17] Former German Bundestag President Rita Süssmuth was on the Board of the Gülen movement's *Forum für Interkulturellen Dialog* (FID) or Forum for Intercultural Dialogue in Berlin. Hessen Justice Minister

The US-based Gülen Movement has a network of schools worldwide, including in Germany.

Jörg-Uwe Hahn (FDP), CDU's Ruprecht Polenz, and Berlin Senator Ehrhart Körting (SPD) had been guests at events of the Gülen Movement.

In April 2013, in Dortmund's Westfalen Hall, Sabine Christiansen, a former very popular German TV talk show hostess, moderated an event with some 8,000 people attending. The event's official patron was represented by State Minister (*Staatsekretarin*) of the Foreign Ministry, Cornelia Pieper of the Liberal Party (FDP). The organizer of the event, which celebrated Turkish, as well as German, culture, was a little-known Academy Association for Education Advise (*Academy Verein für Bildungsberatung*), registered in Frankfurt along with media partner World Media Group in Offenbach. Both organizations were part of the network of Fethullah Gülen.[18]

According to former members who had escaped the Gülen sect and spoke on condition of anonymity about the inner life in the German Gülen "Light Houses," far from a happy, religiously tolerant brotherhood of love, the reality inside was anything but brotherly love. They described it as an arch-conservative, strict discipline similar to the Scientology sect. The key teaching was reportedly *Hizmet,* or "to serve," as in slavery. As the former members described it, one served Allah by serving the dictates of Gülen and his lieutenants.

The Koran was at the center, and no disagreement with the commands of Gülen, who communicated via the Internet from his retreat in Pennsylvania, or of his lieutenants, was tolerated. Former members of the Gülen sect have described how Gülen himself was regarded as a sort of "new Messiah," whose writings gave the path to understand the Koran and true Islam. The professed secret aim was creating a new era in which their absolutist brand of Islam would rule over the entire Western world. Like their close brothers in the Egyptian Muslim Brotherhood, they worked to that goal with a deceptive façade of moderation.[19]

According to a German *Der Spiegel* magazine series on the Gülen organization, in one sermon in Turkey, Gülen told his disciples:

> You must penetrate the arteries of the System, without anyone noticing your existence until you reach all the power centers. . . until the conditions are ripe, you must continue like this. If you do something prematurely, the world will crush our heads, and Muslims will suffer everywhere. . . You must wait until such time as you have gotten all the state power. . . Until that

time, any step taken would be too early — like breaking an egg without waiting the full 40 days for it to hatch. It would be like killing the chick inside.[20]

Dutch sociologist Martin van Bruinessen likened the Gülen organization, with its international network of schools, businesses, banks, TV, and newspapers, to the Roman Catholic secret society, Opus Dei. Respected German Islamic scholar Professor Ursula Spuler-Stegemann of Marburg University called the Gülen movement, "the most important and most dangerous Islamic movement in Germany. They're everywhere."[21]

US Embassy cables leaked in 2010 by *Wikileaks* included a note from the US Embassy in Ankara to Washington on the influence of Gülen's organization in Erdogan's Turkey. The memo described them as the most powerful Islamic group in Turkey, controlling major branches of trade and key parts of the economy, and that they had deeply penetrated into state political institutions.[22]

When four members of the Turkish Parliament from the opposition party, CHP, visited Gülen-critic Hanefi Avcı in prison after he had written of Gülen's takeover of the Turkish national police institutions, they issued a press statement. They stated, "We knew that the Movement was especially well organized within the police. However further revelations were a shock for us. The Turkish intelligence and KOM (Division of Smuggling and Organized Crime) had been removed from state control, and were no longer answerable under state laws."[23] (author's translation).

Some in Turkey and elsewhere suspected that the vast funds to finance the worldwide Gülen Movement could have come from proceeds of Turkish organized crime, including their heroin transit from Afghanistan.[24] Whatever the source of their funds, it was clear that Gülen's people were spreading their networks deep into German society.

Gülen's followers did not organize openly for Jihad or give away Korans on the streets of Germany or other countries. They had no headquarters in Germany or even in Turkey. Gülen himself operated his worldwide network, said to be worth more than €80 billion, from a vast remote estate in eastern Pennsylvania, where two former senior CIA officials organized his "self-imposed" exile from Turkey in 1999. Gülen's people operated well under the radar, and far more dangerously, behind the exterior façade of tolerance and interfaith dialogue.

The former head of Russian Intelligence called the international Gülen Movement a "CIA front." Former head of Turkish Intelligence Osman Nuri Gundes claimed in his memoirs that Fethullah Gülen's worldwide Islamic movement based in Saylorsburg, Pennsylvania, had been providing cover for the CIA since the mid-1990s, and that in the 1990s the movement "sheltered 130 CIA agents" at its schools in Kyrgyzstan and Uzbekistan alone.[25]

That was just after the collapse of the Soviet Union when the CIA and US State Department were engaged in widespread operations to subvert the old Moscow-loyal authorities and create pro-US and pro-NATO regimes across former Soviet republics. Turkey's Gülen played, and continues to play, a most important and little-understood role in that subversion. Gülen will appear in these pages numerous times as the enormous extent of his powerful network comes to light in other countries.

Before 2001 and the ensuing chaos in the region of Central Asia and the former Soviet Union, Salafism was barely on the official radar screens of German or other EU governments, with exception of a handful of secret intelligence services. What had happened to transform a once-passive fundamentalist Islamic Salafist dogma into a radical Salafist Jihadism? The answer was to be found in Washington and the CIA's agenda for radicalization of the Islamic world, beginning with Afghanistan and Iraq. Washington had decided to make its former Muslim Brotherhood assets into a new "enemy image" in a US War against Terror. The Iraq War in 2003 was to mark this radical shift in CIA Islam policy.

Endnotes

1   In 1982, during a confidential meeting in Bonn with British Prime Minister Margaret Thatcher, Chancellor Helmut Kohl confided privately his plan to send some half of the then 1.5 million Turkish immigrants back to their homeland, deeming that, unlike Portuguese or Italian or east Europeans, Turks came from a distinctly different culture that did not integrate well. "Chancellor Kohl said . . . over the next four years, it would be necessary to reduce the number of Turks in Germany by 50 percent—but he could not say this publicly yet," state the secret minutes of the meeting dated Oct. 28, 1982. Thatcher's record of the talks, labeled "Secret," were released by the UK State Archives in August 2013 and declassified. See Claus Hecking, *Secret Thatcher Notes: Kohl Wanted alf of Turks Out of Germany*, 1 August 2013, Spiegel, accessed

in http://www.spiegel.de/international/germany/secret-minutes-chancellor-kohl-wanted-half-of-turks-out-of-germany-a-914376.html.

2   Federal Ministry of the Interior, *Enforcement measures against Salafist associations*, Berlin, June 14, 2012, accessed in http://www.bmi.bund.de/SharedDocs/Kurzmeldungen/EN/2012/06/salafismus.html;jsessionid=FF79FDDBBCEB235925D8027EB8B1DA16.2_cid231.

3   N-TV, *„Deutschland ist ein Kriegsgebiet": Salafist droht mit Anschlägen*, n-tv, 3. September 2012, accessed in http://www.n-tv.de/politik/Salafisten-drohen-mit-Anschlaegen-article7125141.html.

4   Frank Jansen, *Europäische Islamisten zunehmend in Syrien*, Der Tagesspiegel, 22.02.2013, accessed in http://www.tagesspiegel.de/politik/salafisten-europaeische-islamisten-zunehmend-in-syrien/7824314.html.

5   David Rising, *Millatu Ibrahim German Salafist Organization Banned Amid Raids*, HuffingtonPost, 14 June 2012, accessed in http://www.huffingtonpost.com/2012/06/14/millatu-ibrahim-german-salafist-organization-banned_n_1596127.html.

6   DTN, *Großrazzia in NRW und Hessen gegen Salafisten: Deutsche Sicherheitsbehörden greifen durch*, Deutsch Türkische Nachrichten, 13 March,2013, accessed in http://www.deutsch-tuerkische-nachrichten.de/2013/03/470809/grossrazzia-in-nrw-und-hessen-gegen-salafisten-deutsche-sicherheitsbehoerden-greifen-durch/.

7   Ian Johnson, *A Mosque in Munich: Nazis, the CIA, and the Rise of the Muslim Brotherhood in the West*, interview with New America Foundation, accessed in http://newamerica.net/events/2010/a_mosque_in_munich.

8   Ian Johnson and Zarinés Negrón, *Interview on A Mosque in Munich: Nazis, the CIA, and the Rise of the Muslim Brotherhood in the West*, May 13, 2010, accessed in https://www.carnegiecouncil.org/studio/multimedia/20100513b/0287.html/_res/id=sa_File1/A_Mosque_in_Munich.pdf.

9   Soren Kern, *Germany: Radical Salafism is Like a Hard Drug*, June 19, 2012, accessed in http://www.gatestoneinstitute.org/3121/germany-radical-salafism.

10   Bruce Livesey, *The Salafist Movement*, accessed in http://www.pbs.org/wgbh/pages/frontline/shows/front/special/sala.html.

11   Florian Flade, *Salafisten verteilen 25 Millionen Korane*, Die Welt, 10 April 2012, accessed in http://www.welt.de/print/die_welt/article106165597/Salafisten-verteilen-25-Millionen-Korane.html.

12   Katharina Iskandar, *Salafisten Einen Koran in jeden Haushalt*, 3 April 2012, Frankfurter Allgemeine Zeitung, accessed in http://www.faz.net/aktuell/ politik/inland/salafisten-einen-koran-in-jeden-haushalt-11705989.html.

13   Ibid.

14   Maximilian Popp, Altruistic Society or Sect? The Shadowy World of the Islamic Gülen Movement, SpiegelOnline, http://www.spiegel.de/international/ germany/guelen-movement-accused-of-being-a-sect-a-848763.html.

15   Ibid.

16   Ibid.

17   Günther Lachmann, *Islam Bewegung breitet sich in Deutschland aus*, 21 May 2011, Die Welt, accessed in http://www.welt.de/politik/ausland/article13384879/ Islam-Bewegung-breitet-sich-in-Deutschland-aus.html.

18   Nick Brauns, *Gülen: Schattenhafter Puppenspieler*, 08 August 2013, accessed in http://www.armenieninfo.net/nick-brauns/5532-fethullah-gulen-und-sein-einfluss-auf-die-akp-justiz-und-polizei.html.

19   Maximilian Popp, op. cit.

20   Ibid.

21   Ibid.

22   Ibid.

23   Cited in Wikipedia.de, under *Fethullah Gülen*, accessed in http:// de.wikipedia.org/wiki/Fethullah_G%C3%BClen#cite_note-Hali. C3.A7.27de_ya.C5.9Fayan_Simonlar-37.

24   Sibel Edmonds, *Connecting the Dots: Afghan Heroin, NATO, Azerbaijan Hub & Cargo Business*, 7. March 2013, http://www.boilingfrogspost.com/2013/03/07/ connecting-the-dots-afghan-heroin-nato-azerbaijan-hub-cargo-business/.

25   Sibel Edmonds, *Turkish Intel Chief Exposes CIA Operations via Islamic Group in Central Asia*, 6, January 2011, accessed in http://www.boilingfrogspost.com/2011/01/06/ turkish-intel-chief-exposes-cia-operations-via-islamic-group-in-central-asia/.

CHAPTER TWO

IRAQ AND WASHINGTON'S CRUSADE AGAINST ISLAM

*"It is imperative that no Eurasian challenger emerges, capable of domi-
nating Eurasia and thus of also challenging America. . . . For America,
the chief geopolitical prize is Eurasia. . . America's global primacy is
directly dependent on how long and how effectively its preponderance
on the Eurasian continent is sustained."*

—Zbigniew Brzezinski, a key architect of
US Mujahideen war against Soviets in Afghanistan

Preventing a Eurasian Rival

The rise of Salafist Jihad militant Islamic groups since the CIA and Saudi
creation of Mujahideen in Afghanistan in the 1980s to defeat the Soviet army
and, especially, after the US War on Terror after September 11, 2001, was a
direct and indirect consequence of the actions of the Western intelligence
agencies, especially Washington. It resulted in the growing militancy and
prominence of political Islam across the Muslim world, from Afghanistan
to Mali and beyond.

What few understood was the necessary and deliberate interplay between
an American War on Terror and the rising power of that Islamic Jihad
terrorism. Without the brutal interventions of US military forces in Iraq
or Afghanistan and elsewhere after September 2001, organizations such
as those of Osama bin Laden's al Qaeda, the Muslim Brotherhood, or
Fethullah Gülen's Movement, would have had little likelihood of success
in recruiting new fanatics.

Under the rubric of "fighting terrorism," and, "deterring the resurrection of Islamic fundamentalism," the Pentagon and the military–industrial complex behind it could easily lobby for more US bases in the Middle East, Africa, and Central Asia. That increased US military presence acted, in turn, as a red cape in the face of an Islamic Jihadist bull. The spreading chaos, fighting, and instability sweeping across the Islamic world was, in turn, further justification for increased US and NATO military presence in those very strategic areas. And that US military presence, with its deliberate drone attacks on civilians and brutal treatment of ordinary citizens, made the recruitment by Salafists of young militants—ready to commit suicide for what they were told was the holy cause of Jihad—much easier.

Targeting Eurasia

The area from North Africa across the Middle East and through Central Asia also happened to be the strategic, economic lifeline of the only grouping of nations in a possible position to challenge America's sole superpower hegemony. Those nations were the members of the Shanghai Cooperation Organization (SCO). The SCO, created in 2001 in the aftermath of the collapse of the Soviet Union, joined China, Russia, Kazakhstan, Uzbekistan, Kyrgyzstan, and Tajikistan in a loose union for economic and partial military security cooperation. Later, cooperation combating terrorism became part of the SCO agenda.

By 2012, India, Pakistan, Iran, Belarus, Pakistan, and Mongolia had all requested SCO official Observer status. A look at the map reveals a contiguous land area that incorporated well over one half the entire world's population. It was the world's fastest growing economic space, with every conceivable raw material it needed to fuel that development and to create a new economic magnet for the world. Eurasian nations could in every sense, "make it on their own," without dependence on the West. That was highly alarming for Washington.

No rival economic bloc could be allowed to challenge American hegemony. That was the core of US foreign policy after the end of the Cold War. Former Obama foreign policy adviser Zbigniew Brzezinski, a most influential person in the US power establishment, summed up the position as seen from Washington. He noted that following the collapse of the Soviet Union, the only conceivable long-term challenge to America's sole superpower status was the possible coming together of the nations of

SHANGHAI COOPERATION ORGANIZATION
Founded in Shanghai in 2001, the SCO is comprised of China, Russia, Kazakhstan, Kyrgyzstan, Tajikistan and Uzbekistan

Timeline

2001 Shanghai, China	Signed the founding manifesto of SCO
2002 St. Petersburg, Russia	Signed the Charter of SCO, elaborating the principles, organization and other related issues
2003 Moscow, Russia	Hold their first joint anti-terrorism military training
2004 Tashkent, Uzbekistan	Mongolia was involved as an observer of SCO and the launch of secretariat in Beijing
2005 Astana, Kazakhstan	Confirmed the observer status of Pakistan, Iran and India
2006 Shanghai, China	Release of five-year manifesto
2007 Bishkek, Kyrgyzstan	Signed good-neighborly cooperation agreement
2008 Dushanbe, Tajikistan	Signed dialogue partner regulation
2009 Yekaterinburg, Russia	Signed anti-terrorism pact
2010 Tashkent, Uzbekistan	Agreed on rules of accepting new members
2011 Astana, Kazakhstan	10th anniversary of the SCO's founding

Except for Uzbekistan, the other countries had been members of the **Shanghai Five, founded in 1996.** After its inclusion in 2001, the members renamed the group as Shanghai Cooperation Organization.

Source: Xinhua   CHINA DAILY

The nations of Eurasia in the Shanghai Cooperation Organization pose the only potential challenge to America's sole superpower status. Source: China Daily.

Eurasia. That was precisely what the Shanghai Cooperation Organization threatened to do. Brzezinski wrote in his 1997 book, *The Grand Chessboard: American Primacy and It's Geostrategic Imperatives,*

> It is imperative that no Eurasian challenger emerges, capable of dominating Eurasia and thus of also challenging America. . . .[1] For America, the chief geopolitical prize is Eurasia. . . . America's global primacy is directly dependent on how long and how effectively its preponderance on the Eurasian continent is sustained.[2]
>
> Eurasia is the globe's largest continent and is geopolitically axial. A power that dominates Eurasia would control two of the world's three most advanced and economically productive regions. A mere glance at the map also suggests that control over Eurasia would almost automatically entail Africa's subordination, rendering the Western Hemisphere and Oceania geopolitically peripheral to the world's central continent. About 75 per cent of the world's people live in Eurasia, and most of the world's physical wealth is there as well, both in its enterprises and underneath its soil. Eurasia accounts for 60 per cent of the world's GNP and about three-fourths of the world's known

energy resources...[3] The most immediate task is to make certain that no state or combination of states gains the capacity to expel the United States from Eurasia or even to diminish significantly its decisive arbitration role.[4]

Creating the Conflict

Preventing just such a combination of states from expelling the USA from Eurasia, or even diminishing its decisive role, was a strategic priority of US foreign and military policy since the collapse of the Soviet Union. It took many different guises to achieve that aim of divide and rule.

To prevent the emergence of an economically prosperous Eurasian land space after the collapse of the Soviet Union, Washington and its NATO allies fostered separatism across the former parts of Soviet-dominated Eurasia. They did so by wooing countries such as Poland, Czechoslovakia, Hungary, Bulgaria, and others, to join NATO, feeding tension between those states and Russia. They seduced oil-rich Central Asian countries, such as Azerbaijan and Kazakhstan, by bringing in major US and British oil companies and offering a share in the oil riches that could flow if they were to distance themselves from their former Soviet masters and join the Anglo-American oil economy. Tension between Moscow and its former satellites was central to US strategy after 1990.

US intelligence agencies and Washington's NATO allies also used narcotics trafficking to weaken the societies of Eurasia, much as the CIA had done during the Vietnam War.[5] US intelligence agencies protected and fostered the cultivation of opium in Afghanistan to record levels after the US occupation in 2001. That opium found its way, under protection of US military aircraft in many cases, into Russia, Iran, and other Central Asian countries, creating major social unrest.[6] That was a vital part of Washington's divide and rule strategy to prevent the rise of a coherent, prosperous Eurasia.

By 2013, Iran, with a porous border to Afghanistan, reported having at least two million youth addicted to Afghani heroin.[7] A similar Afghan heroin plague among unemployed and rootless Russian young people took place after 2002. In Russia in 2006 alone, eighty-seven thousand people were arrested for drug related crimes—an increase of 24 percent over the year before.[8] By 2010, the UN Office on Drugs and Crime estimated that the net profit pocketed by criminals trafficking Afghan heroin into the Russian Federation was around US$ 1.4 billion.[9]

Weaponizing Religion

But by far, the most effective of the various methods to sow division and conflict in the Eurasian space was the weaponizing of religion, using the little-understood deployment by the US military of techniques of irregular warfare in Afghanistan, Iraq, and elsewhere.

Taking a term from Sir Halford Mackinder, the British founder of the theory of geopolitics, General David Petraeus, former Commander of the US Central Command that encompassed all Eurasia, including Afghanistan, declared, in 2009, that "Central Asia constitutes a pivotal location on the Eurasian continent between Russia, China, and South Asia."[10] For Mackinder a geopolitical pivot was a unique strategic land base enabling a power to control vast regions.

Petraeus introduced methods of irregular warfare, termed earlier by the British as Low Intensity Warfare, into US tactics in Iraq, Afghanistan, and Central Asia, first as head of Central Command and second as Director of the CIA, until he was forced to resign around a sex affair in November 2012.

The irregular warfare method was sometimes referred to as deploying "Gang/Counter-Gang." The essence was that the orchestrating intelligence agency or military occupying force, whether the British Army in Kenya in the 1950s against the Mau Mau rebellion or the CIA in Afghanistan, effectively controlled the actions of both sides in an internal conflict.

The irregular warfare cadre deliberately created small civil wars, gang wars, or broader regional wars, as in Syria after March 2011. The aim was to divide a target population with violence, thereby creating the pretext for outside military force in what the US deceptively renamed as "Peace-Keeping Operations," or PKOs. Grant Hammond of the US Air War College gave the game away when he referred to those US-led Peace Keeping Operations as "war by another name."[11]

Petraeus and USA military specialists targeted the divisions between various branches of Islam for their war by another name.

Rumsfeld, Petraeus, and Iraq's "Dirty War"

That method of creating a militant Jihadist terror climate across the Muslim world was used in Iraq after the US military occupation in 2004. It was introduced by then Defense Secretary Donald Rumsfeld. Rumsfeld ordered the leading American "dirty war" experts into Iraq to work with General Petraeus to foster internal civil war between different religious groups—Sunni against Shi'ite and Shi'ite against Sunni and Kurd—in order to entrench a firm US military control over Iraq.

It mattered not which side the CIA and Pentagon backed as long as the result was terror and more chaos. The aim was to foster permanent instability that would justify permanent US military presence, a presence that could stir the hornet's nest of hatreds at any time.

In May 2011, several years after leaving Washington, Rumsfeld delivered a speech on the War on Terrorism to an influential organization of right-wing Christian Fundamentalists called the Council of National Policy. He said, "We are going to have to be willing to engage in the battle of ideas. . . . We are going to have to screw up our courage and develop better skills at identifying our enemy—and our enemies are radical Islamists, let there be no doubt."[12]

In 2004, Rumsfeld personally ordered Colonel James Steele into Iraq to incite Low Intensity Warfare, or "Gang/Counter-Gang," in a program that was to do little other than to help create more "radical Islamists."

Steele, a US Special Forces veteran, was called to help organize paramilitary groups in Iraq. At the time, the CIA and Pentagon wanted to build up Shi'ite militias in Iraq as a force against secular Ba'ath Party nationalists loyal to Saddam Hussein by allowing them to join Iraqi security and police forces, including a Special Police Commando (SPC). The SPC included numerous members of the trained Badr brigades that had been set up in Iran in 1982 as the military wing of the Supreme Council for Islamic Revolution in Iraq (SCIRI).

US Army Special Forces Colonel James Steele trained Iraqi Shi'ite Jihadi Death Squads to torture and kill thousands of Iraqi Sunni Muslims for Washington, reporting only to Defense Secretary Don Rumsfeld.

Steele was a veteran of creating bloody, dirty wars in El Salvador and elsewhere. As US military adviser in El Salvador in 1980, he organized what was called the "Dirty War." In that war, a right-wing government backed by Washington fought a leftist insurgency in a 12-year carnage beginning in 1980, which cost more than 70,000 people killed in a country of only six million, most of them civilians.

Right-wing "Death Squads" organized by Steele and US Special Forces carried out most of the killing and torturing in El Salvador, including, according to an Amnesty International report in 2001, "extrajudicial executions, other unlawful killings, 'disappearances' and torture. . . . Whole villages were targeted by the armed forces and their inhabitants massacred." James Steele led a team of 55 US Special Forces "advisers" to the Salvador army.[13]

In 2004, Colonel Steele reappeared in Iraq, personally invited by US Defense Secretary Don Rumsfeld to again deploy his gruesome skills. Steele reported directly to Rumsfeld, a highly unusual practice, rather than through the command chain. He was also a long-time friend and associate of David Petraeus, who was then in charge of the Iraqi irregular warfare operations and, as later emerged, of the torture centers in Iraq including Abu Ghraib.

Adnan Thabit, commander of Iraq's Special Police Commandos, was in charge of the torture and killing machine Steele had organized. Petraeus ordered that Adnan's commandos should receive whatever arms, ammunition, and supplies they required and assigned Steele to work with them. It was only years later in a 2013 newspaper article that the truth emerged that Petraeus and Washington had been fully aware of the creation by Adnan and Steele of a network of torture centers, such as Abu Ghraib, across Iraq. Those torture centers did virtually nothing to yield valuable intelligence as claimed, but they very effectively fostered deep hatred and resentment of the US force presence in Iraq. They also laid the seeds for the later Sunni-Shi'ite war, Washington's longer-term goal of spreading chaos and dis-order across the oil-rich Middle East.

Muntadher al-Samari, an Iraqi General who worked with Steele, later recalled, "I remember a 14-year-old who was tied to one of the library's columns. And he was tied up, with his legs above his head. Tied up! His whole body was blue because of the impact of the cables with which he had been beaten."[14]

Rumsfeld was fully aware of the existence of the torture centers and endorsed them. It was Pentagon policy to foster religious civil war in Iraq using torture and US military terror against innocent civilians. The powerful faction of Washington neoconservatives and US Christian Fundamentalist right were creating their own Jihadist "enemy" in Iraq, deliberately.[15]

From 2004 until he was removed in 2006, General Adnan Thabit led the most feared counterinsurgency force, the Special Police Commandos, with some 5,000 troops under him. They murdered and tortured both Sunni insurgents and Shi'ite militias.

Adnan ordered videos of the torture of prisoners by his commandos to be aired on the American-financed *Al Iraqiya* national TV. The prisoners were shown with cuts and bruises from their torture. In one show, a former policeman with two black eyes confessed to killing two police officers in Samarra; a few days after the broadcast, the former policeman's family told reporters his corpse was delivered to them.[16]

The TV shows created a phenomenon that could only be described as a 21st century Roman *Circus Maximus*, where prisoners were filmed confessing to various crimes, from contract murders to sodomy, feeding the population's desire for revenge. Adnan was a Sunni, the Iraqi minority, as were most of the Iraqi insurgents.

Even by the criteria of the neoconservative Washington hawks and the CIA, their Iraq project was a devastating failure. At a US taxpayer cost of almost one trillion dollars, the human and economic costs were incalculable. More than a million US troops were deployed to Iraq, 4,483 were killed, 33,183 were wounded, and more than 200,000 came home with post-traumatic stress disorder. The number of Iraqi civilians killed—the final number is still unknown—counted at least 121,754 to have been killed directly during the US war, with hundreds of thousands more having died from crippling sanctions, diseases caused by dirty water when the US destroyed the water treatment system, and the inability to get medical help because of exploding violence from Petraeus' irregular war tactics—the "dirty war."[17]

That failure was simply ignored as the Pentagon moved General Petraeus, now deemed the "hero of the Iraq surge," on to Afghanistan to deal with the Taliban insurgency as the "architect of Iraqi success."

"Soldiers of Christ" Kill Islamic "Infidels"

Driving the fanaticism of the US military wars against Islamic terrorism was a US military that was saturated with Christian right-wing fundamentalist fanaticism and hate groups.

One of the most influential was a well-financed organization called Military Ministry, an affiliate of Campus Crusade for Christ. The Military Ministry had an annual budget of nearly $500 million. They had branch offices at all the main US Army bases, as well as overseas Bible study programs globally, a mirror of Gülen's Koran study groups. The Military

Ministry group's mission statement was "To Win, Build, and Send in the power of the Holy Spirit and to establish movements of spiritual multiplication in the worldwide military community."[18]

In 2005, at the peak of the Iraqi insurgency operations of Petraeus and Steele, Military Ministry's executive director, retired Army Major General Bob Dees, said the group, "must pursue our. . . means for transforming the nation—through the military. And the military may be the most influential way to affect that spiritual superstructure."[19] Indeed they had a deeper agenda than mere prayer meetings or church picnics.

Military Ministry inside the US military spread a crusader fanaticism. They cited the Bible to sanction killing in combat by "God's servant, an angel of wrath, to punish those who do evil." Military Ministry leaders would frequently refer publicly to US soldiers as "government-paid Missionaries for Christ." In one incident, it was revealed that a private contractor was supplying rifle scopes to the Defense Department imprinted with coded references to Christ-related biblical verses.[20]

The cocktail of hate and death was well mixed in Iraq by this select network out of Washington. They used a fanatical brew of fundamentalist Christianity to go against an equally fanatical Salafist Jihadism which US military destruction and torture in Iraq and Afghanistan was fostering. It was the trial application of a secret Pentagon plan to take military control of the entire oil-rich, strategically vital Middle East using the War on Terror as the means. That then would be spread across the entire Muslim world, from Afghanistan and Pakistan to Xinjiang in China, to Uzbekistan, to Chechnya and Dagestan in Russia, to Syria, Egypt, and Iran, and on to North Africa.

Secret Pentagon Plan

Using both Christian and Islamic militant fundamentalism was central to a secret Pentagon war plan developed inside the Rumsfeld Defense Department during the Bush-Cheney Administration.

In October 2007, Wesley Clark, retired US General and former military head of NATO, gave a talk at the Commonwealth Club in San Francisco. It was some four years after George W. Bush and the cabal of neoconservative war hawks around Paul Wolfowitz had made the decision to invade Saddam Hussein's Iraq. Clark revealed to his audience that the US occupation of Iraq was no spontaneous reaction to the attacks of September

11, 2001. He told his listeners that there had been a "policy coup" by the neoconservative hawks, together with Vice President Cheney and defense Secretary Don Rumsfeld.

In October 2001, a decade before the misnamed Arab Spring, Clark said that he had been shown a classified Pentagon memo from the Office of Defense Secretary Don Rumsfeld: "It says we're going to attack and destroy the governments in seven countries in five years—we're going to start with Iraq, and then we're going to move to Syria, Lebanon, Libya, Somalia, Sudan and Iran," Clark explained.[21] That was the secret Pentagon plan in October 2001. The ensuing fourteen years of events in those countries assumed a new dimension when viewed in that light.

Clark described the aim of the Pentagon neoconservatives' plot: "They wanted us to destabilize the Middle East, turn it upside down, make it under our control."[22] The role of the US military, Clark said, was to start conflicts, not prevent them. It went contrary to every precept of international law, the UN Charter, and contrary to what most Americans believed that their Constitution, that the American rule of law, and that their Government were about.

What General Wesley Clark described as a coup was indeed the hijacking of the massive American war machinery and, in fact, the entire foreign policy machinery by a private cabal of very powerful interests, above all the combined power of the military–industrial complex, a handful of Washington neoconservative think-tanks, and their close cousins in the major US and British oil companies.

With the end of the Cold War in 1990 and the ensuing collapse of the Soviet Union, the same cabal of aggressive policymakers urged then President George H. W. Bush to launch a push. Their aim was to, in effect, dominate the entire world. There was now no rival on the scene, they argued. The key figure pushing that aggressive agenda for a global US hegemony then was Paul Wolfowitz. The same Wolfowitz later reemerged as Deputy Defense Secretary in 2001 in the George W. Bush administration, architecting the Iraq invasion and shaping the Administration's War on Terror.

Paul Wolfowitz had worked in the Pentagon from 1989 to 1992, when Dick Cheney was Defense Secretary under President George H. W. Bush. During the later Clinton administration, Wolfowitz formulated a new foreign policy with regard to Iraq and other "potential aggressor states," dismissing containment in favor of "preemption"—strike first to eliminate even theoretically possible threats, a version of the old Wild West "shoot first and ask questions later."

In early 2002 Deputy Defense Secretary Wolfowitz and Defense Secretary Rumsfeld formulated and defined the Bush Doctrine. In effect, the doctrine legitimized unilateral aggression, which, in reality, was a doctrine of aggression to prevent what might or might not ever become a threat to the United States. Iraq, as was confirmed after the war, had never been a threat to the United States and had no weapons of mass destruction, nor had Afghanistan ever threatened the United States, regardless of whether or not the Afghan Taliban regime had given sanctuary to Osama bin Laden.

The US, according to the logic of the Bush Doctrine, was the only nation with power to decide to launch war or not, regardless of the UN Charter, the UN Security Council, or precepts of international law or diplomacy. It was an inherently dangerous doctrine: "Bomb them back to the stone-age before they even have time to think about asserting their power" was the implicit message.

In the aftermath of the end of the Soviet Union, Wolfowitz had authored an earlier version of his preventive war doctrine. In March 1992, the *Washington Post* printed a sensational story based on a leaked Pentagon document:

> In a classified blueprint intended to help "set the nation's direction for the next century," the Defense Department calls for concerted efforts to preserve American global military supremacy and to thwart the emergence of a rival superpower in Europe, Asia or the former Soviet Union. . . .
>
> In particular, the document. . . contemplates use of American military power to pre-empt or punish use of nuclear, biological or chemical weapons, "even in conflicts that otherwise do not directly engage US interests." Wolfowitz was the architect of that proposed 1992 policy. . . . The central strategy of the Pentagon framework is to "establish and protect a new order" that accounts "sufficiently for the interests of the advanced industrial nations to discourage them from challenging our leadership," while at the same time maintaining a military dominance capable of "**deterring potential competitors from**

even aspiring to a larger regional or global role."[23] (author's emphasis).

When that statement was properly understood, the entirety of United States military and foreign policy since the end of the Cold War began to take on an entirely different hue than the publicly proclaimed role of "America as world champion of democracy and human rights."

By the last decade of the 20th century, America's foreign policy architects were preoccupied with, in effect, creating a de facto global empire, even though they clothed the goal under the rubric of "spreading democracy and the free market." The Pentagon termed that Pax Americana "Full Spectrum Dominance."

The expansion of NATO into the countries of the former Soviet Union and Warsaw Pact was an integral part of that global strategy. The installation of aggressive US missile bases in Poland and of US ballistic missile-detecting radar in the Czech Republic and Turkey to monitor Russia's nuclear silos was a part of that global strategy. The creation of a new Pentagon command, AFRICOM, to block Chinese and Russian economic advances in Africa was also a part of that global strategy.

The most ambitious part of that Washington strategy outlined first in 1992 by Wolfowitz in order "to thwart the emergence of a rival superpower," however, was to emerge out of the US invasions of Afghanistan in 2001, of Iraq in 2003, and the covert US support for what came to be known as the Arab Spring in 2010. The Washington War on Islamic Terror, on Jihad, was the new "enemy image" for Washington war hawks and their Christian right supporters. Islamic Fundamentalism was to become, for some, the new crusade to replace the Cold War crusade against "Godless Communism."

Only a small handful of people in and around Washington policy circles fully grasped the explosive power inside the Muslim world that the US War on Terror would ignite. That US War on Terror was a coldly calculated strategy by a group of very bad and very powerful people in Washington and elsewhere to poke a very big, sharp stick into a giant hornet's nest.

The hornet's nest was built on decades of Muslim rage going back to the First World War almost a century before. Washington, or rather some very powerful circles in Washington, believed they could weaponize militant Jihadist Islam and aim it directly at the states of Eurasia, as well as at

Europe, to divide and rule the Eurasian space in order to prevent the rise of what Brzezinski called the Eurasian Challenge.

Endnotes

1   Zbigniew Brzezinski, *The Grand Chessboard: American Primacy And It's Geostrategic Imperatives*, 1997, Basic Books, p. xiv.

2   Ibid., p. 30.

3   Ibid., p. 31.

4   Ibid.

5   Alfred W. McCoy et al., 1972, *The Politics of Heroin in Southeast Asia: CIA complicity in the global drug trade*, 1972, New York, Harper & Row, p. 464 ff.

6   F. William Engdahl, *Kyrgyzstan's* . . . op. cit.

7   The Economist, *Drug addiction in Iran: The other religion—Why so many young Iranians are hooked on hard drugs*, Economist August 17, 2013, accessed in http://www.economist.com/news/middle-east-and-africa/21583717-why-so-many-young-iranians-are-hooked-hard-drugs-other-religion.

8   UNODC, *Illicit Drug Trends in the Russian Federation* (UNODC Regional Office for Russia and Belarus, April, 2008), p. 20, accessed in http://www.unodc.org/documents/regional/central-asia/Illicit%20Drug%20Tr...

9   United Nations Office on Drugs and Crime, *Opiate Flows Through Northern Afghanistan and Central Asia: A Threat Assessment*, (UNODC Afghan Opiate Trade Project of the Studies and Threat Analysis Section (STAS), Division for Policy Analysis and Public Affairs, May 2012), p. 85, accessed in http://www.unodc.org/documents/data-and-analysis/Studies/Afghanistan_nor...

10 General David H. Petreus, US Army, Commander US Central Command, *Statement to Senate Armed Services Committee on the Afghanistan-Pakistan Strategic Posture Review and the Posture of US Central Command*, April 1, 2009, accessed in http://www.centcom.mil/en/countries/aor/kazakhstan/.

11 F. William Engdahl, *Kyrgyzstan's "Roza Revolution": Washington, Moscow, Beijing and the Geopolitics of Central Asia*, 26 May 2010, accessed in http://www.engdahl.oilgeopolitics.net/print/Kyrgyzstan%20Part%20II.pdf.

12   Donald Rumsfeld, *Known and Unkown*, CNP, May 2011, accessed in http://www.cfnp.org/Page.aspx?pid=445.

13   Mona Mahmood, et al., *Revealed: Pentagons link to Iraqi torture centres—Exclusive: General David Petraeus and 'dirty wars' veteran behind commando units implicated in detainee abuse*, The Guardian, 6 March 2013, accessed in http://www.theguardian.com/world/2013/mar/06/pentagon-iraqi-torture-centres-link.

14   Mona Mahmood et al., *Revealed: Pentagon's link to Iraqi torture centres*, The Guardian, 6 March 2013, accessed in http://www.theguardian.com/world/2013/mar/06/pentagon-iraqi-torture-centres-link.

15   Elisabeth Braw, *Donald Rumsfeld On bin Laden Iraq torture Pakistan*, May 18, 2011, accessed in http://www.metro.us/newyork/news/international/2011/05/18/donald-rumsfeld-on-bin-laden-iraq-torture-pakistan/.

16   Peter Maass, *The Way of the Commandos*, New York Times magazine, May 1, 2005, accessed in http://www.nytimes.com/2005/05/01/magazine/01ARMY.html?_r=0&pagewanted=print&position=.

17   Phyllis Bennis, *Way Worse Than a Dumb War: Iraq Ten Years Later*, The Nation, March 18, 2013, accessed in http://www.thenation.com/blog/173396/way-worse-dumb-war-iraq-ten-years-later#.

18   Stephen Glain, *Backward Christian Soldiers*, The Nation, February 28, 2011, accessed In http://www.thenation.com/article/158462/backward-christian-soldiers?page=full#axzz2ePPujziS.

19   Ibid.

20   Ibid.

21   Wesley Clark, *Winning Modern Wars* (New York: Public Affairs, 2003), p. 130.

22   Ibid.

23   Barton Gellman, *Keeping the U.S. First; Pentagon Would Preclude a Rival Superpower*, Washington Post, March 11, 1992.

CHAPTER THREE

ROOTS OF ISLAMIC RAGE: SYKES-PICOT, BALFOUR AND BRITISH PERFIDY

"All political leadership of the time depended on Islam for legitimacy and all political leaders were pro-British. Islam was a tool to legitimize the rule, tyranny and corruption of Arab leaders. To the West, Islam was acceptable; it could be and was used."

> —Said K. Aburish, Palestinian historian, on Islam's relationship with the West after the Great War

"One nation solemnly promised to a second nation the country of a third. More than that, the country was still part of the Empire of a fourth, namely Turkey."

> —Arthur Koestler, Jewish author, on the Balfour Declaration between England and Lord Rothschild for a Palestinian Jewish homeland

"I risked the fraud on my conviction that Arab help was necessary to our cheap and speedy victory in the East, and that better we win and break our word, than lose."

> —T.E. Lawrence (Lawrence of Arabia) on the perfidy of Sykes-Picot secret accord to carve up the Arab Middle East as he advised Hussein's forces in the successful Arab Revolt.

Decay of the Ottoman Empire

The modern wellspring of Arab Muslim rage against the Christian West that George W. Bush's War on Terror was able to tap into, his "holy crusade" as he termed it, had deep roots. It went back to the Great War of 1914–1918, when certain Arab Muslim clan leaders trusted the promise of the Christian—at least from their Muslim point of view—British Empire. British politicians and military officials had promised leading Arabs within the Ottoman Turkish Empire that they would win their independence from foreign rule were they to help England defeat Germany and the German-allied Ottoman Empire of Sultan Mehmed V.

The Turkish Ottoman Empire had been one of the most powerful and successful empires in the world for more than six centuries. They had maintained their rule over disparate cultures, ethnic groupings, and religious peoples by allowing subjected peoples in the peripheral conquered lands to retain their religion, language, and customs. They did so by carefully cultivating the ruling elites from the various religious minorities throughout the empire and by dominating the religious establishment.[1]

However, in the decades up to the outbreak of World War I, as the Ottoman state fell into deeper and deeper debt to European bankers, the governments of Britain and France, the two largest creditors, used that foreign indebtedness to bind the Ottoman state and take control over the vast wealth of Empire. The Ottoman Empire became debt slaves of the Europeans. One consequence was higher taxes across the empire. Another was centralized control to collect those taxes and elimination of the ethnic and language and religious freedoms of before. The Sultan and his court began to impose Turkish language and culture on their subjects, something that grated deeply on the Arabs.

Into this decay of the Ottoman Empire and growing resentment of the states on the periphery toward the Sultanate in Istanbul, the British were cunning and unscrupulous in taking every opening through deceit and perfidy to gain large parts of the empire for its own.

British Prime Minister Benjamin Disraeli had promised to support restoration of Ottoman territories on the Balkan Peninsula during the 1878 Congress of Berlin in return for winning from Turkey the control of the vital island of Cyprus. It was an empty British promise as Cyprus became a British naval base.

Then, in 1882, the British told the Ottoman government it was sending British troops into Egypt to "restore order for Constantinople (Istanbul)" by putting down the Urabi military officers' revolt. Army officers led by Ahmed Urabi had begun to take control of the government, and soon Egypt was in the hands of nationalists opposed to European domination of the country. The new army-controlled revolutionary government began nationalizing all assets, especially those of the Europeans living in Egypt. The British retook control of Egypt only to use their military presence to take Egypt and the strategic Suez Canal from the hapless Ottoman Sultan.[2]

The perfidious British were under no apparent moral constraint to change their habit of using deceit and lies to win their wars of conquest as the Empire spread across the globe. After all, they reasoned, they were the world's greatest imperial power and its greatest "benefactor."

As the British imperialist poet Rudyard Kipling expressed it in his 1899 poem of the same name, it was the British colonial "white man's burden." The burden, as Kipling justified bloody British imperial rule, was, in fact, a moral "duty" of the English to "civilize" the more brutish and barbaric parts of the world. Civilize them with bayonets and mass killings if needed.

Kipling originally wrote his poem "White Man's Burden" for the British Queen's Jubilee. He later rededicated it to a United States elite that had just completed its first imperial conquest, the Philippines, taking it from a bankrupt Spain in the Spanish-American war of 1898. In his reworked poem, Kipling implored the Americans not to recoil from accepting that "white man's burden" of "civilizing the barbarian peoples" of the less-developed world. He described the captured natives as "new-caught, sullen peoples, half devil and half child."[3]

That haughty attitude was endemic in the leading figures of the British Empire and increasingly with their American cousins. It implied a religious superiority of European Christian culture to that of what they saw as the inferior peoples of the under-developed colonial world of the south. If you lorded over races and peoples who you regarded as sub-human slaves, you need not have moral pangs of conscience. Anything was possible.

British imperialists were also pragmatists who used whatever ruse necessary to win gains of new imperial conquest, and in the 1914 Great War, no potential conquest was greater for the British Empire than capturing the crown jewels of the Ottoman Empire, especially the oil rich fields of

Mesopotamia, or modern-day Iraq, and the strategic Palestine lands as spoils of war.

Ottoman Empire into Debt Slavery

Sultan Abdul Hamid II, the spiritual and political head of the Ottoman Empire, a religious Islamic Caliphate, had been maneuvered in 1881 by British and French creditor banks and governments into accepting creation of foreign bankers' control over the national debt through something called the Public Debt Administration. Housed in Istanbul, the new European debt collection agency—acting in every respect as the International Monetary Fund was to act a century later to collect the debts of the Third World—held virtual control over Ottoman state revenues. It had a board representing British, Dutch, German, Austro-Hungarian, Italian, and other Turkish bondholders. The administration had power to collect directly from tax revenues to repay the debt of the Ottoman state to the foreign creditor banks, independently of the Ottoman government.[4]

The debt bondage was draining Turkish finances to repay French and City of London banks and, in the process, was weakening the financial ability of Istanbul to control its far-flung empire. In fact, that weakening was precisely the aim of the British to prepare for the looting of the vast wealth of the Ottoman Empire.

In 1899, Britain took advantage of the growing financial troubles of the Sultan and defiantly signed a secret 99-year treaty with the Sheikh of Kuwait, making Britain, in effect, the Sheikh of Kuwait's colonial protector and ruler. In 1901, British warships off the Kuwait coast dictated to the Turkish government that, from then on, they must consider the Persian Gulf port below the Shaat al-Arab, today's Kuwait, controlled by the Anaza tribe of Sheikh Mubarak al-Sabah, to be a "British protectorate." Turkey was too economically and militarily weak at that point to do anything.[5]

The Ottoman debt collection model of a foreign banker controlled Public Debt Administration was used again after World War I by the British and French against defeated Germany under control of an Allied Reparations Committee that, in 1924, took control over German state finances under the American-authored Dawes Plan to ensure payment of war reparations to Britain, France, and, ultimately, to J.P. Morgan bank in New York.[6]

Owing to her huge foreign debt burdens and economic troubles, the Ottoman Empire had declined in extent to a territory consisting of only modern-day Turkey, the Middle East, and the Arabian coast. It had lost territories of the Caucasus, Crimea, the Balkans, and the Mediterranean islands. . . and the tax revenues that they had paid to the Sultanate.

Lawrence and the Arab Revolt

Under financial stress, the Sultanate abandoned their successful policy of cultural autonomy in the empire. Increasing financial pressure from the European bank creditors on Istanbul resulted in sharply increasing taxes across the Arab and other parts of the empire. Earlier successful Turkish policies of allowing cultural and language autonomy ended under the growing financial pressures, and Istanbul rule became more brutal. That squeeze sowed the seeds of the Arab revolt against Ottoman Turkey.

As a reaction to the increased severity of life under Istanbul rule, the Arabs in the Ottoman Empire began organizing secret Arab nationalist societies to oppose Istanbul oppression. Sherif Hussein ibn Ali was Emir of the Muslim holy city of Mecca. Mecca was the birthplace of the Prophet Muhammad and revered across the Islamic world as the site of Muhammad's first revelation of the Quran. It was a city in the Hejaz, the western strip of the Arabian Peninsula near the Red Sea. Some of Sherif Hussein's fellow Arab tribal leaders asked him to lead an Arab revolt against the increasingly oppressive Sultanate rule. Hussein sent his son Abdullah to meet with Arab nationalists in Syria and then to Cairo to determine whether the British would aid such an Arab uprising.

The reply was positive. British Secretary of State for War Lord Kitchener appealed to Hussein to fight with the British, French, and Russian Triple Entente against Ottoman Turkey, which had joined the Great War on the side of the German Empire.

In letters with British High Commissioner in Egypt Henry McMahon, Hussein demanded and got a written promise of recognition of an Arab nation that included the Hejaz and other adjacent territories, as well as approval for the proclamation of an Arab Caliphate of Islam independent from the Turkish Sultanate. McMahon had promised that, in return for Hussein's fighting on the British side to overthrow Ottoman rule, Hussein would be rewarded by an Arab empire encompassing the entire span between Egypt and Persia, with the exception of British imperial possessions and interests in Kuwait, Aden, and the Syrian coast.[7]

Hussein thereby began what would become known as the Great Arab Revolt against Ottoman control in 1916. Soon, he was approached by an enigmatic British military intelligence agent named T.E. Lawrence, later known in popular news accounts as Lawrence of Arabia. Lawrence, a highly unconventional figure, trained Hussein's ragtag contingent of Bedouins and other desert nomads how to use dynamite in their attacks on the Hejaz railway that brought Turkish soldiers and munitions into the Arab lands of the Arabian Desert.

Initially, the Ottoman forces, advised by the German military General Liman von Sanders, had a significant superiority owing to German arms and air power. Their Achilles heel, however, was the long logistics supply line via the Hejaz Railroad, or the Damascus-Medina Railway, and that was precisely where the daring Lawrence aimed his deadly sabotage with Hussein's Bedouins with great success.[8]

At the same time the British were promising Hussein and his Hashemite tribesmen their rule over a new Arab Caliphate in return for their joining England's war against the Ottoman empire, they were making similar promises of independence to the bitter rival of Hussein, Ibn Saud, a Bedouin tribal leader of legendary ferocity against his desert foes. In reality the perfidious British were selling the same horse twice to gain their goal.

Major General Percy Cox, British Colonial Administrator in the Middle East, was sent to determine if England should back Ibn Saud's nomadic forces as a second flank in their proxy war against the Ottoman rule. After meeting with the Bedouin leader, Cox signed an Anglo-Saudi Friendship Treaty with Ibn Saud, a deeply fundamentalist follower of a merciless and harsh sect known as Wahhabi within Sunni Islam.

The treaty, signed in December 1915, explicitly acknowledged Ibn Saud as head of a Saudi state and gave the Arab leader the guarantee of British "protection" in any revolt against Istanbul, promising him rifles and money to buy the services of fellow Bedouins. The only problem was that Ibn Saud's bitter foe, Hashemite Sherif Hussein of Mecca, had just declared himself "King of the Arabs," of all Arabs, including Ibn Saud and his Bedouin Wahhabis.[9]

The British foreign office made no attempt to unite the two Arab leaders. Instead, they sent different agents to handle each separately: St John Philby, father of Kim Philby, to handle Ibn Saud, and T.E. Lawrence for Hussein.

Sykes-Picot and British Perfidy

Not only did the British knowingly back two bitter Arab foes in order to defeat the Turkish forces, but at the same time they secretly signed an agreement with the French and Czarist Russia to later divide those "newly independent" Arab lands among themselves after the war.

In February 1916, ignoring the many promises to their new Arab allies in the war, the British Foreign Office's Sir Mark Sykes and French diplomat Georges Picot worked out a secret postwar deal. It called for the carving up of the lands of the Arab Muslim Middle East. Under the secret agreement, later known as Sykes-Picot for its two authors, Russia would take northern Turkey, including Persia; Italy got southern Turkey and the Dodecanese Islands. Modern Syria and Lebanon went to France, and pretty much everything else, especially the oil-rich lands of Iraq and Kuwait, were to be British colonies. Outside of the vast desert lands of the Arabian Peninsula, the Arabs were not to be allowed to keep the lands their blood had liberated.[10]

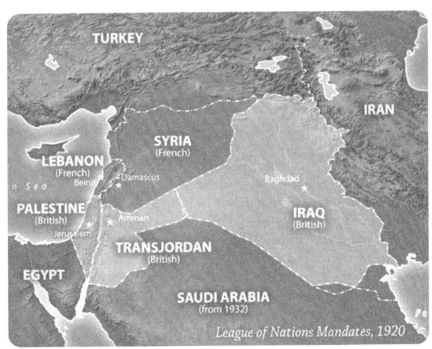

The secret Sykes-Picot British–French pact to carve up the Middle East was a Great Betrayal for the Arabs.

Following the Bolshevik Revolution of November 1917, Russia ended the British-French alliance against Germany. At that point, the new government in Moscow discovered the secret Sykes-Picot Agreement and immediately made it public, showing—for all the world to see—that the Arabs were double-crossed for their support of the British and French war. Sykes-Picot placed the most educated and most developed areas of the Arab world, which were hungry for independence, into the grips of the European colonial powers, sowing a mistrust and hate toward the West that lasted until the 21st century.

T.E. Lawrence (Lawrence of Arabia) knew about the perfidy as he advised Hussein's forces in the successful Arab Revolt but kept it secret. Later he wrote, "I risked the fraud on my conviction that Arab help was necessary to our cheap and speedy victory in the East, and that better we win and break our word, than lose."[11]

A few weeks after the Bolsheviks released the text of the Sykes-Picot betrayal of the Arabs, London also changed its policy of support for Ibn Saud, cutting his supply of promised guns and funds. As he watched British forces leave Arabia, he bitterly remarked, "Who after this will put their trust in you?"[12] The British double cross in Sykes-Picot against Ibn Saud cut deep, perhaps even deeper than that against Hussein.

Lord Balfour's Bizarre Declaration

The next betrayal of England's Arab allies came almost immediately after the exposure of the secret Sykes-Picot text.

On October 31, 1917, some 150,000 British forces led by General Allenby had captured Beer Sheba, thereby opening all of Palestine to British military occupation. Once news reached London, Britain's Foreign Secretary Arthur Balfour reportedly reached into his desk to pull out a secret letter that had been drafted earlier. He then published the letter with an altered date of November 2, 1917. More curiously, he addressed it to the powerful London banking scion, Walter Lord Rothschild, with a request it be sent on to the World Zionist Federation, whose head was Chaim Weizmann. It became known as the Balfour Declaration and read:

Foreign Office, November 2nd, 1917

Dear Lord Rothschild,

I have much pleasure in conveying to you on behalf of His Majesty's Government the following declaration of sympathy with Jewish Zionist aspirations, which has been submitted to and approved by the Cabinet:

"His Majesty's Government view with favour the establishment in Palestine of a national home for the Jewish people, and will use their best endeavours to facilitate the achievement of this object, it being clearly understood that nothing shall be done which may prejudice the civil and religious rights of existing non-Jewish communities in Palestine or the rights and political status enjoyed by Jews in any other country."

I should be grateful if you would bring this Declaration to the knowledge of the Zionist Federation.

Yours sincerely,
Arthur James Balfour[13]

The text of the letter was published in the press one week later, on November 9, 1917. The "Balfour Declaration" was later incorporated into the 1920 Sèvres Peace Treaty with the Ottoman Empire as the British claimed a League of Nations Mandate for Palestine. As Jewish historian and author Arthur Koestler noted of the declaration between Balfour and Rothschild, "one nation solemnly promised to a second nation the country of a third. More than that, the country was still part of the Empire of a fourth, namely Turkey."[14]

Humiliation of Sèvres

In August 1920, the governments of Great Britain, France, and Italy met at Sèvres in France to carve up the defeated Ottoman Empire as spoils of victory. Russia was excluded because the German-financed Bolshevik Revolution of 1917 had put Russia into a hostile camp. The United States had withdrawn into isolationism, leaving Sevres to become a carving up of the Arab Middle East by European imperial powers. The agreement among

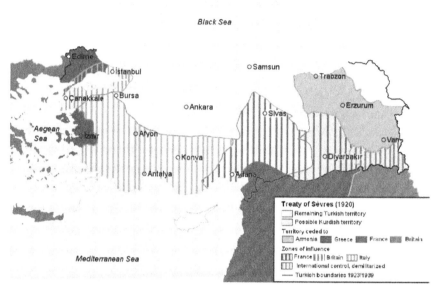

The 1920 Treaty of Sèvres, in broad respects, defined the tensions of Muslim Middle East for almost a century after World War I.

the victors, largely following the secret Sykes-Picot map, sealed the fate of millions of Arab Muslims for the following century, if not more.

Britain and France had already decided what would happen to the area generally referred to as the "Middle East." Britain took control of Palestine in the form of a League of Nations Mandate, as intended by the Balfour Declaration.

France took Syria, Lebanon, and land in southern Anatolia. East and West Anatolia were declared "areas of French influence." This had already been decided some three years before the Treaty of Sèvres in the secret Sykes-Picot Agreement. Britain also took over Iraq and got generous oil concessions there via the Turkish Petroleum Company which the British grabbed from the Germans as spoils of war. It was later renamed the Iraq Petroleum Company.

The Kingdom of Hejaz—Saudi Arabia—was given formal international recognition as an independent kingdom, with Mecca and Medina as its most important cities. Oil had not yet been discovered there. Armenia was recognized as a separate sovereign state.

The treatment of defeated Turkey under the treaty was comparable to the Allied victors' treatment of Germany at Versailles, with the entire finances of Turkey placed in control of Britain and France. The Treaty of Sèvres by design failed to deal with the issue of an independent Kurdistan as the Kurdish population, while concentrated inside the new borders of Turkey, also spilled over into Iran, Iraq, and Syria, leaving one of the world's largest ethnic groups with no national borders, convenient to the British and French occupiers as a source of unending tensions. And British troops occupied large parts of western Iran, which was not part of Ottoman Empire but was where they had extracted a 99-year lease on the vast oil riches for the British government-owned Anglo-Persian Oil Company, later to be known as British Petroleum, or BP.

No other power had managed to emerge from the postwar carve-up of the Ottoman Empire with more gain than the British. England had won the vast known oilfields of the newly formed Iraq. Britain had already de facto annexed Kuwait in 1899 well before the war for its oil. Britain had de facto annexed Egypt when she formally declared her Protectorate over Egypt in 1914 at the outbreak of the war and her control over the vital Suez Canal and Sudan.

And Great Britain had also managed to get what Lord Balfour promised to Lord Rothschild, "the establishment in Palestine of a national home for the Jewish people." In 1917, British forces had taken Jerusalem. The Versailles Peace Conference concluded agreements that as well founded a new international organization, the League of Nations, whose bureaucracy would be British-dominated. As a result, Great Britain got governing control of Palestine as a League of Nations Mandate territory.

Sir Halford Mackinder, founder of British imperial geopolitics and a fervent backer of the Balfour Declaration, wrote at the time that the Arab world, which he termed a "passage-land," was central to the British project of a global Empire, their new world order. In prose with deep religious, mystical overtones, Mackinder remarked, "the hill citadel of Jerusalem has a strategic position with reference to world-realities, not differing essentially from its ideal position in the perspective of the Middle Ages, or its strategic position between ancient Babylon and Egypt."[15]

Mackinder believed that the "ideal position" of Jerusalem as the center of the world in medieval Crusader maps was no religious quirk but an inspired understanding of the unique geopolitical nature of the place. In his words,

"In a monkish map, contemporary with the Crusades, which still hangs in Hereford Cathedral, Jerusalem is marked as at the geometrical centre, the navel, of the world, and on the floor of the Church of the Holy Sepulchre at Jerusalem they will show you to this day the precise spot which is the centre. . . The medieval ecclesiasts were not far wrong."[16]

In his book *Democratic Ideals and Reality*, written in 1919 as a roadmap for the geopolitical world domination strategy of the postwar British Empire, Mackinder declared,

> There are certain strategical positions in the Heartland and Arabia which must be treated as of world importance, for their possession may facilitate or prevent a World domination. . . It follows, therefore, that Palestine, Syria, and Mesopotamia, the Bosporus and the Dardanelles, and the outlets from the Baltic must be internationalized in some manner. In the case of Palestine, Syria, and Mesopotamia, it has been understood that Britain and France would undertake international trusts.
>
> The Jewish National seat in Palestine will be one of the most important outcomes of the War. That is a subject on which we can now afford to speak the truth. The Jew, for many centuries shut up in the Ghetto, and shut out of most honourable positions in Society. . . Therefore a National Home, at the physical and historical centre of the world, should make the Jew "range" himself. Standards of judgment, brought to bear on Jews by Jews, should result, even among those large Jewish communities which will remain as Going Concerns outside Palestine. This, however, will imply the frank acceptance of the position of a Nationality, which some Jews seek to forget.[17]

Indeed, that Balfour Jewish homeland in Palestine would prove to be a cause of seemingly unending conflict between Muslim Arabs and Palestinian Jews, a trigger for countless wars and revolts. It would provide a new source of Muslim Arab rage against not only Palestinian Jews as they settled there in the 1920s but also against Christian Europe for enabling that incursion. As Arabs and, especially, Ibn Saud of the new Saudi Arabia saw it, it was an unholy incursion, a theft of Muslim homelands. With their Palestine

Mandate, Britain had at its control means to explode the simmering tensions in the Middle East as it chose.

British Model of Islamic Despotism

By the end of the First World War, London and the British oil companies—Anglo-Persian Oil Co. and Royal Dutch Shell—had largely achieved their combined goals of carving up the vast territories of the Ottoman Empire in order to balkanize and dominate the Arab oil lands at the dawn of the petroleum era. Now, they had to make sure of their continued control.

To insure that continued control, the British directly chose and installed in power corrupt and ruthless despots dependent on British financial and, above all, military backing. They were hand-picked despots who used the most reactionary form of the Islamic religion as their legitimation to suppress any and all dissent. Here began a fascination of the British Secret Intelligence Services with how they might use that force of reactionary Islamic ideology as a political force against any indigenous democratic and intelligent future threats to their domination.

In the first years after World War I, despite the humiliating fact that the Arab leaders Ibn Saud and Sherif Hussein had been cheated and betrayed, they were still dependent on the British support to allow them any type of rule over the Arab masses. Ibn Saud was the leader of the Wahhabi sect. The British used his influence as a religious and military figure and funded his conquest of all of Arabia with a band of British-financed Bedouin Wahhabite mercenaries.

Ibn Saud had come to control the vast deserts of Saudi Arabia through leading a group of warriors called the Ikhwan, Arabic for "brothers," a Wahhabite Islamic religious militia made up of Bedouin tribes whose ultra-strict version of Islam went back to the 1700s.

Approximately the year 1745, Muhammad bin Abd al-Wahhab, a religious extremist with a radical interpretation of the Koran, found refuge in an oasis in the Najd desert controlled by the Al Saud clan. There clan leader Muhammad bin Saud adopted al-Wahhab's strict interpretation of Islam and his literal interpretation of the Sharia, or Koranic law. For al-Wahhab, all forms of poetry, music, jewels, tobacco, or any novelties were strictly prohibited. Any other cult or faith believing in saints or intermediary spirits was condemned. Adulterous women were stoned to death. The hands of thieves were cut off and the Wahhabites enforced five daily prayer sessions.

The militant Wahhabism, bound in alliance with the warriors of bin Saud, spread by the sword to Shi'ite regions of Oman, into Qatar, into Kuwait and Bahrain. Some forty years later, they conquered Yemen, the Syrian desert, and what is today southern Iraq, fighting against the forces of the Ottoman Empire, or Caliphate. Some one hundred years later, ibn Saud would join a new crusade, this time with the British, to regain territories lost to Ottoman Constantinople in 1811.[18]

The Saudi Ikhwan, under the command of Ibn Saud since 1915, declared that they were dedicated to the purification and the unification of all Islam under their strict observance of Sharia.[19]

At that time the Hashemites of Sherif Hussein were the strongest traditional Arab force, but their back was broken when Ibn Saud threw them out of the Muslim holy cities of Mecca and Medina. In their "pity," the British then placed Hussein's sons, Abdallah and Faisal, in control as British puppets over Jordan and Iraq.

These Hashemite princes were outsiders to the peoples there, to say the least, but the British played the religion card for all it was worth and justified their actions to the Arab people through the Hashemite lineage that claimed it traced back to Mohammed.[20]

In 1921 the British used Islam in Palestine as well when they manipulated the election of their man, Haj Amin al-Husseini, to the post of Grand Mufti of Jerusalem. They backed al-Husseini, a cunning opportunist, in order to give an Islamic façade to their control to quell unrest once the Bolsheviks had leaked the secret details of the French-British Sykes-Picot Agreement. In Palestine, almost all of the elite Arab families quickly found it profitable to be pro-British. The Grand Mufti was as well, at least until 1936, when the imminent establishment of a Jewish Israel forced him to organize a murderous campaign of terror against the new Jewish settlers.

On Islam's relationship with the West after the Great War, Palestinian historian Said K. Aburish noted, "All political leadership of the time depended on Islam for legitimacy and all political leaders were pro-British. Islam was a tool to legitimize the rule, tyranny and corruption of Arab leaders. To the West, Islam was acceptable; it could be and was used." [21]

After 1919 that British imperial model was one of an informal, sometimes hidden colonialism by controlling brutal, reactionary, dependent

Arab despots. And the British and French colonial rulers had made certain that they were despots whose legitimacy over the newly created artificial Arab states depended entirely on the military power behind them from London or Paris.

The Arab despots acted as British surrogates in the British League of Nations Mandate territories, or British "areas of influence." Britain used the Arab despots to politically control the region and its vast oil riches, as well as guarding the Suez Canal in Egypt as the route to India.

Through various manipulations the British and French imperial regimes had made certain after World War I that there were no legitimate popular Arab regimes under their dominion but rather a group of dictatorships representing small minorities with no claim to genuine, popular legitimacy. Ibn Saud was given British money and guns to impose the rule by his Bedouins adhering to the ultraconservative Wahhabite Islamic sect, even though they represented a mere twenty percent of all Saudis. The French applied a similar regime in the Levant, imposing a Maronite Christian minority rule which banned any non-Maronite from high office, even though the Maronites composed a mere twenty percent of the largely Muslim land.[22] Iraq, Syria, and the other lands of Arab Middle East grabbed from Ottoman Turkey after the First World War were controlled in a similar way.

That calculated strategy of foreign domination ensured that those Arab dictators were utterly dependent on support from the more powerful European imperial powers to maintain their grip on power contrary to the wishes of the vast majority of their Arab peoples to develop genuine, legitimate representative governments responsive to the majority of the populations.[23]

The British-dependent Arab despots used religion in the form of an ultraconservative brand of Islam. None was more repressive than the sect of Wahhabism in Saudi Arabia. That repression in the name of Islam created a climate of simmering rage.

That rage was instrumentalized and politicized by the cultivation of an increasingly intolerant brand of political Islam that soon began to spread under the harsh conditions of postwar Egypt. It was a secret society to become known as the Society of the Muslim Brothers, or, in Arabic, *al-'Ikhwān al-Muslimūn*. That Muslim Brotherhood survived into the 21st century as the most powerful organized force in the Muslim world. Its origins were revealing as they were alarming.

Endnotes

1   Şerif Mardin, *Center-Periphery Relations: A Key to Turkish Politics?*, Daedalus, Vol. 102, No. 1, Post-Traditional Societies (Winter, 1973), pp. 169–190.

2   A.J.P. Taylor, *The Struggle for mastery in Europe, 1848–1918*, Oxford: Oxford University Press (1955), pp. 228–54.

3   Rudyard Kipling, *The White Man's Burden: The United States & The Philippine Islands, 1899*, Rudyard Kipling's Verse: Definitive Edition (Garden City, New York: Doubleday, 1929).

4   Encyclopedia of the Ottoman Empire, *Debt and the Public Debt Administration in the Ottoman Empire*, accessed in http://www.fofweb.com/History/Hist RefMain.asp?iPin=EOE172&SID=2&DatabaseName=Modern+World+ History+Online&InputText=%22Mahmud+II%22&SearchStyle=& dTitle=debt+and+the+Public+Debt+Administration+in+the+Ottoman+ Empire&TabRecordType=Subject+Entry&BioCountPass=16&Sub CountPass=56&DocCountPass=0&ImgCountPass=1&MapCountPass= 0&FedCountPass=&MedCountPass=1&NewsCountPass=0&RecPosition =52&AmericanData=&WomenData=&AFHCData=&IndianData=& WorldData=Set&AncientData=&GovernmentData=.

5   F. William Engdahl, *A Century of War: Anglo-American Oil Politics and the New World Order*, 2010, edition.engdahl, Wiesbaden, pp. 24–25.

6   Ibid., pp. 69–73.

7   Avi Shlaim, *Lion of Jordan*, page 2, London, Penguin Books, Ltd.

8   O'Brien Browne, *Creating Chaos: Lawrence of Arabia and the 1916 Arab Revolt*, MHQ magazine, August 10, 2010, accessed in http://www.historynet.com/ creating-chaos-lawrence-of-arabia-and-the-1916-arab-revolt.htm

9   Robert Lacey, *The Kingdom: Saudi Arabia and the House of Saud*, 1983, Avon Books, New York, pp. 124–127.

10 Ibid., pp. 134–5.

11 T.E. Lawrence, *Seven Pillars of Wisdom*, London, Cape, 1935, p. 24.

12 Quoted in Elizabeth Monroe, *Britain's Moment in the Middle East: 1914–56*, London, Chatto, 1963, p. 93.

13   Yapp, M.E. , *The Making of the Modern Near East 1792–1923*, England, Longman, p. 290.

14   Arthur Koestler, cited in, *Britain's Zionists Prepare the Ground*, accessed in http://www.1948.org.uk/preparing-the-ground/

15   Halford Mackinder, cited in Israel Shamir, *Why Palestine is Important*, accessed in http://www.israelshamir.net/English/Why_Palestine.htm

16   Ibid.

17   Halford J. Mackinder, *Democratic Ideals and Reality: A Study in the Politics of Reconstruction*, 1919, London, Constable & Co., pp. 223–227.

18   Jean-Charles Brisard and Guillaume Dasquie, *Forbidden Truth*, 2002, Nation Books, New York, pp. 64–65.

19   Wilfred Thesiger, *Arabian Sands*, Penguin, 1991, pp. 248–249.

20   Said K. Aburish, *A Brutal Friendship: The West and The Arab Elite*, London, 1998, St Martins' Griffin, p. 57.

21   Ibid.

22   Ibid., pp. 14–16.

23   Ibid., pp. 13–14.

CHAPTER FOUR

"DEATH IN THE SERVICE OF ALLAH": THE MUSLIM BROTHERS ARE BORN

"Allah is our goal; The Prophet is our Leader; The Qur'an is our Constitution; Jihad is our Way; Death in the service of Allah is the loftiest of our wishes; Allah is Great; Allah is Great."

—Credo of the Society of Muslim Brothers of Egyptian Hassan al-Banna

"Victory can only come with the mastery of the 'Art of Death.' A martyr's death fighting for establishment of the new Caliphate is the shortest and easiest step from this life to the life hereafter."

—Hassan al-Banna, founder of the Muslim Brotherhood

British Egypt

Onset of demonstrations and protests in Tunisia in December 2010 set into motion something later termed by the popular mainstream western media as the "Arab Spring." Those protests spread rapidly across the entire Muslim world. Millions of disaffected students, intellectuals, trade unionists, ordinary men and women, took to the streets to demand freedom, democracy, and a better life. Many demanded an end to the dictatorships they had lived under since the end of the First World War, when the colonial powers artificially carved out vassal states across the Middle East.

Little noticed, initially, was the fact that behind every Arab Spring regime change, from Tunisia to Egypt, to Libya, and later to Syria, one organization invariably emerged out of the shadows to push aside the poorly organized democratic protestors and to take center stage. That organization was the Muslim Brotherhood, or al-'Ikḥwān al-Muslimūn.

The Muslim Brotherhood enjoyed direct Washington support right up to the Obama White House. Yet until after the fall of the Mubarak dictatorship in February 2011, when Mohammed Morsi was installed as President of Egypt, few outside the Islamic world had ever heard of the Brotherhood. It was a highly secret, totally disciplined organization created out of the resentment and rage against British colonial occupation of Egypt after the First World War and loss of the power of traditional Islam over the population.

The British, as noted, had illegally occupied Egypt, then still part of the Ottoman Caliphate, since the uprising of 1882. They had used Egypt's huge foreign debt to grab control of the Suez Canal and turn the country into a British "protectorate," a euphemism for "colony" in all but name. The protectorate meant a de facto British vassal country with British troops and British control of state finances to "guarantee" repayment of the state debt to City of London and Continental European banks. Ottoman Turkey had been dissolved after 1919, and the British filled the vacuum, tossing a few pieces of Ottoman real estate, including Lebanon and Syria, to the French to ensure their acquiescence as an echo of the Sykes-Picot deal.

Even though Egypt had not been a theater of fighting in the First World War, Egyptians were forced to support the British war effort. English soldiers flooded the country, creating shortages of basic food staples, rationing, soaring food prices, and famine. Egyptians responded, much as they were to do almost a century later against an American presence under the Mubarak dictatorship. They took to the streets and burned British buildings. Strikes, riots, and terrorism brought the country virtually to a halt.

Egypt underwent almost daily protests against the British control. The first mass demonstrations began in 1919, protests which—to the shock of the British—included thousands of Egyptian women, as well as men. The British, for their part, treated the Egyptians with imperial contempt and derision. They tried to suppress the protests with violence, leading to the deaths of hundreds and fomenting even more protest and resentment of the occupiers. Finally, in 1922, the British agreed to pull out and grant Egypt independence—with certain conditions.

The conditions the British imposed were to insure that their control be continued with a figurehead Egyptian government under King Fouad, who owed his job to the British.

London's terms were harsh. The British demanded of Fouad the power to dictate Egyptian foreign and military policy and to force Egypt to go to war in order to protect British interests, such as the Suez Canal. The Canal, the link of the British Empire to India, was to remain firmly in British control on the grounds the canal was "the security of the communications of the British Empire." British citizens were to be allowed to keep all their business and strategic holdings in Egypt. Britain and Egypt would jointly be responsible for the administration of the Sudan protectorate.[1] In short, Egyptian independence was a sham. The British had again betrayed.

Birth of a Sinister Brotherhood

The growing anti-British nationalist sentiment in Egypt culminated in the coming to power of the pro-independence Wafd Party in the 1924 elections. The rising anti-British nationalist tide also created the backdrop in which an obscure Sunni Muslim school teacher named Hassan Al-Banna created the Society of the Muslim Brothers, or, as it became known in the West, the Muslim Brotherhood.[2]

Over the ensuing decades, the Muslim Brothers grew into one of the most powerful secret societies in modern history, in many respects, not unlike the Society of Jesus, or Jesuit Order of the Catholic Church, that was created by Ignatius Loyola to counter the Protestant reformation in the 16th century Europe, concentrating on a special education of youth and presenting the outside world with a façade of charity and good works while concealing a deadly and ruthless inner agenda of power.

Al-Banna's society sought to fill the vacuum created by the collapse of the Islamic Caliphate under the Ottoman Empire. The Caliphate, after a long struggle between republicans and traditionalist Muslims in the newly declared Turkish Republic, had been formally dissolved in 1924 by the Turkish National Assembly on the initiative of reformer Kemal Ataturk.

Hassan al-Banna created a death cult called Muslim Brotherhood.

Al-Banna, son of an Imam, sought an alternative to the secular Wafd movement, one that would turn the clock way back. Almost from the outset, his secret society had the sole aim, no matter how difficult and long the task, to reestablish a Caliphate, to establish a new Islamic rule over not just Egypt but also the entire Muslim world, a kind of worldwide City of Allah as opposed to St. Augustine's Roman Catholic City of God. It was based on Al-Banna's interpretation of Islamic *Shari'a* law that had evolved from the time of the death of the Prophet Mohammed in the 7th century until approximately the 10th century.

For the project, again as the infamous Jesuit Order of the Catholic Church since the 16th century, Al-Banna instructed his followers that secrecy and deception to the world outside were a necessary part of devotion to achieving the goal. The Westernized Ataturk, in the eyes of the Brotherhood, had committed a sacrilege in dissolving the Caliphate and ending the rule by Shari'a. They were out to change that by whatever means necessary.[3]

Al-Banna, a charismatic organizer who turned his sights to disaffected youth as potential recruits, built his secret organization on the argument that Egyptian poverty, powerlessness, and lack of dignity resulted from failing to adhere to Islam and from adopting Western values and culture. The oath he and his co-founders swore was an oath to Allah to be "soldiers for the message of Islam. . . . We are brothers in the service of Islam; hence we are the Muslim Brothers." His motto was simple: *"Islam hooah al-hal"*—Islam is the solution to all of Egypt's and mankind's ills.[4]

All in the "Family"

Al-Banna set up a system of branches or cells across Egypt in the 1930s, each running a mosque, a school, and a sporting club. The sport clubs were aimed to physically bind the men closer. The Egyptian Brotherhood started as a religious social organization preaching the Qur'an, teaching the illiterate, setting up hospitals, and launching businesses, including an independent press. They planned their strategy carefully.

After initial experiments with how to control the Society and keep it from being subverted from without, Al-Banna finally organized the Brothers around the concept of a system of "families" (*nizam al-usar al-ta' awuni*). The families defined internal relations and made the cells of the secret organization virtually impenetrable to outsiders.

Each all-male cell or "family" was limited to five brothers, later changed to ten. The separate families met weekly to discuss personal, social, and financial problems. Each family elected its chief to represent them in a larger Clan, or *Ashira*, of four families also headed by a chief. Five Clans constituted a Group and five Groups a Battalion. Leadership at each level rotated, with a High Command led by Al-Banna controlling the entire complex pyramid of the organization, making it largely impervious to infiltration or destruction from outside.[5]

The purpose of the families was to indoctrinate. Indoctrination included insistence on absolute obedience to the leadership, the accepting of Islam as a total system, as the final arbiter of life. Indoctrination taught that Islam was based on only three sources—the Qur'an, the Sunna or deeds and customs dating from the Prophet, and the *Hadith*, or sayings of the Prophet Mohammed—and that Islam was applicable at all times and in all places.[6]

Al-Banna's Muslim Brotherhood inculcated in its members the goal of a return to the original meaning of *islam*, the Arabic word meaning "submission." However for Al-Banna's sect the submission was to something far from love of Allah or their fellow man. It was a submission in every respect similar to the kind of total submission the Führer demanded of his Nazi followers during the Third Reich.

Brothers were indoctrinated to be strictly obedient to the rituals of Islam, to avoid evils, including drink, gambling, usury, and adultery, and to bring Islamic obedience into their own families, with their wives and children. Finances within the male Brotherhood "family" were pooled, with one-fifth going to the headquarters for a Society for Islamic Social Insurance.[7] All of this bonded members with an incredible loyalty.

The Society of the Muslim Brothers under Al-Banna's control cultivated a cult of obedience analogous to the severe monastic obedience demanded of monks in a Roman Catholic Cistercian monastery trying to replicate monastic life exactly as it had been in Saint Benedict's time or the discipline of the Society of Jesus of Ignatius Loyola.

Al-Banna realized that, in the Islam of his day and the culture of the Arab world over centuries, no better enforcer of blind obedience existed than the father-dominated, authoritarian Islamic family, bound by enforced study of the Qur'an and Shari'a law as the Brotherhood dictated. Al-Banna wrote tracts to the members telling which parts of the Qur'an were to be read and, more crucially, how they were to be interpreted so no deviant thinking arose.[8]

Hassan Al-Banna and his Muslim Brothers successfully manipulated such obedience in order to cultivate a desire to recreate in the 20th century an Islamic religious fundamentalism going back to a world that had emerged from the severity of the deserts of Saudi Arabia in the 7th century. That, if nothing else, was a tribute to his pathological genius. He realized that the heart of any such total obedience or submission lay in getting his members to desire to make the ultimate sacrifice in the name of Allah—death.

"Death Is Art"

In 1936, the Brotherhood became politically active for the first time as it began to openly oppose British rule in Egypt. As his numbers and potential power grew, Al-Banna set up the Special Section, as it was known internally (*al-nizam al-khass*), or, as it was known to the British and other outsiders, the Secret Apparatus (*al-jihaz al-sirri*). It was the military wing of the Brotherhood, in effect, the "assassination bureau." Al-Banna's brother, Abd Al-Rahman Al-Banna, became the head of the Secret Apparatus.[9] Nazi agents came from Germany to Egypt to help train the Special Section cadres and provide money as well. Both the Nazis and Al-Banna shared a deep anti-Jewish hatred and the Brotherhood's *Jihad*, or Holy War, was aimed, in large part, at Jews in Egypt and Palestine.[10]

The proclaimed virtues of martyrdom and a "fighting for the true faith," or *Jihad*, were taught as central to the moral foundation of Al-Banna's Muslim Brothers. He taught that "*Jihad* is an obligation of every Muslim" and that, as he wrote, Allah grants a "noble life to that nation which knows how to die a noble death."[11]

Hassan Al-Banna introduced the idea of a special kind of death cult into Islam in the 20th century. This aspect of the Brotherhood became the petri dish or wellspring which later, in the 1990s and after, served for virtually all Sunni Islamic terrorist organizations to spread Salafist *Jihadism*. That included radical Islamic groups such as Al Qaeda or ISIS or al-Nusra. In many respects, Al-Banna's Sunni Islamic death cult was a revival of the murderous Assassins Cult, or Islamic *hashshāshīn*, during the Holy Crusades of the 12th century.

Al-Banna variously termed it "the Art of Death" (*fann al-mawt*) or "Death is Art" (*al-mawt fann*). He preached to his followers that it was a kind of saintly martyrdom to be devoutly honored. He claimed, falsely, that it was based on the Qur'an.

His doctrine commanded people to love death more than life. "Unless the philosophy of the Qur'an on death replaces the love of life which has consumed Muslims," then they will reach naught, he argued. Al-Banna insisted, "Victory can only come with the mastery of the '*Art of Death*.'"

Hassan Al-Banna taught his fellow Muslim Brothers that militant *Jihad* and a martyr's death fighting for establishment of the new Caliphate was "the shortest and easiest step from this life to the life hereafter."[12]

The credo of his Society of Muslim Brothers was incorporated into a chant of six short phrases:

> *Allah is our goal; The Prophet is our Leader; The Qur'an is our Constitution; Jihad is our Way; Death in the service of Allah is the loftiest of our wishes; Allah is Great, Allah is Great.*[13]

By the 1930s the Muslim Brotherhood in Egypt had been able to set up secret guerrilla training camps in the hills outside Cairo. Training was done by young officers in the Egyptian army who were also, secretly, members of the Brotherhood.

The Brotherhood established an internal court, or Shari'a judiciary, that issued *fatwas*, or legal judgments, against those whom they judged to have betrayed faith and country. Once the Society's court had condemned a person, the Brotherhood's militant arm carried out the sentence.

During the 1940s, as they became better trained and far more numerous, they bombed shopping center complexes, assassinated internal security officials of King Farouk, and murdered Prime Minister Noqrashi Pasha to advance their Caliphate restoration agenda.[14]

German Jewish psychologist Arno Gruen, who fled to New York as a child with his family during the Third Reich, made a lifelong study of the family roots of fascism. In an analysis of the relationship between a dysfunctional childhood and those men who crave war and are fascinated by death, Gruen noted, "If death is what offers the greatest safety to such a man, then that is what he longs for. It is no accident that ideologies that express the deepest contempt for compassion and pay the greatest homage to the male mythology of strength and heroism have been and continue to be the fascist ones. And every one of them glorifies death."

Al-Banna's Society of the Muslim Brothers was based on such a fascist ideology.[15]

Al-Banna's Muslim Brotherhood, in that sense, was an explosively dangerous and powerful sect using Islam to glorify death. It was, therefore, not surprising that it was to join forces with the most powerful death cult of its day, a death cult which used another religion to glorify death in the name not of Allah, but of *Der Führer.*

Endnotes

1   University of Texas, *20th Century Cairo: 1882 to Present*, accessed in http://www.laits.utexas.edu/cairo/history/modern/modern.html.

2   Richard P. Mitchell, *The Society of the Muslim Brothers*, Oxford University Press, New York, 1969, p. 8.

3   Mark Curtis, *Britain and the Muslim Brotherhood Collaboration during the 1940s and 1950s*, 18 December 2010, accessed in http://markcurtis.wordpress.com/2010/12/18/britain-and-the-muslim-brotherhood-collaboration-during-the-1940s-and-1950s/.

4   Richard P. Mitchell, op. cit., p. 8.

5   Ibid., pp. 197–198.

6   Ibid., p. 198.

7   Ibid., pp. 14, 198.

8   Ibid., p. 198.

9   Ibid., pp. 30–4, 55.

10 Ian Johnson, *A Mosque in Munich: Nazis, the CIA and the Rise of the Muslim Brotherhood in the West*, Houghton, Mifflin, Harcourt, Boston, 2010, p. 112.

11 Richard P. Mitchell, op. cit. p. 206.

12 Ibid., pp. 206–207.

13 Ibid., pp. 193–194.

14 Youssef H. Aboul-Enein, *Al-Ikhwan Al-Muslimeen: the Muslim Brotherhood*, Military Review, November 12, 2005, accessed in the official web-site of Al-Ikhwan Al-Muslimeen, http://www.ikhwanweb.com/article.php?id=5617&ref=search.php.

15 Arno Gruen, *The Insanity of Normality: Toward Understanding Human Destructiveness*, Human Development Books, Berkeley California, 2007, p. 48.

CHAPTER FIVE

THE MUSLIM BROTHERHOOD JOINS HITLER'S "HOLY WAR" AGAINST THE JEWS

"Our fundamental condition for cooperating with Germany was a free hand to eradicate every last Jew from Palestine and the Arab world. I asked Hitler for an explicit undertaking to allow us to solve the Jewish problem in a manner befitting our national and racial aspirations and according to the scientific methods innovated by Germany in the handling of its Jews. The answer I got was: The Jews are yours."

—Grand Mufti of Jerusalem, Muslim Brotherhood ally
of Hassan al-Banna, on his agreement with Hitler

The Grand Mufti's Obsession

During the 1930s, Al-Banna's Muslim Brothers and their close ally, the Grand Mufti of Jerusalem, collaborated in a gruesome alliance with an elite group in Germany during the Third Reich known as the Waffen-SS or *Schutzstaffel* ("Protective Squadron"), the feared armed wing of Hitler's Nazi party under Heinrich Himmler.[1]

At the beginning of the 1930s, the Al-Banna organization was still limited to a relatively small cadre of some 800 members across Egypt, with a scattering in Palestine, Syria, and other Arab lands. That was to change dramatically in 1936, when they teamed up with the Grand Mufti's campaign of Jihad against the Jews of Palestine.

Within two years, the Society of the Muslim Brothers had more than 200,000 members and was expanding rapidly. They had declared Jihad against the Jews who were being settled in ever greater numbers in Palestine. As well they extended their Jihad to a war against the British, whose Balfour Declaration and League of Nations Palestine Protectorate were encouraging worldwide Jewish immigration into Palestine, especially from Nazi Germany.

In April 1936, a Higher Arab Committee was formed in Palestine during the onset of a series of violent protests by Palestinian Arabs. It marked the start of the 1936–39 Arab revolt. Mohammed "Haj" Amin al-Husseini had earlier been named by the British as Grand Mufti of Jerusalem, the supreme spiritual authority. It was done as a ploy to quell Arab unrest over the Balfour Declaration. Al-Husseini headed the Higher Arab Committee. The Higher Arab Committee demanded an end to Jewish immigration, called on Arabs to refuse payment of taxes, and endorsed a general strike of Arab workers and businesses.

As Grand Mufti, the highest Islamic authority in the British mandate, Al-Husseini also presided as the Imam of the Al Aqsa mosque in Jerusalem, considered the third most holy site in the Islamic world, where the Prophet Mohammed was said to have been taken up to Heaven. Al-Husseini was also president of the Supreme Muslim Council, the political authority of Palestine.[2] In other words, he was the man to do business with in Palestine.

During the three years of the Arab Revolt Al-Banna's Egyptian Brotherhood collected funds to support the Grand Mufti and his Palestinian actions. The Muslim Brothers printed select passages from the Qur'an hostile to Jews combined with anti-Semitic propaganda borrowed from Hitler's Third Reich. That fueled a boycott of Jewish and British stores in Palestine and violent demonstrations under the slogan "Jews out of Egypt and Palestine!"[3]

A year earlier, in 1935, Hassan Al-Banna had quietly dispatched his brother Abd al-Rahman Al-Banna, head of the Brotherhood's secret Special Section, to Jerusalem to meet with the Grand Mufti to cement a close collaboration with Al-Banna's Muslim Brotherhood, a collaboration and friendship which was to last until Amin al-Husseini's death in 1974. The result was that the Muslim Brothers in Egypt began distributing anti-British and anti-Jewish propaganda while sending funds to support Al-Husseini's revolt.[4]

Al-Husseini was not the naïve Palestinian nationalist that later historical accounts attempted to portray him as. He was an intense, obsessed anti-Semite who had been implicated in instigating riots and in the killings of Jewish residents in Hebron and across the British Palestine Mandate since 1920. In March 1933, just after the Nazi seizure of power, Grand Mufti Al-Hussieni wrote to Adolf Hitler expressing his unconditional support for the Nazis' struggle against the Jews.[5]

In a telegram to Berlin's Foreign Ministry, Heinrich Wolff, German Consul General in Jerusalem, met with the Grand Mufti Amin Al-Hussieni. He sent a telegram after his meeting to Berlin dated March 31, 1933 where Wolff wrote:

> The Mufti explained to me today at length that Muslims both within Palestine and without welcome the new regime in Germany and hope for the spread of fascist, anti-democratic forms of government to other countries. Current Jewish economic and political influence is harmful everywhere and has to be combated. In order to be able to hit the standard of living of Jews, Muslims are hoping for Germany to declare a boycott [of "Jewish" goods], which they would then enthusiastically join throughout the Muslim world.[6]

In the first years of the Third Reich, the official policy, backed by people such as Deputy Foreign Minister Ernst von Weizsäcker, was that immigration of German Jews to Palestine represented a tolerable "solution to Germany's Jewish problem." Beginning in August 1933, the Third Reich made possible Jewish immigration into Palestine under terms of the so-called *Haavara*, or "Transfer," Agreement. The Haavara Agreement allowed selected German Jews to transfer part of their wealth to Palestine and favored German exports to the region—the latter aspect earning it the support of the Economics Ministry.[7]

That policy was to change by 1941, as it became clear to Berlin that Britain was in no way interested in dividing the world with Hitler's Reich. The outbreak of the War had brought the Haavara Agreement to an end. The Grand Mufti played a major role in that policy change, which became known to history as the Jewish Holocaust.

Peel Plan Changes Palestine Issue

In 1937, the Arab Revolt took on a new quality when the British released the Peel Report, recommending establishment of two separate states—one Jewish and one Arab—in the territory of the British Palestine Mandate. At that point, relations between Grand Mufti Amin Al-Husseini, Al-Banna's Egyptian Muslim Brotherhood, and the Third Reich intensified.

Nazi Berlin saw a chance to cultivate Arab rage against British interests in Egypt and the Middle East, as well as advancing their own anti-Semitic agenda. The Third Reich Foreign Minister at the time, Konstantin von Neurath, remarking on the British plan for formation of a Jewish state, declared, "it is not in Germany's interest." Such a state, he said, "would create an additional position of power under international law for international Jewry. Germany therefore has an interest in strengthening the Arab world as a counterweight against such a possible increase in power for world Jewry."[8] He meant in so many words that the German Reich was interested in using political Islam as a "counterweight against such a possible increase in power for world Jewry."

German foreign policy changed from cautious neutrality to one of active support of the Muslim Brotherhood in Egypt and the Grand Mufti in Jerusalem. By then, the Grand Mufti had been forced to flee from the British to Beirut to carry on his revolt. Al-Husseini himself later said that it was only because of German money that it had been possible to carry through the uprising in Palestine. From the outset, he made major financial demands on the Nazis which were significantly met by Berlin.[9]

Before 1936, there had been little visible anti-Semitism in Egypt. Jews were influential in economic and political life. The anti-Jewish pamphlets that the NSDAP's local group in Cairo had initially spread fell on deaf ears. In a letter to Berlin in 1933, the local NSDAP group wrote to Berlin that further leaflets and pamphlets would be of no avail and that, instead, attention should be turned to where "real conflicts of interests between Arabs and Jews exist: Palestine. The conflict between Arabs and Jews there must be transplanted into Egypt."[10]

The Muslim Brothers of Al-Banna were to become the vehicle for that conflict. As Al-Husseini's 1936 Arab Revolt in Palestine took fire, Al-Banna's Muslim Brothers called for a boycott of all Jewish businesses in Egypt. In mosques and factories, the rumor was spread that the Jews and British were destroying the holy places of Jerusalem. Further false reports that hundreds of Arab women and children had been killed by the Jews and British were spread by the Brotherhood to inflame passions of the ignorant Muslim populations.

After publication of the British Peel Plan for creation of a Jewish Palestine state, anti-Jewish agitation was stepped up. Cries of "Down with the Jews!" and "Jews out of Egypt and Palestine!" were chanted in violent student demonstrations in Cairo, Alexandria, and across Egypt. A column titled "The Menace of the Jews of Egypt" appeared in the Brotherhood's magazine, *Al- Nadhir.* Al-Banna's Muslim Brotherhood was growing in numbers like a prairie fire as they fomented the hatred.

Norwegian historian Brynjar Lia recounted the following in a monograph on the Muslim Brotherhood:

> Documents seized in the flat of Wilhelm Stellbogen, the Director of the German News Agency (Deutsches Nachrichtenbüro) affiliated to the German Legation in Cairo, show that prior to October 1939 the Muslim Brothers received subsidies from his organisation. Stellbogen was instrumental in transferring these funds to the Brothers, which were considerably larger than the subsidies offered to other anti-British activists. These transfers appear to have been coordinated by Haj Amin el-Husseini and some of his Palestinian contacts in Cairo.[11]

The Nazi funds enabled the Muslim Brotherhood to set up a printing plant to get their message out more widely. The Muslim Brotherhood also got the assistance of German Third Reich officers in constructing their military organization.

Berlin's foreign language Arab station in Zeesen just outside Berlin beamed Arab-language, anti-Jewish messages daily from one of the world's most powerful shortwave transmitters. The broadcasts lasted from 1939 to the end of the war. Of all the foreign-language services, the Oriental Service at Radio Zeesen had "absolute priority" for Berlin. It reached out to Arabs, Turks, Persians, and Indian Muslims, skillfully mixing anti-Semitic propaganda with quotes from the Qur'an and Arabic music.[12]

The key man of the Muslim Brotherhood in Berlin responsible for all Arab-language Nazi broadcasting at Radio Zeesen was the Grand Mufti of Jerusalem, Haj Amin el-Husseini.

The Mufti Joins Himmler and Hitler

While Hassan Al-Banna was occupied organizing in Egypt during World War II— building both the public and the secret sides of his Society of the Muslim Brothers and campaigning against the British and against the Jews, Al-Banna's now close friend and, reportedly, by then fellow Muslim Brother, Haj Amin Al-Husseini, had landed in Berlin. He had managed a "miraculous" escape from Jerusalem to Lebanon, then to Iraq, and, eventually, to Nazi Germany, where he was welcomed with open arms in 1941.

In Berlin, the Grand Mufti played one of the least-known and most gruesome roles in the Nazi extermination of millions of Jews. He became close friends with Heinrich Himmler, *Reichsführer* of the dreaded Nazi death cult known as *Schutzstaffel* (SS). Himmler was the one perhaps most directly responsible for the Third Reich's implementation of the Holocaust.

The Grand Mufti shaking hands with Himmler in 1943.

In his Memoirs written after the War, Grand Mufti Amin Al-Husseini declared shamelessly the basis of the collaboration between the Nazis and the Muslim Brotherhood in Palestine, Egypt, and the Arab world: "Our fundamental condition for cooperating with Germany was a free hand to eradicate every last Jew from Palestine and the Arab world. I asked Hitler for an explicit undertaking to allow us to solve the Jewish problem in a manner befitting our national and racial aspirations and according to the scientific methods innovated by Germany in the handling of its Jews. The answer I got was: The Jews are yours."[13]

At his Nuremburg trial testimony after the War, Dieter Wisliceny, deputy to Adolf Eichmann, testified before being sentenced to hang for crimes against humanity: "The Mufti was one of the initiators of the systematic extermination of European Jewry and had been a collaborator and adviser of Eichmann and Himmler in the execution of this plan. . . He was one of Eichmann's best friends and had constantly incited him to accelerate the extermination measures."[14]

Eichmann, one of the major organizers of the Holocaust against Jews after 1941, had been charged by Reinhard Heydrich, SS-*Obergruppenführer*, with managing the logistics of mass deportation of Jews to ghettos and extermination camps in German-occupied Eastern Europe.[15]

The Mufti, as he was known in Berlin—even though the British had taken back his title for his incitements to riot in Palestine years before—was the key link between the Muslim Brotherhood and allied Islamist Jihad groups in the Arab world and in the core of the Third Reich.

Grand Mufti Al-Hussieni meets with Hitler in Berlin in 1943.

According to documents in German national archives, Adolf Hitler was introduced to the Grand Mufti in Berlin, where the Mufti had been received as a special VIP guest. He remained in Berlin until the end of the war in 1945. At their first meeting in 1941, Hitler, "enjoining him to lock it in the uttermost depths of his heart," told Al-Husseini that once his armies had reached the southern exit of the Caucasus, he would proclaim to the Arab world that its hour of liberation had arrived. Germany's goal would then be what he termed the "destruction of Jewry living in Arabia."[16]

In November 1941, after their first meeting, Hitler wrote to the Grand Mufti:

> Germany stands for an uncompromising struggle against the Jews. It is self-evident that the struggle against the Jewish national homeland in Palestine forms part of this struggle, since such a national homeland would be nothing other than a political base for the destructive influence of Jewish interests. Germany also knows that the claim that Jewry plays the role of an economic pioneer in Palestine is a lie. Only the Arabs work there, not the Jews. Germany is determined to call on the European nations one by one to solve the Jewish problem and, at the proper moment, to address the same appeal to non-European peoples.[17]

The Grand Mufti, based in Berlin from 1941 until 1945, played the lead role in fomenting Jihad against the Jews in Egypt and Palestine and across the Arab Muslim world. He was treated as royalty by the Third Reich, as the symbol of an Arab-German alliance in the war against the Jews. The German government put Al-Husseini in charge of the Nazi's Arab-language broadcasts at Radio Zeesen outside Berlin. From there, he called out to the Arab brothers who heard his daily tirades to declare Jihad against all Jews. Nobody promoted hatred of Jews among Muslims more effectively than the Mufti.[18]

The anti-Semitism of Al-Husseini and the Muslim Brotherhood did not come from the Nazis. The race hatred and anti-Semitism were there on both sides, Nazi and Muslim, the one feeding the other, according to serious historical accounts.[19]

In December 1942, the Nazis appointed Al-Husseini honorary chairman of their newly founded Islamic Central Institute in Berlin. In his acceptance speech, the Grand Mufti showed the depth of his hatred of Jews:

The Jews and their accomplices are to be counted among the bitterest enemies of the Muslims. . .Every Muslim knows all too well how the Jews afflicted him and his faith in the first days of Islam and what hatefulness they displayed toward the great Prophet—what hardship and trouble they caused him, how many intrigues they launched, how many conspiracies against him they brought about—such that the Qu'ran judged them to be the most irreconcilable enemies of the Muslims. . .In England as in America, it is the Jewish influence alone that rules; and it is the same Jewish influence that is behind godless Communism. . .And it is also this Jewish influence that has incited the nations into this grueling war.[20]

Amin Al-Husseini's loathing of Jews was so virulent that when he learned, in 1943, that the pro-German government of Bulgaria planned to allow some 4,000 Jewish children and 500 adult companions to immigrate to Palestine rather than send them to the concentration camps, the Mufti wrote a letter to the Bulgarian Foreign Minister dated May 6, 1943, demanding the operation be stopped. The Grand Mufti cited a,

Jewish danger for the whole world and especially for the countries where Jews live. If I may be permitted, I would like to call your attention to the fact that it would be very appropriate and more advantageous to prevent the Jews from emigrating from your country and instead to send them where they will be placed under strict control: e.g. to Poland. Thus one can avoid the danger they represent and do a good deed vis-à-vis the Arab peoples that will be appreciated.[21]

The reference to Poland was a reference to Auschwitz, Treblinka, and the other death camps the Nazis had built in Poland for the extermination of the Jews. In remarks after the war, a former German Foreign Ministry official who had dealt with the Grand Mufti stated, "The Mufti was a sworn enemy of the Jews, and he made no secret of the fact that he would have preferred to see them all killed."[22]

Not even SS head Heinrich Himmler, the man responsible for execution of the Jewish extermination's "final solution," was as extreme in the Bulgarian issue as the Grand Mufti. According to German historical archives, Himmler's Reich Security Central Office (RSHA), directly responsible for implementing the Final Solution, had indicated it was willing to tolerate the Bulgarian Jewish rescue action if it was part of a trade involving the release of some 20,000 Germans interred by the Allies in exchange for the Jewish children.[23]

The Mufti's SS Muslim Brigade

In Nazi Berlin, the Grand Mufti also worked with a group under Gerhard von Mende in the *Ostministerium* of Nazi ideologist Alfred Rosenberg. The *Ostministerium*, or the Ministry for Occupied Eastern Territories, was at the heart of Hitler's strategy for eastern Lebensraum.

Von Mende was head of the Ministry's Caucasus Division responsible for recruiting fighters from the Muslim regions of the Soviet Union willing to make Jihad, or battle, against their own Soviet Union side by side with the German troops. Von Mende's efforts at propaganda inside the Soviet Caucasus and beyond led to recruitment of more than 20,000 Tatar volunteers willing to fight with the Nazis against their Soviet masters.[24]

Erich Von Mende won the thousands of Muslim volunteers, willing to fight and die side by side with the German Reich, based on a false promise that they would win freedom for their ethnic nationalities after the final Nazi "victory." Ethnic radio stations, newspapers, and "liaison offices" that were portrayed as quasi governments in exile were set up by von Mende's *Ostministerium*.

As the German *Wehrmacht* took control of the Caucasus, the recruitment of Muslim volunteers from Azerbaijanis, Volga Tatars, Turkestanis, Uzbek, and Kyrgyz areas of the USSR advanced as well. The Nazi project of recruiting Central Asian Muslim peoples to wage Jihad against Moscow was the harbinger of a project that was revived consciously by the CIA in the years of the US-Soviet Cold War. Some three decades Islamic Jihadists were used by US intelligence in Afghanistan to help bring down the Soviet Union and, a half-century later, to destabilize Russia and all Central Asia, including China, from Chechnya to Dagestan, to Uzbekistan, to Kyrgyzstan, and beyond, after the collapse of the Soviet Union.

The Grand Mufti of Jerusalem, Amin Al-Husseini, worked closely with von Mende, giving his official endorsement to von Mende's new Islamic brigades. In gratitude, von Mende even offered to appoint Al-Hussieni as Mufti for the Crimean Muslims.[25]

The Mufti of Jerusalem salutes the Bosnian SS division.

In 1943, the Grand Mufti was invited to Sarajevo in Bosnia-Herzegovina in former Yugoslavia, where the Nazi occupation was in a bitter battle with Josef Tito's communist partisans. Himmler was convinced of the ruthlessness of Muslims as fighters of Jihad. In Sarajevo, Amin Al-Husseini played a crucial role in organizing and recruiting Muslims into the *Handschar*, or Scimitar, the 13th Waffen-SS Division. It was the first non-German Waffen-SS division and it was the largest. The SS Handschar Division, composed of largely Bosnian Muslims, were active accomplices in the genocide of Serbian, Jewish, and Roma (gypsy) populations.[26]

The official logo of the Muslim Brothers(l), cross scimitars as in the Ottoman Caliphate, and the Logo of the Waffen SS handschar Division(r) in Bosnia.

British and French Protect Nazi Brotherhood

The Nazis had done pioneer work in developing ways of steering Islamic Jihad, as spread by the Muslim Brotherhood, as a weapon of war against their enemy, the Soviet Union. The Muslim Brotherhood and, especially, the Grand Mufti had played a central role in that war.

After the war, the Grand Mufti and Al-Banna's Muslim Brotherhood were wanted for war crimes and genocide against Jews. Their German intelligence handlers were captured in Cairo. The whole network was rolled up by the British Secret Service.

Then, instead of being put on trial, the British Secret Service, MI6, hired the Brotherhood. They brought all the fugitive Nazi war criminals of Arab and Muslim descent into Egypt and trained them for three years on a special mission. The British Secret Service wanted to use the Muslim Brotherhood to strike down the infant state of Israel in 1948, an Israel which had successfully revolted from British control. Many of the members of the Arab Armies and terrorist groups that tried to strangle the infant State of Israel, including the Grand Mjufti himself, now back in Palestine, were the Arab Nazis of the Muslim Brotherhood.

The French intelligence services cooperated with the British by releasing the Grand Mufti and smuggling him into Egypt so that all of the Arab Nazis could be brought together. From 1945 to 1948, the British Secret Intelligence Services protected every Arab Nazi they could. But they failed to quash the State of Israel.[27]

CIA Buys the Brotherhood

What the British did then was to offer to "sell" the Muslim Brotherhood leaders they had trained to the newly created CIA.[28] Great Britain had been financially exhausted by the costs of war and reconstruction, and London began to realize that the sun was indeed "setting" on her Empire.

After the Second World War ended in the total defeat of Hitler's Germany, Gerhard Von Mende of the Ostministerium, Grand Mufti Amin Al-Husseini's old anti-semitic friend, was one of the Nazi survivors who went on to build a significant career in US-occupied Germany. Von Mende offered his skills to both West German intelligence, the British, and the CIA. They all wanted to use his abilities in directing the wrath of Jihad Islam against the Communist Soviet Union. It was to develop into one of the most significant black chapters in postwar history, one whose fateful consequences are still shaking the world today.

Endnotes

1   Matthias Küntzel, *National Socialism and Anti Semitism in the Arab World*, Jewish Political Studies Review, 17:1–2 (Spring 2005), accessed in http://jcpa. org/phas/phas-kuntzel-s05.htm.

2   Jacob Norris, *Repression and Rebellion: Britain's Response to the Arab Revolt in Palestine of 1936–39*, The Journal of Imperial and Commonwealth History, 2008, 36(1):25–45.

3   Klaus-Michael Mallmann, Martin Cüppers, *"Elimination of the Jewish National Home in Palestine": The Einsatzkommando of the Panzer Army Africa*, 1942, Yad Vashem Studies 35.1, Edited by David Silberklang, Yad Vashem, Jerusalem, p. 15, accessed in http://www.yadvashem.org/about_holocaust/studies/vol35/ Mallmann-Cuppers2.pdf.

4   Richard P. Mitchell, *The Society of the Muslim Brothers*, Oxford University Press, USA, reprint July 1993, p. 55.

5   *Deutsches Generalkonsulat Jerusalem an AA*, v. 31.3.1933, PAAA, R 78325, cited in Klaus-Michael Mallmann, op. cit., p. 22.

6   John Rosenthal, *The Mufti and the Holocaust*, Policy Review, Stanford University, March 28, 2008, No. 148, accessed in http://www.hoover.org/publications/ policy-review/article/5696.

7   Ibid.

8   Matthias Küntzel, op. cit.

9   Kurt Fischer-Weth, *Amin el-Husseini. Grossmufti von Palästina*, Berlin, Walter Titz Verlag, 1943, p. 83.

10 Matthias Küntzel, op. cit.

11 Ibid.

12 Ibid.

13   Cited in David Storobin, *Nazi Roots of Palestinian Nationalism*, New York Jewish Times, March 8, 2005, accessed in http://www.nyjtimes.com/cover/03-08-05/nazirootsofpalestiniannationalism.htm

14   Ibid.

15   Wikipedia, Adolf Eichmann, accessed in http://en.wikipedia.org/wiki/Adolf_Eichmann.

16   Adolf Hitler, *Documents on German Foreign Policy 1918–1945*, Series D, Vol. XIII no. 515, quoted in http://www.fpp.co.uk/Himmler/Judenfrage/Mufti_memoirs.html.

17   Klaus Gensicke, *Der Mufti von Jerusalem und die Nationalsozialisten*, Darmstadt, Wissenschaftliche Buchgesellschaft, 2007, pp. 60–61.

18   Matthias Küntzel, *National Socialism and Anti Semitism in the Arab World*, Jewish Political Studies Review 17:1–2, Spring 2005, accessed in http://jcpa.org/phas/phas-kuntzel-s05.htm.

19   Klaus Gensicke, op. cit.

20   John Rosenthal, op. cit.

21   Cited in John Rosenthal, op. cit.

22   Ibid.

23   Ibid.

24   Ian Johnson, op. cit., pp. 25–26.

25   Ibid., p. 31.

26   Seán Mac Mathúna, *The Role of the SS Handschar division in Yugoslavias Holocaust*, accessed in http://www.fantompowa.net/Flame/yugoslavia_collaboration.htm.

27   John Loftus, *The Muslim Brotherhood, Nazis and Al-Qaeda*, Jewish Community News, April 10, 2006.

28   Ibid.

CHAPTER SIX

FROM MUNICH TO THE SOVIET STEPPES: THE CIA FINDS THE MUSLIM BROTHERS

"The fusion of ultra-conservative Saudi Wahhabite Islam with the Muslim Brotherhood's fanatical political activism was a deadly and highly shrewd combination that never lost sight of its goal of building a new global Islamic Caliphate that would become the world religion. The alliance of the Brotherhood with Saudi Wahhabism was to remain from the early 1950s for more than seven decades."

—F. William Engdahl

A Fateful Regrouping in Munich

The end of the Second World War and the defeat of Nazi Germany were by no means the end of the influential circle of Nazis who had spent the war collaborating with Grand Mufti Al-Husseini and Al-Banna's Muslim Brotherhood. Ironically, deeply Roman Catholic Munich became the center of the regrouping of the Islamic *Jihad* cadre assembled by Gerhard von Mende's wartime *Ostministerium*, the Ministry for Occupied Eastern Territories.

In the chaos of collapse of order in the last days of the war, von Mende managed to see to it that numbers of his valued Islamist cadre who had fought alongside the *Wehrmacht* against their Soviet rulers during the war would get captured in the American, British, or French zones of what, in 1948, became the Federal Republic of (West) Germany. Soviet capture he knew meant certain death. His Jihadists were his bargaining chip to begin a new career working for the former enemy, the West.

The Soviet exiles had concentrated in Munich in southern Germany, coming from the ethnic Turkic regions of Tatarstan, Uzbekistan, Chechnya, and other Muslim territories of the Soviet Union. It was a fraternity of bitter anti-communist war veterans but of a very odd sort.[1]

While von Mende was working to bring together his Muslim friends in the Bavarian zone, where the US military was in control, the newly-created Central Intelligence Agency was trying to build a new propaganda capacity to beam US propaganda into the Soviet Union. It was ultimately named Radio Liberty, and its sister propaganda arm was called Radio Free Europe. Von Mende's Muslims were destined to play a key role in the CIA's propaganda operations out of Munich.

Rockefellers Join Billy Graham's Crusade

By the early 1950s, the US-Soviet Cold War was in full force. Both sides used propaganda to try to win neutral third countries to the side of American capitalist free enterprise or to Soviet communism. Early on, the Rockefeller family, the most influential family in America emerging out of World War II, together with the newly founded CIA, decided that Christian fundamentalism could be used as an instrument to help demonize Soviet communism in the eyes of ordinary churchgoing Americans.

Abraham Vereide, an evangelical Norwegian-American minister, among other feats, claimed responsibility for converting a former Nazi SS officer, Netherlands' Prince Bernhard, to Christ in the early 1950s. It was around the time Bernhard became the nominal founding head of the Anglo-American Bilderberg Group meetings. Vereide would play a key role in the politicization of Christian groups for the Cold War.

Together, Vereide and Frank Buchman, founder of the Oxford Movement, which was influential in German "re-education" after 1945, secured sponsorship for something they called the Prayer Breakfast movement. It was very political, their praying and breakfasting. The two men soon founded a Fellowship House in Washington, DC, as a "spiritual service center" for members of Congress.

By the end of the 1940s, Vereide had about a third of the entire US Congress attending his weekly prayer meetings. In the early 1950s, he got President Eisenhower's support as Vereide came to play a major role in the US government's anti-communist activities.[2]

The *Los Angeles Times* described the process:

> Pentagon officials secretly met at the group's Washington Fellowship House in 1955 to plan a worldwide anti-communism propaganda campaign endorsed by the CIA, documents from the Fellowship archives and the Eisenhower Presidential Library show. Then known as International Christian Leadership, the group financed a film called "Militant Liberty" used by the Pentagon abroad.[3]

Christianity, at least a US government version of it, was on the way to becoming a weapon in the Cold War.

In 1953, the Fellowship Foundation held the first Presidential Prayer Breakfast in the White House.

The Reverend Billy Graham was a regular speaker at the Washington "Prayer Breakfasts." Graham preached a fire and brimstone sort of anti-communism that was strongly promoted by the US government and America's mainstream establishment. Billy called his large outdoor rallies the Billy Graham Crusades. Images of a new "holy crusade against Godless Soviet Communism" were beamed over US television and radio to millions of American homes.[4] By the early 1950s, Billy Graham's revival marathons across the United States were converting tens of thousands of stirred up ordinary Americans to "accept Jesus Christ as their personal savior."

In 1957, the Rockefeller brothers discreetly gave $50,000, a huge sum in that day, to launch Graham's New York Crusade. It was a booming success, propelled by the then novel use of television and the hidden support and corporate connections of the Rockefellers. The result was that, for the first time since the infamous 1925 Scopes Monkey Trial, Christian Fundamentalism was able to raise its head again in public, re-clothed in fiery Madison Avenue anti-communist garb.[5]

The evangelical revivalist and Rockefeller friend Reverend Billy Graham preaches to a stadium of tens of thousands in Duisburg, Germany, 1954.

The titans of American business—including Phelps Dodge copper heir Cleveland Dodge, Jeremiah Milbank and George Champion of the Rockefeller's Chase Manhattan Bank, Henry Luce of *Time-Life* (the author of the famous 1941 *Life* magazine editorial proclaiming the dawn of the "American Century"), Thomas Watson of IBM, and Laurance Rockefeller's partner at Eastern Airlines, Eddie Rickenbacker—were all among the select backers of the new Graham evangelical movement.[6]

They clearly had motives other than the promotion of the Christian faith or supporting of brotherly love.

The American establishment, at least the faction close to the Rockefeller family, had decided by 1957 that a worldwide "revival" of religion was necessary to "assert the United States' moral leadership in the Free World." The revival was, however, to be carefully nurtured and, when necessary, financed, to advance those interests of the powerful US banking and corporate interests.

CIA finds Von Mende's Muslims

The newly created US Central Intelligence Agency, directed by Allen Dulles under the conservative presidency of Dwight D. Eisenhower, was also eager to find other ways than Billy Graham's aggressive Christian anti-communist tirades to undermine the Soviet Union. Religion was to be the key again, but this time, it would be political Islam.

The CIA had discovered a group of political Islamists that von Mende had managed to gather in and around Munich as refugees after the war.

Thousands of former Soviet Muslims, who had fought with the Nazis against the Soviet Red Army, had sought refuge in West Germany, building one of the largest Muslim communities in 1950s Europe.

In April 1951, the CIA first learned that von Mende had collected key Muslims in the Munich area and was setting up a think-tank in an attempt to rebuild his Nazi *Ostministerium*, this time on behalf of the Konrad Adenauer and the Christian Democratic German government rather than for Adolf Hitler.[7] The CIA was interested in co-opting von Mende's group for their own aims.

The CIA discovered that these seasoned Muslim "warriors of Allah," who had been cultivated and deployed by von Mende, had invaluable language skills, as well as invaluable contacts back in the Soviet Union. They began a project to recruit them as warriors for America's anti-communist crusade.

During the war, von Mende and his *Ostministerium* had organized a project with a plan approved by Hitler to free prisoners who would take up arms against the Soviets. They set up "*Ostlegionen*"—Eastern Legions—made up primarily of non-Russian, mainly Muslim, minorities willing to wage *Jihad* against the Soviet communist leadership as revenge for decades of Soviet oppression. Up to a million Soviet Muslims had joined Hitler's *Ostlegionen*, and a select group had landed in Munich, the site of the CIA's new Radio Liberty project. The CIA was soon recruiting them to work against the Soviet communists in various forms of Cold War activity. The new American intelligence service was learning how to work with political Islam for the first time.[8]

Brotherhood Joins with CIA

As the former Muslim Nazi fighters began to work for the CIA in Munich, the Muslim Brotherhood in Egypt also found a new "home" with the CIA. In 1957, the Eisenhower Doctrine was announced, promising armed US and NATO intervention against any threatened aggression in the Middle East, making the region into a de facto US sphere of interest. The Eisenhower Doctrine was aimed at the growing inroads that the Soviets were making, especially in Egypt, where a reformist military coup led by Colonel Gamal Abdel Nasser had dethroned Britain's puppet, King Farouk, in 1952.

In 1948, as an instructor in Egypt's Royal Military Academy, Nasser had sent emissaries to try to negotiate an alliance of his Free Officers group, an anti-British, anti-monarchy group of young colonels and officers, with

Hassan Al-Banna's Muslim Brotherhood. He soon realized that the rigid theocratic agenda of the Brotherhood was antithetical to his nationalist secular reform agenda. Nasser then decided to takes steps to limit Muslim Brotherhood influence within the military. It was the beginnings of a bitter hostility between Nasser and Al-Banna's Brotherhood.[9]

Nasser had been the architect of the 1952 officers' revolt by the Egyptian Army that overthrew the monarchy. During the 1940s, the very pro-British Egyptian King Farouk had financially subsidized the Muslim Brotherhood as a counter to the power of nationalists and communists. That made them a direct ideological opponent of Nasser's reformist nationalism.

By 1949, the King, however, also began to have doubts about working with Al-Banna's organization as the influence of the Brothers grew greatly. His Prime Minister, Mahmud al-Nuqrashi, was assassinated by a member of the Muslim Brotherhood's "secret apparatus." The King responded with massive repression, arresting over one hundred leading members. In February 1949, Brotherhood founder Hassan al-Banna himself was assassinated. The killer was never found, but it was widely believed that the murder had been carried out by members of the Egyptian political police on orders of the King. An MI6 report was unequivocal, stating, "The murder was inspired by the government, with Palace approval."[10]

By 1953, with the Egyptian monarchy formally abolished and the Muslim Brotherhood on the run, Nasser's Free Officers were able to govern as the Revolutionary Command Council (RCC), with Nasser as vice-chairman. He soon grabbed leading power as chairman and proceeded to ban all political parties. No communist himself, Nasser became a leading spokesman for Arab nationalism and joined the emerging Non-Aligned Movement, with Tito's Yugoslavia and India's Nehru. The Non-Aligned group of nations sought to define a "middle way" between Soviet communism and American capitalist free markets.[11]

In 1953, Nasser introduced far-reaching land reforms and was taking steps to renationalize the British-controlled Suez Canal Company. London was not happy with the emergence of Nasser. In fact, British MI6 secret intelligence tried repeatedly to assassinate him.[12]

Brotherhood's Failed Assassination

On October 26, 1954, Mohammed Abdel Latif, a Muslim Brotherhood member, also attempted to assassinate Nasser while Nasser was delivering a speech in Alexandria to celebrate British military withdrawal from Egypt. The strong suspicion was that British intelligence stood behind the Brotherhood's attempt on Nasser. Nasser's speech was being broadcast to the entire Arab world via radio. The gunman missed after firing eight shots. In response, Nasser ordered a massive crackdown on Al-Banna's Society of Muslim Brothers, as well as against leading communists. Eight Brotherhood leaders were sentenced to death. Thousands went underground.[13]

By 1956, Nasser had gained enough popular support that he felt able to nationalize the Suez Canal in retaliation for US and British cutoff of promised financial aid for construction of the Aswan Dam. He also recognized Communist China and made arms deals with communist East Bloc countries. Nasser, never a communist but rather a strong-willed anti-colonialist and Arab nationalist, was becoming a major problem for the US Cold War agenda in the Middle East.

Saudis meet the Brothers in A Marriage Made in Hell

The Eisenhower administration began to look to the arch-conservative monarchy of King Ibn Saud in Saudi Arabia as a counter within the Arab world to the growing influence of Nasserism. That was to result in a fateful marriage of political Islam in the form of exiled Egyptian Brotherhood members and the Saudi monarchy. CIA Cairo Station Chief Miles Copeland officiated at the marriage ceremony, organizing the escape of Egyptian Brotherhood members into Saudi Arabia in what was to transform over the next decades the political map of the world.

Saudi Arabia was perhaps the most conservative, strictest Muslim country in the world. The desert land, only decades earlier an undeveloped land ruled by nomadic Bedouins, practiced a unique form of Islam called Wahhabism. It was named after Muhammad ibn Abd al-Wahhab, who died in 1792, the first modern Islamic fundamentalist extremist.

Abd al-Wahhab made the principle that absolutely every idea added to Islam after the third century of the Muslim era, about 950 AD, was false and should be eliminated. That was the central point of his movement. Muslims, in order to be true Muslims, insisted al-Wahhab, must adhere solely and strictly to the original beliefs set forth by Muhammad. And of course, only those who followed the strict teachings of al-Wahhab were true Muslims because only they still followed the path laid out by Allah.

Accusing someone of not being a true Muslim was significant because it was forbidden for one Muslim to kill another; but if someone was not a "true Muslim" as defined by Wahhabism, then killing them in war or in an act of terrorism becomes legal.[14]

There, in the words of John Loftus, a former US Justice Department official charged with prosecuting and deporting Nazi war criminals, with the joining of Egypt's Muslim Brothers and Saudi strict Islam, "they combined the doctrines of Nazism with this weird Islamic cult, Wahhabism."[15]

Allen Dulles' CIA secretly persuaded the Saudi monarchy to help rebuild the banned Muslim Brotherhood, thereby creating a fusion with Saudi fundamentalist Wahhabi Islam and vast Saudi oil riches to wield a weapon across the entire Muslim world against feared Soviet incursions. A young man named Osama bin Laden was later to arise out of this marriage in Hell between the Brotherhood and Wahhabite Saudi Islam.[16]

In a 1957 meeting with the CIA Director of Covert Operations, Frank Wisner, Eisenhower declared the US should engage the "Holy War" aspect of Arab Muslims in order to get them to fight communism. The Muslim Brothers were willing to oblige, and there began an unholy alliance of US intelligence with the death cult called the Muslim Brotherhood.[17]

By 1954, Saudi Arabia had become the center of worldwide Muslim Brotherhood activity. The Saudi monarchy had struck a grand bargain with the Brotherhood: in return for unheard-of financial support from Saudi oil revenues, the Brotherhood would focus their political activity abroad outside the Saudi Kingdom, spreading their influence in countries such as Egypt, Afghanistan, Pakistan, Sudan, and Syria. They would not organize politically inside Saudi Arabia, where the Monarchy had banned all political parties.[18]

Leading figures of the Muslim Brotherhood such as Dr Abdullah Azzam, became the teachers in the Saudi madrassas, the religious schools. The Brothers retained their secret organizational "family" structure inside Saudi Arabia and established successful businesses, even becoming editors of influential Saudi newspapers, such as *El Medina*.

By 1961, the Muslim Brothers were able to persuade the Saudi King to create the Islamic University of Medina, where dozens of Egyptian scholars that were secretly Muslim Brothers, established themselves. Significantly, the university, a center of Islamic rightwing ideologues of Saudi Wahhabism, combined with the political militancy of the Egyptian Brotherhood, became the petri dish for training the next generation of Islamic Jihadists and Salafists. Notably, some 85 percent of the students at the Medina university came from outside the Saudi Kingdom. That internationalism enabled the Muslim Brotherhood to spread the cadre of the Brotherhood throughout the entire Islamic world.[19]

The vehicle for their worldwide mission that the Saudi-exiled Muslim Brothers used was the Muslim World League (MWL). In 1962, a year after the Brotherhood's success in founding of the Islamic University of Medina, they convinced the Saudi Royal family to finance and support their league as well.

The Muslim World League was headquartered in Mecca, Saudi Arabia, with the Saudi government as the official sponsor. It described itself as an Islamic, non-governmental organization involved in "the propagation of Islam, and refutation of dubious statements and false allegations against the religion." Their stated goal was "to help to carry out projects involving propagation of the religion, education and culture, and to advocate for the application of the rules of the Shari'a either by individuals, groups or states."[20] In reality the Muslim World League represented the fusion of Wahhabite strict interpretation of the teachings of the Prophet Muhammed with the activist political Jihad of the Brotherhood—a very dangerous combination.

The Saudi-based Muslim World League was set up by the Muslim Brotherhood in the 1960s to spread their radical message to the entire Islamic world.

The Muslim World League created offices throughout the Muslim world, as well as in non-Muslim majority regions in the West with offices in Washington, New York, and London. The organization reportedly used its network and Saudi money to fund Islamic centers and mosques and to distribute materials promoting its fundamentalist interpretation of Islam. Its Secretary General was always a Saudi national.

The Saudi fusion of ultraconservative Wahhabite Islam with the Muslim Brotherhood's fanatical political activism was a deadly and extremely shrewd combination that never lost sight of its long-term goal of building a new global Islamic Caliphate that would become the world religion. The alliance of the Brotherhood with Saudi Wahhabism was to remain from the early 1950s until around 2010, when the Saudi monarchy, amid the upheavals of the Arab Spring, began to increasingly fear the Brotherhood, at some point, would turn against the monarchy that had fed them so long.

Princeton Celebrates Ramadan

While many leading exiled Muslim Brothers were brought with aid of the CIA into Saudi Arabia, Hassan Al-Banna's son-in-law and ideological heir, Said Ramadan, was invited to Princeton in the early 1950s to meet US intelligence, shake hands in a personal meeting with President Eisenhower, and discuss what was to become a fateful and deadly collaboration.

Said Ramadan had been in Damascus, Syria, for a conference on the day of the assassination attempt against Nasser and, thereby, escaped the Egyptian police roundup of Brotherhood members. He finally ended up in exile in Geneva, Switzerland, under protection of the Swiss Government, who saw his anti-communism as useful during the Cold War. Declassified Swiss Archives documents revealed that the Swiss regarded Ramadan as an "intelligence agent of the English and the Americans."[21]

From his Islamic Center in Geneva, Ramadan maintained his influence around the world with his fellow Brothers in the aftermath of the murder of his father-in-law, Al-Banna. He traveled frequently to Pakistan, where he helped organize a fanatical Jihadist Islamic Student Society, IJT, fighting leftist students at the universities. His IJT was organized by Ramadan on the Egyptian Brotherhood model.[22] The student IJT group was the forerunner of radical Islamic *Jihadism* that later would train the Muslim Brotherhood's Taliban project in Afghanistan with aid of the Pakistani ISI secret intelligence agency.

In September 1953, Said Ramadan was invited to attend an "Islamic Colloquium" to be held with leading Islamic intellectuals from around the world at the prestigious Princeton University in New Jersey. The invitation and the idea to organize a meeting between Said Ramadan and President Eisenhower came from the co-founder and Deputy Director of the CIA-linked US Information Agency (USIA), Abbott Washburn. Washburn was liaison between USIA and the White House.[23]

Washburn had convinced C.D. Jackson, Eisenhower's psychological warfare expert of the importance of the idea. Jackson was a senior CIA officer sitting in the White House as liaison between the President, the CIA, and the Pentagon.

The Princeton conference was cosponsored by Washburn's USIA, the State Department, Princeton University, and the US Library of Congress. Washburn wrote Jackson that his goal in the conference and with a Presidential meeting with Ramadan and others was "that the Muslims will be impressed with the moral and spiritual strength of America." Washburn and the CIA had other unspoken goals in mind than trying to impress Ramadan of the moral and spiritual strength of America.[24]

President Eisenhower in a 1953 White House meeting with Muslim Brotherhood members, including Hassan al-Banna's son-in-law, Said Ramadan, on far right holding papers.

John Foster Dulles, a fanatical Cold War conservative Republican and former Wall Street lawyer for the Rockefeller interests, who had been an open Nazi sympathizer at the beginning of the Second World War, was Secretary of State. His brother, Allen Dulles, another Rockefeller family lawyer, was CIA Director. They were both ready to test the Muslim Brotherhood as a force to damage Soviet influence.

CIA files on this part of Cold War history are still closed for reasons of "national security," but what is known is that Radio Liberty executive Robert Dreher, a militant CIA agent who believed not in containment but in an active "rollback" of Soviet influence in Eastern Europe, invited Said Ramadan to Munich in 1957 to become part of the board of the Islamic Center of Munich. There Ramadan would go on to become the key architect of the Munich mosque as a future center for spreading Islam through Europe and the World.

Ramadan was charismatic, highly intelligent, and urbane, a perfect spokesman for the CIA's operations against the Soviet Union. That same year, the CIA's Operations Coordinating Board created an Ad Hoc Working Group on Islam that included top officials from the Government's US Information Agency, the State Department, and the CIA.[25]

The relations between the Muslim Brotherhood and the CIA over the ensuing decade and into the 1970s were mainly focused on countering Soviet influence in the Arab Middle East, where Nasser's Arab Socialism had become a major influence in Iraq, Syria, and across the Arab world, threatening the Islamist agenda of the Brotherhood.

Nasser's nationalization of the Suez Canal and his charismatic presence made him a magnetic personality across the Arab world. The fact that he had turned to Moscow for aid, while remaining non-aligned, gave him further appeal. Saudi Arabia's alliance with the Muslim Brotherhood became the major vehicle—aside from the customary CIA orchestrated coups, such as that against Mossadegh in Iran, or assassinations—for Washington to indirectly and secretly counter the appeal of Nasserism and nationalism in the Arab world of the 1950s and 1960s.

Jihadist political Islam was now firmly on the CIA radar. The marriage of the two—US covert intelligence agencies and fanatical Muslim Brothers and Jihadist Islam—were to form a main pillar of US secret intelligence and secret foreign policy for more than seven decades. Until the shocking events of September 11, 2001 and revelations that Osama bin Laden had been trained in Afghanistan during the 1980's by the CIA, few had the slightest idea of the sinister alliance.

In 1979, the had CIA turned more actively to what was now Said Ramadan's Muslim Brotherhood when the Soviet Union invaded Afghanistan. Their project was called *Mujahideen*, or people doing Jihad, and one of their young recruits was a Saudi who had been educated in Saudi Arabia by the Brotherhood. His name was Osama bin Laden.

Endnotes

1   Ian Johnson, *The Beachhead: How a Mosque for Ex-Nazis Became Center of Radical Islam*, The Wall Street Journal, July 12, 2005, accessed in http://www.moralgroup.com/NewsItems/Islam/p20.htm.

2   Lisa Getter, *Showing Faith in Discretion*, The Los Angeles Times, Sep 27, 2002.

3   Ibid.

4   William Martin, *The Riptide of Revival*, Christian History and Biography (2006), Issue 92, pp. 24–29.

5   Gerard Colby, Charlotte Dennett, *Thy Will Be Done: The Conquest of the Amazon: Nelson Rockefeller and Evangelism in the Age of Oil*, Harper Collins,1996, pp. 292–295.

6   Ibid.

7   Ian Johnson, *A Mosque in Munich: Nazis, the CIA and the Rise of the Muslilm Brotherhood in the West*, Houghton, Mifflin Harcourt, Boston, 2010, p. 69.

8   Ibid., p. 129.

9   Said K. Aburish, *Nasser, the Last Arab*, 2004, New York, St. Martin's Press, p. 26.

10 Mark Curtis, *Britain and the Muslim Brotherhood Collaboration during the 1940s and 1950s*, 18 December 2010, accessed in, http://markcurtis.wordpress.com/2010/12/18/britain-and-the-muslim-brotherhood-collaboration-during-the-1940s-and-1950s/.

11 Steven A. Cook, *The Struggle for Egypt: From Nasser to Tahrir Square*, 2011, New York, Oxford University Press, p. 66.

12 Robert Dreyfuss, *Devil's Game*, 2005, New York, Metropolitan Books, p. 104.

13 Richard P. Mitchell, *The Society of the Muslim Brothers*, 1969, New York, Oxford University Press, pp. 151–155.

14 Austin Cline, *Wahhabism and Wahhabi Islam: How Wahhabi Islam Differs from Sunni, Shia Islam*, accessed in http://atheism.about.com/od/islamicsects/a/wahhabi.htm.

15 John Loftus, *The Muslim Brotherhood, Nazis and Al-Qaeda*, April 10, 2006, Jewish Community News.

16 Robert Dreyfuss, op. cit., pp. 121–126.

17 Ian Johnson, *A Mosque in Munich . . .* , p. 127.

18 Robert Dreyfuss, op. cit., pp. 126–127.

19 Ibid.

20 Pew Center, *Muslim World League and World Assembly of Muslim Youth*, September 15, 2010, accessed in http://www.pewforum.org/2010/09/15/muslim-networks-and-movements-in-western-europe-muslim-world-league-and-world-assembly-of-muslim-youth/.

21 Cited in Dreyfuss, op. cit., p. 79.

22 Ibid., p. 75.

23 Ian Johnson, *A Mosque in Munich . . .* , pp. 116–117.

24 Ibid., pp. 116–117.

25 Ibid., pp. 127–136.

CHAPTER SEVEN

THE CIA'S AFGHAN CRUSADE: OPIUM WARS, BIN LADEN, AND MUJAHIDEEN

"When the operation started in 1979, this region grew opium only for regional markets and produced no heroin. Within two years, however, the Pakistan-Afghanistan borderlands became the world's top heroin producer.... CIA assets again controlled this heroin trade. As the Mujahideen guerrillas seized territory inside Afghanistan, they ordered peasants to plant opium as a revolutionary tax."

— **Alfred McCoy, author, The Politics of Heroin in Southeast Asia**

A Soviet "Vietnam"

By far the most influential voice in the US Administration of President Jimmy Carter was his National Security Adviser, Zbigniew Brzezinski. Brzezinski's influence drew largely from the fact that he had one of the most influential patrons in the United States at the time. David Rockefeller, then chairman of the family's Chase Manhattan Bank, one of the most influential banks internationally, had taken Brzezinski under his wing.

In 1973, Rockefeller had founded an elite, secretive policy group called the Trilateral Commission. It was created to "coordinate" political and economic policy between Washington, Western Europe, and, for the first time, Japan, hence the "tri" in the name. Rockefeller selected his trusted friend Brzezinski to be the first Executive Director of the Trilateral Commission, who was charged with selecting the group's three hundred powerful international members. The "coordination" envisioned by Rockefeller and Brzezinski involved not an exchange of ideas among equals but rather bringing the major areas of the industrial world under the control of a Rockefeller agenda.

Rockefeller's group of handpicked Trilateral members was so influential that it was decisive in making a previously unknown Georgia peanut farmer, Jimmy Carter, President of the world's most powerful nation in 1976. Carter had been chosen by Brzezinski to join Rockefeller's exclusive Trilateral Commission in 1973. It was Brzezinski, in fact, who first identified Carter as presidential potential and tutored him in economics, foreign policy, and world politics.[1]

When Carter got elected President in 1976, with more than a little help from Rockefeller's significant influence, he chose Brzezinski as his National Security Adviser and, de facto, his main foreign policy adviser.[2] Brzezinski, an ardent anti-Soviet cold warrior from an anti-Russian Polish nobility background, was a disciple of the British founder of Geopolitics, Sir Halford Mackinder, like Henry Kissinger was before him. Brzezinski had been trained to look at how to most effectively manipulate the global power nexus to Washington's advantage.

By 1979, Washington's geopolitical world was in a terrible flux. The Dollar, a pillar of US hegemony in global finance, was in steep decline against the strong currencies of Japan, Germany, and France. Severely high oil prices in the wake of the Iranian Khomeini revolution were driving the US economy deep into recession. Western Europe, notably Germany and France were increasingly opposed to what they felt was a unilateral de facto imperial arrogance on the part of Washington in world affairs.

In the oil-rich Middle East, Iran had undergone a theocratic revolution that ousted America's puppet dictator and Rockefeller crony, Shah Reza Pahlevi. The Ayatollah Khomeini was consolidating power and establishing a rigid Shi'ite Muslim theocratic state. Initially open to maintaining friendly relations with Washington, Iran under the Shi'ite rule soon distanced herself from her earlier US alliance. By 1980, Turkey, which had been torn between right and leftist parties for several years, underwent a CIA-backed General's Coup, but the growing distrust of the US among Turkish leading circles was always simmering in the background.

Against this background of global instability, Brzezinski initiated a far-reaching policy decision. He authorized and organized the recruitment of Islamic Jihadists from all over the world and smuggled them into Soviet-controlled Afghanistan through US-friendly Pakistan. The aim of his little Jihad, as Brzezinski wrote in a classified internal memo to President Carter, would be to create "the Soviet Vietnam." In other words, Washington and the CIA manipulated events inside Afghanistan to force a Soviet response—a military occupation. Afghanistan was far too strategic to Soviet security, Brzezinski reckoned, and his actions were a trap to bog them down in an endless war against US-trained and armed Jihadist guerrillas.

The global consequences of Washington's attempt to instrumentalize Muslim Jihadists, contemptuously referred to later by Brzezinski as "some stirred-up Muslims," were to haunt and terrorize the world and the US in the decades after.[3] Brzezinski was obsessed with giving the Soviets their Vietnam, and anti-communist Muslim Brotherhood "freedom fighters," as Washington propaganda named them, seemed the perfect way.

Afghanistan: the New Great Game in an "Arc of Crisis"

In the 19th century, there was an ongoing struggle between Czarist Russia and the British Empire over who would control Afghanistan, a geo-strategically central land straddling Central, Southern, and Southwestern Asia. The stakes were huge. With control of Afghanistan, a major power could control or destabilize all Central Asia through Afghanistan. It was the Soviet Union's "soft underbelly." Rudyard Kipling popularized the struggle between Russia and the West over Afghanistan as "the Great Game," a geopolitical rivalry for control of the Eurasian landmass by controlling the Afghan space.

During the Cold War, that Great Game for control of Afghanistan underwent a changing cast of players. Initially the Soviet Union acted as protector of the non-aligned regime of socialist President Nor Mohammed Taraki. Taraki became President in 1978 by ousting Mohammed Daoud, the cousin of deposed King Mohammed Zahir Shah. Moscow was determined to prevent any possible Western attacks from her Afghan underbelly.

This time around, however, the United States played the lead role that the British Empire had played a century before, using Afghanistan to drive a dagger into the heart of Soviet Central Asia in order to force Moscow into its own "Vietnam" quagmire and more.

In 1978, Carter's National Security Adviser, Zbigniew Brzezinski, was already speaking of an "arc of crisis." The arc, he declared, went "along the shores of the Indian Ocean, with fragile and social and political structures in a region of vital importance to us, threatened with fragmentation. The resulting political chaos could well be filled by elements hostile to our values and sympathetic to our adversaries."[4] His clear message was that the United States' "national security interests" dictated US intervention to stem that "chaos" from "adversaries," shorthand for the Soviets.

What Brzezinski deliberately did *not* say was that he and US intelligence networks were actively stirring up that chaotic Arc of Crisis in order to destabilize the Islamic perimeter of the Soviet Union.

Brzezinski's remarks were aimed at preparing the American public for a coming confrontation with the Soviet Union across its Islamic underbelly. Washington intelligence networks were quietly preparing the crisis that was to give the excuse to finance the most costly covert operation in US history, the Afghan Mujahideen war against Soviet-occupied Afghanistan, with the CIA discreetly directing all from behind the stage.

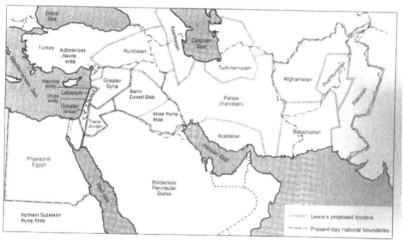

The Bernard Lewis plan for the Middle East

Brzezinski's "Arc of Crisis" was adapted from a proposal of British intelligence operative and Islam expert, Sir Bernard Lewis. Lewis, who was then at Princeton University in the US, proposed new borders for the Middle East: the Bernard Lewis Plan. Brzezinski's Arc of Crisis was composed of the nations across the southern flank of the Soviet Union from the Indian subcontinent to Turkey, south through the Arabian Peninsula to the Horn of Africa, with Iran as its center of gravity.[5]

At a confidential April 1979 meeting of the US-European Bilderberg Group in Baden, Austria, Lewis elaborated his notion of using this Arc of Crisis to destabilize the Soviet Union. He called on NATO countries to "endorse the radical Muslim Brotherhood movement behind Khomeini, in order to promote balkanization of the entire Muslim Near East along tribal and religious lines."[6] At that point, many in US intelligence circles, including even Brzezinski, believed they could control Khomeini's revolution as a weapon against the Soviets.[7]

Anglo-American strategy in the region made a radical shift based on the plans of Lewis and Brzezinski. State Department Middle East official Henry Precht later recalled, "There was this idea that the Islamic forces could be used against the Soviet Union. The theory was, there was an arc of crisis, and so an arc of Islam could be mobilized to contain the Soviets. It was a Brzezinski concept."[8]

Bernard Lewis argued that the West should encourage autonomous groups, such as Kurds, Armenians, Lebanese Maronites, Ethiopian Copts, Azerbaijani Turks, and so forth. The ensuing chaos would spread in what he termed "an 'Arc of Crisis,' which would inevitably spill over into the Muslim regions of the Soviet Union."[9]

Aside from a tiny handful of US Middle East experts, however, almost no one inside the Washington Administration really understood the internal dynamics of political Islam. They were like small children playing with an undetonated bomb they had unearthed from the war. The bomb was soon to explode.

Ramadan in Afghanistan

Said Ramadan was perhaps the most influential man in the Egyptian Muslim Brotherhood in the years just after the death of his father-in-law, Hassan al-Banna. Ramadan spent the 1960s and 1970s in exile in Geneva. From there, with overt and mostly covert political support from the CIA, he traveled regularly between Munich, where the Munich Mosque had become one of the main bases of spreading the Muslim Brotherhood internationally, and Asia. He was very often in Pakistan and Afghanistan, where the CIA had a special Cold War interest in pressuring the Soviet Union as noted.[10]

Ramadan and the Grand Mufti of Jerusalem—the old anti-Semitic friend of Hassan al-Banna and of SS-leader Heinrich Himmler—had revitalized the moribund Muslim World Conference in Jerusalem. Mohammad Amin al-Husayni, the Grand Mufti of Jerusalem, was President of the Congress. It was tightly controlled by the Muslim Brotherhood. Ramadan turned the focus of the Muslim World Conference into a forum for condemning the plight of Muslims forced to live under communist rule, an agenda that fit nicely with the CIA's Cold War strategies.[11]

In 1962, Said Ramadan had gone to Mecca to launch what was to become the most important international organization of political Islam and of the Muslim Brotherhood—the Muslim World League (MWL). Ramadan drafted the League's bylaws.

The Muslim World League became the de facto world center for spreading the Salafist Jihad ideology of the Egyptian Muslim Brotherhood of Hassan al-Banna through his son-in-law, Ramadan. Its founding members included the elite of global Jihadist Islam. It included Al-Banna's old friend from World War II, pro-Nazi Haj Amin al-Husseini, Grand Mufti of Jerusalem, who, by then, was enjoying Saudi financial largesse instead of Hitler's. It included Abul-Ala Mawdudi, the founder of *Jamaat e-Islamiya*, Pakistan's de facto Muslim Brotherhood organization. Mawdudi orchestrated the Salafist dictatorship of Pakistan's President, Zia-ul-Haq.[12]

Ramadan's Muslim World League also included Muhammad Sadiq al-Mujaddidi of Afghanistan, who worked closely with the CIA and whose protégés would form the core of the CIA's Mujahideen. The Muslim World League founding board also included the Grand Mufti of Saudi Arabia, Muhammad ibn Ibrahim al-Shaikh, the senior religious spokesman for the ultra-fundamentalist Saudi Wahhabism, and a person who enjoyed enormous influence within the Saudi Royal House.[13]

In effect, the Muslim World League represented a marriage of the Egyptian Muslim Brotherhood's political Salafism with the ultra-traditional Saudi Wahhabite ideology. A more deadly political cocktail would have been hard to imagine. By all indications, virtually no one at the senior levels of US intelligence bothered to look closely at the new organization of Said Ramadan and what its ultimate goals might be beyond the simple fact that Ramadan's Muslim World League was devoutly anti-communist.[14]

The League, by tradition always headed by a Saudi national—usually from the Royal family—was financed by Saudi oil dollars. It combined the feudal Islamic obedience of Saudi Wahhabite Sunni Islam with the Brotherhood's agile, politically opportunist Islamic Jihadism. The League basically took whatever public profile was useful in order to advance their global Caliphate agenda, much like the Catholic Church's Society of Jesus since their founding by Ignatius of Loyola and Francis Xavier.[15]

The Muslim Brotherhood's development and expansion of the Muslim World Conference in Jerusalem and the Muslim World League in Mecca created the low-profile organizational infrastructure of what was soon to be called a "Global Jihad."

In the 1960s and up well into the 1970s, the CIA seemed content to give Ramadan and the Muslim Brotherhood a large degree of freedom so long as their focus was anti-communism and against troublesome Arab nationalism of the Nasserite brand. As a consequence Said Ramadan helped build up the Pakistani Muslim Brotherhood local organization, *Jamaat e-Islamiya*, and founded madrassas and other religious schools across Afghanistan.[16] Those organizations of the Muslim Brotherhood in both Afghanistan and neighboring Pakistan were soon to gain greater attention from the CIA and Western intelligence.

Afghanistan and the Soviets

In 1973, Afghan Prince Muhammad Daoud ousted his cousin, the Afghan king, with help from the Soviet Union. He then established an Afghan republic of sorts.

As President, Daoud embarked on a cautious land reform program to try to win poor Afghan sharecroppers. Washington was alarmed that they had not anticipated the Daoud coup and began to actively encourage the Muslim Brotherhood networks they knew from Ramadan and other assets to make resistance to the Daoud presidency. Earlier, as Prime Minister to the King, Daoud had strongly opposed the Brotherhood, making the two bitter enemies from the start.[17]

However, soon after seizing power in 1974, Daoud began to distance himself from overreliance on the Soviet Union for military and economic support. He opened stronger ties with non-aligned India and the pro-US Shah in Iran. Daoud also turned to other oil-rich Muslim nations, such as America's strongest Middle East Muslim allies, Saudi Arabia, Iraq and Kuwait, for financial assistance, bringing him still closer to the US influence.

During a March 1978 visit to Islamabad, Pakistan, Daoud reached an agreement with Pakistan's US-backed Sunni military dictator, President Mohammad Zia-ul-Haq.

As Daoud turned closer to the West and Washington's Persian Gulf allies, he distanced his regime from the Soviets. He began to purge his government of communists, removed Soviet military advisers, and shifted military training from the Soviets to the pro-US Egypt of Anwar Sadat. His new cabinet contained several staunch anti-communists. By spring of 1978, he announced plans to fly to Washington for high level talks with the Carter Administration.[18]

Daoud had failed to improve Afghanistan's economy, and his increasingly dictatorial one-man rule alienated most of his earlier allies. When he arrested leaders of the communist PDPA (the People's Democratic Party of Afghanistan), communist leaders Nor Mohammed Taraki and Tabizullah Amin, along with a group of anti-Daoud military officers, staged a coup that ended in the killing of Daoud and the installing of Mohammed Taraki as new President.

The PDPA military putsch brought major land reform intended to weaken powerful landlords who were closely tied to fundamentalist Sunni Islam. Taraki's goal was to win the peasants to the new Taraki regime by aiding poor Afghan sharecroppers traditionally forced to work land owned by the king and his cronies. Taraki also built schools for women who had been banned from education under the religiously strict Sunni monarchy. He opened Afghan universities to the poor and introduced free health care.[19]

The land reforms and the education of women represented a red flag for the Muslim Brotherhood and other reactionary fundamentalist Muslim organizations in Afghanistan, who had flourished among wealthy landowners and in the universities since the time of Ramadan. These fundamentalist Islamic networks began inciting riots and protests against the Taraki regime, charging them with violating fundamental precepts of Islam.

It was widely said within Afghanistan and in Moscow that well before the December 25, 1979, Soviet occupation of Afghanistan, Washington had covertly encouraged the protests against Taraki's socialist government. It was a cruder, earlier version of the tactics later perfected in the 2011 "Arab Spring" revolts.

In March 1979, a CIA memorandum to Brzezinski stated that the fundamentalist attacks on the Kabul regime, burning of girls' schools, and other acts of violence had "achieved surprising successes."[20] In February 1979, against the wishes of Moscow and of the Taraki government, pro-Taraki militants kidnapped and assassinated CIA Kabul Station Chief and then US Ambassador Adolf "Spike" Dubs, conveniently enough, further justifying strong action from Washington.

The man named by Taraki to carry out his land reform, Tabizullah Amin, Cabinet Minister, was suspected by Soviet KGB Chief Yuri Andropov to be a CIA deep cover agent. Amin had launched a brutal campaign of terror against political opponents that turned world opinion against the Taraki government. Andropov believed the CIA had Amin infiltrate the Kabul government with the intent of discrediting the Taraki revolution.[21]

If that was so, he did a brilliant job for his Washington sponsors.

Taraki flew to Moscow to consult with Brezhnev on a strategy to get rid of Amin. The day he returned to Kabul, Amin had Taraki executed and immediately seized power himself. Weeks later, CIA-backed warlords massacred dozens of Afghan government officials in the western city of Herat. The combination of these two events finally convinced a reluctant Brezhnev to send troops into Afghanistan on December 25, 1979.

Falling into Brzezinski's Trap

With Moscow's friend, Nor Mohammed Taraki, murdered and Tabizullah Amin a suspected CIA agent in control in Kabul, Moscow realized they were in danger of losing the strategic Great Game for control of Afghanistan to the West, a devastating strategic catastrophe were it to cope to pass. On December 25, 1979, after initially rejecting direct military intervention as too dangerous, Soviet Premier Leonid Brezhnev ordered Soviet tanks to roll into Afghanistan across the Panjshir Valley while KGB operatives and Soviet Special Forces troops stormed the Royal Palace in Kabul.

The Soviet forces assassinated Tabizullah Amin and installed Babrak Karmal as the new leader of Afghanistan. The original intent of Moscow was to stabilize the situation and leave within a few months. Instead, they would be caught in Afghani political and tribal quicksand, as would the US military itself in Afghanistan after 2001.[22]

A Soviet-organized government led by Babrak Karmal was hastily organized in an effort to try to fill the power vacuum. Soviet troops were deployed in substantial numbers to stabilize Afghanistan under Karmal, although the Soviet government, naively, did not expect to do most of the fighting in Afghanistan. As a result of their intervention, however, the Soviets were directly involved for the first time in what had been a domestic war in Afghanistan.

Brzezinski now had the excuse he'd been looking for to begin overtly arming a USA-backed counter-revolution in Afghanistan. Moscow had taken the bait.[23]

"Birthing" Mujahideen

In April 1979, eight months before the Soviet intervention, US officials had secretly begun meeting with Mujahideen guerrillas and as a result of the talks, asked a Pakistani military official to recommend that Mujahideen organizations receive US support. Brzezinski was laying his trap, and the Islamic fundamentalists were his bait.

Unbeknownst to the American public, on July 3, 1979, well before Soviet tanks and paratroopers rolled into Afghanistan, President Carter—at Brzezinski's recommendation—had signed the first national security directive authorizing secret US aid to Afghan warlords to fight the Afghan regime. Brzezinski said years later he had convinced Carter that, in his "opinion this aid was going to induce a Soviet military intervention."[24]

Brzezinski was right, and everything Washington covertly did was to make sure it happened that way.

Initially, the principle Islamic Jihad organization which the CIA used against Soviet Afghanistan was *Hezbi Islami*. It was a neo-feudal Islamic Jihad organization modelled on Ramadan's Muslim Brotherhood. Like the Brotherhood in Egypt, it set out to create a pure Islamic State, deploying a highly disciplined organization built around a small cadre of educated elites.[25]

CIA's Mujahideen Islamic Jihadists defeated the Soviet Army in Afghanistan in 1980s.

Hezbi Islami had been founded in 1977 by Gulbuddin Hekmatyar. Hekmatyar was a psychopathic Sunni fundamentalist whose unrestrained acts of murder and terror won him the attention of the CIA and of Pakistan's US-trained military dictator, General Zia-ul-Haq.

Hekmatyar's *Hezbi Islami* had murdered hundreds of left-wing students in Afghanistan universities. Hekmatyar ordered his followers to throw acid into the faces of Afghan women who refused to wear their *burkas*. He was brutally serious about his Sharia fundamentalism.

Gulbuddin Hekmatyar had come out of Kabul University in 1973 as leader of the CIA-financed Organization of Muslim Youth, the student organization of Said Ramadan's *Jamiat-e-Islami*, a Muslim Brotherhood affiliate.[26] Hekmatyar later became President Reagan's favorite Mujahideen "freedom fighter" in the CIA's secret war against the Soviets.

Even as a student at Kabul University, Hekmatyar was no mere academic intellectual or theoretical Jihadist. He joined the Brotherhood there and put his beliefs into practice. While a student in charge of the secret military wing of the Brotherhood's Kabul student organization, he was sentenced to prison for murdering his university rival, a Maoist student.[27] He and his *Hezbi Islami* followers then fled to Peshawar across the border in Pakistan, where he soon caught the attention of Pakistan's equally brutal Jihadist President, Zia-ul-Haq.[28]

The so-called Mujahideen were a ragtag assortment of various tribal gangs from inside Pakistan, together with Islamist foreign Jihad volunteers. Hekmatyar's *Hezbi Islami* was the most powerful of seven such gangs which constituted the Peshawar Seven alliance of Sunni Mujahideen forces.

One such foreign Jihad volunteer to the Mujahideen Jihad was Osama bin Laden, the 22-year-old son of a Saudi construction billionaire whose family had made their fortune as the Saudi Royal constructor. Young Bin Laden arrived in Peshawar, Pakistan, from Saudi Arabia in 1979 with money and many Arab Jihad volunteers. Osama bin Laden had been sent to Afghanistan, with US approval, by then Saudi intelligence chief Prince Turki bin Faisal.[29]

Osama Bin Laden became part of the CIA's *Operation Cyclone*, the code name for Brzezinski's project to use Islamist fighters against the Soviet forces in Afghanistan to give the Soviet Union their own "Vietnam." He proceeded to set up something innocuously called the Services Office, together with his teacher and mentor from the university in Jeddah, Muslim Brotherhood member Abdullah Yusuf Azzam, a Palestinian Sunni Muslim known as the "Father of Global Jihad."[30]

Part of the Afghan Mujahideen financing was organized through Osama bin Laden. In 1984, bin Laden and Azzam established *Maktab al-Khidamat (MAK)*, which funneled money, arms, and fighters from around the Arab world into Afghanistan. The Saudi monarchy had agreed to match dollar-for-dollar every sum Washington put into the Afghan proxy war against the Soviet Union.[31] Bin Laden, the MAK, and the Afghan Mujahideen received in total about half a billion dollars a year from the CIA and roughly the same from the Saudis, funneled through Pakistan's Inter-Services Intelligence (ISI).[32]

Through Maktab al-Khidamat or MAK, bin Laden became one of the financiers of the Afghan Mujahideen Holy War against Moscow. His MAK paid for air tickets to bring thousands of Arab fighters for the Afghan Holy war against Communism.

Bin Laden also collaborated closely with Hekmatyar's *Hezbi Islami*. Bin Laden established camps across the Afghan border inside Khyber Pakhtunkhwa in Pakistan near Peshawar. There, the ISI and allied intelligence services trained Jihadi volunteers from across the Muslim world, so-called "Afghan Arabs," to fight against the Soviet puppet regime: the Democratic Republic of Afghanistan.[33] After the Soviet withdrawal from Afghanistan in 1989, the key figures in Maktab al-Khidamat, including Osama bin Laden, went on to form what became known as Al Qaeda.[34]

When the Soviet Union invaded Afghanistan in 1979, bin Laden's Palestinian partner, the Muslim Brotherhood's Abdullah Yusuf Azzam, issued a fatwa titled, *Defence of the Muslim Lands, the First Obligation after Faith*. In it he declared that both the Afghan and Palestinian struggles were Jihads in which killing occupiers of their land, no matter what their faith, was a personal obligation for all Muslims. The edict was supported by Abdul al-Aziz bin Baz, Saudi Arabia's Grand Mufti, or highest religious scholar.[35]

CIA Operation Cyclone Launched

Brzezinski's new Mujahideen Jihad project, *Operation Cyclone*, was taking formidable shape.

With US and Saudi money and training done by Zia-ul-Haq's Inter-Services Intelligence (ISI) agency and Pakistani military officers, the Afghan Mujahideen began to take on Soviet occupation troops inside

Afghanistan in a terror campaign that lasted from 1979 until the Soviet withdrawal in 1989. Pakistan's Zia was the main intermediary for doling out the money from US intelligence and Saudi sources—including Osama bin Laden—handing out weapons, and giving military training and financial support to Afghan Mujahideen groups.

General Zia-ul-Haq, Pakistani President, introduced brutal Sharia law in Pakistan and trained the Mujahideen along with CIA and Saudi money.

Zia-ul-Haq was a suitable ideological patron for Hekmatyar and the Afghan Mujahideen. He was a fanatical devotee of the most severe Islamic Sharia. As President, Zia-ul-Haq put more than 15,000 female rape victims in jail because they could not comply with the Islamic condition requiring them to have numerous male witnesses of their victimization. They were charged with fornication, and their rapists were let go free. A Pakistani woman who made an allegation of rape was convicted for adultery, while the rapist was acquitted. Previous Pakistani legal provisions relating to adultery under Zia's Sharia were replaced so the guilty woman and man would be flogged, each with a hundred stripes if unmarried. And if they were married, they would be stoned to death.

Blaspheming Muhammad was punishable with "death, or imprisonment for life," while disrespecting the Quran was punishable by life imprisonment, and disrespecting the family of the Prophet or the Companions of the Prophet was punishable by up to three years in prison. This was the ideology of Washington's man in charge of training and recruiting Afghan Mujahideen "freedom fighters."[36]

Washington's CIA, along with funding from Britain's MI6 and SAS and significant money from Saudi Arabian intelligence, made it possible for the Pakistani ISI to arm and train over 100,000 insurgents between 1978 and 1992.[37] Washington alone spent as much as $20 billion, by some estimates.

Heroin trafficking run by Mujahideen, as in Vietnam in the 1970s, played a major added financial role with more than a little help from their friends in the CIA.[38]

CIA and "Poppy" Bush Take Over

One of the greatest political problems facing President Carter in his reelection bid was the Iranian government's seizure of US embassy personnel as hostages. US news media broadcast the plight daily, making it an albatross around Carter's neck for not finding a solution.

With the assist of a secret deal between the Republicans and Khomeini's Iran, US embassy hostages held since November 1979 in the Teheran Embassy were not released until after the November 1980 US presidential elections. Carter's people had secretly been negotiating such a release before US elections to boost Carter against the Republican team of Ronald Reagan and George H.W. Bush. But Bush, Reagan Campaign Manager and future CIA Director, Bill Casey, and a small circle around G.H.W. Bush secretly offered Iran a sweeter deal if the release took place *after* the US elections. It became known as the "October Surprise."[39]

On January 20, 1981, the same day Reagan and Bush were sworn into office, Iran released the 52 US Embassy hostages. At the same time, in violation of the US Arms Export Control Act—a law prohibiting a recipient country of US arms from transferring "United States-origin" munitions to a third country without written permission from the United States—Israeli Defense Minister Ariel Sharon began to channel what became billions of dollars of US-made weapons to Iran to tilt the war between a US-backed Saddam Hussein regime in Iraq and Khomeini's Iran.[40]

With the Reagan-Bush Administration now in charge of US foreign policy, a dramatic shift took place in what was permitted in terms of covert operations in Afghanistan, as well as in the Iran-Iraq war then underway. The latter had begun as a US-covert encouragement to Iraq's Saddam Hussein to neutralize the growing power of Iran under Khomeini's strict Sharia Islamic rule.

One faction in the Reagan Administration, led by US Secretary of State George Shultz and defense Secretary Casper Weinberger, backed Iraq against Iran for reasons of Western oil supply security. Another faction, led by National Security Adviser Robert C. McFarlane and two members of his national Security Council staff, Howard Teicher and Colonel Oliver North, argued in favor of arming Iran for two reasons: to enhance Israel's security and to facilitate better relations with a post-Khomeini Iran. At the time, Israel depended on Iranian oil and made a nice business selling Israeli arms to Iran.

Vice President and former CIA Director George H.W. Bush shrewdly straddled both camps with the effect of US policy zigzagging between backing for Iraq and then backing for Iran to ensure that the Iran-Iraq war raged for eight years until 1988, costing hundreds of thousands of dead and disabled in both countries. The Iran-Iraq US duplicity and arming of both sides to drag out the conflict was a huge boon to Bush's friends in the military–industrial complex, as well as giving billions in windfall profits for Bush's cronies in the US and British oil industries, who used the war to charge high oil prices.[41]

A key figure who was instrumental in a Reagan Administration shift from arming Iraq to covertly arming Khomeini's Iran in 1985 was Graham E. Fuller, the CIA's National Intelligence Officer for the Middle East. For the previous two years, the Reagan Administration had conducted a program known as *Operation Staunch* to stem the flow of weapons to Iran while it continued to supply Iraq with covert aid, including top-secret satellite photographs.

Fuller argued that it was now time to change course. "Our tilt to Iraq was timely when Iraq was against the ropes and the Islamic revolution was on a roll," Fuller wrote in a May 1985 memo to CIA director Casey. "The time may now have to come to tilt back." Fuller contended that the United States should once again authorize Israel to ship United States arms to Iran.[42]

The Fuller memo initiated the first of what would become repeated US "tilt fro, tilt back" shifts between backing Sunni against Shi'ite or backing Shi'ite against Sunni interests in the Islamic geopolitical space. Fuller's memo laid the seeds for the illegal enterprise later known as the Reagan-Bush Iran-Contra Affair.

Graham E. Fuller was later to play an instrumental role in the CIA's cultivation of another Islamic asset, Fethullah Gülen in Turkey. Step by step, US intelligence was becoming immersed in trying to steer Islamic Jihadists on behalf of the Washington global strategic agenda. The Muslim Brotherhood and its later offshoots, however, had their own global strategic agenda, and it was hardly one supportive of US national interest.

Bush, BCCI, Mujahideen, and Heroin "Fallout"

By the mid-1980s, under Vice president and ex-CIA Director George H.W. Bush and CIA Director Bill Casey, Washington's geopolitical games with fundamentalist Jihad Islam went into high gear in Pakistan and Afghanistan.

The operations were very dirty, involving heroin and opium trafficking and money laundering through a very dirty bank, BCCI. It involved the CIA, Saudi intelligence, and the Mujahideen.

It was perhaps more than ironic that, within the family, George Herbert Walker Bush, father of later president George W. Bush, was known as "Poppy" Bush, a moniker that could refer to opium poppies of Afghanistan just as well as to his being family father. The Bush family was deeply entangled in both Colombian cocaine and Afghan opium and heroin operations. As Reagan's Vice President during the time of the Afghan Mujahideen war, Bush headed a Presidential Task Force on International Drug Smuggling. According to European anti-narcotics officials, Bush used his post to facilitate the inflow of Colombian cocaine via Florida, where his old CIA Cuban buddies controlled organized crime.[43]

With the Republicans now in a second term, Vice President George Bush became bolder. As veteran Washington journalist Robert Parry described the mood then,

A *real-politick Zeitgeist* took hold in Washington. It tolerated drug smuggling by CIA-connected groups, including the Nicaraguan contras and the Afghan Mujahideen. It watched passively as CIA associates plundered the world's banking system, most notably through the corrupt Bank of Credit and Commerce International (BCCI), which also had paid off a key Iranian in the October Surprise mystery.[44]

The CIA and Saudis, through BCCI bank, financed Osama bin Laden's Mujahideen in Afghanistan and laundered their heroin profits.

The financial heart of the CIA's 1980s Mujahideen operation was the Bank of Credit and Commerce International (BCCI), founded in 1972 by Agha Hasan Abedi, a Pakistani financier close to Zia-ul-Haq. The Bank was registered in Luxembourg, with head offices in Karachi and London. It became the bank of choice for laundering profits of Mujahideen heroin sales, financing CIA black operations, and countless other illegal transactions.[45]

In fact, as a later US Senate investigation uncovered, BCCI was intimately tied to the CIA. BCCI head Abedi was on personal terms with former Director of the CIA Richard Helms, Colonel Oliver North, and the CIA operatives loyal to Vice President Bush in the Iran/Contra affair. And Reagan-Bush CIA Director Bill Casey met numerous times with Abedi.[46]

BCCI, in short, was the financial glue linking Afghan Mujahideen, Saudi Arabian intelligence, the CIA, and Pakistani ISI. Its owners included Bank of America, then the largest US bank; Khalid bin Mahfouz, who headed the largest bank in Saudi Arabia, NCB, which handled funds of the Saudi Royal family; and Sheikh Zayed bin Sultan Al Nahyan of Abu Dhabi. Kamal Adham and Abdul Raouf Khalil, the past and the then Saudi intelligence liaisons to the United States, respectively, were shareholders as well.[47] According to Craig Unger's book *House of Bush, House of Saud*, bin Mahfouz donated over $270,000 to Osama bin Laden's Islamist organization to assist the US-sponsored resistance to the Soviet occupation of Afghanistan.

In addition to the CIA, the BCCI client list included Saddam Hussein, Manuel Noriega, the Medellin Cocaine Cartel, and mercenary terrorist-for-hire, Abu Nidal, along with Osama bin Laden. In 1987, BCCI's US bank subsidiary even helped a young Texas oilman, George W. Bush, with financing for his Harken Energy Co.[48]

As the Mujahideen expanded operations in Pakistan across the border and into Afghanistan, opium cultivation and refined heroin traffic grew along with it, as did the global operations of BCCI. Veteran drug researcher Alfred McCoy described how it functioned during the CIA's covert Afghan Mujahideen war:

> When the operation started in 1979, this region grew opium only for regional markets and produced no heroin. Within two years, however, the Pakistan-Afghanistan borderlands

became the world's top heroin producer, supplying 60 percent of US demand. . . . CIA assets again controlled this heroin trade. As the Mujaheddin guerrillas seized territory inside Afghanistan, they ordered peasants to plant opium as a revolutionary tax. Across the border in Pakistan, Afghan leaders and local syndicates under the protection of Pakistan Intelligence operated hundreds of heroin laboratories. During this decade of wide-open drug-dealing, the US Drug Enforcement Agency in Islamabad failed to instigate major seizures or arrests.[49]

McCoy further described the situation at the end of the Afghan Mujahideen war and the time of Soviet withdrawal:

In May 1990, as the CIA operation was winding down, The *Washington Post* published a front-page expose charging that Gulbudin Hekmatyar, the CIA's favored Afghan leader, was a major heroin manufacturer. The *Post* argued . . . that U.S. officials had refused to investigate charges of heroin dealing by its Afghan allies. . . . In 1995, the former CIA director of the Afghan operation, Charles Cogan, admitted the CIA had indeed sacrificed the drug war to fight the Cold War. "Our main mission was to do as much damage as possible to the Soviets. . . . I don't think that we need to apologize for this. Every situation has its fallout. . . . There was fallout in terms of drugs, yes." [50]

McCoy continued his description of the CIA narcotics operations:

Once the heroin left Pakistan's laboratories, the Sicilian mafia managed its export to the United States, and a chain of syndicate-controlled pizza parlors distributed the drugs to street gangs in American cities, according to reports by the Drug Enforcement Agency. Most ordinary Americans did not see the links between the CIA's alliance with Afghan drug lords, the pizza parlors, and the heroin on US streets.[51]

Mujahideen "Freedom Fighters" into "Terrorists"

US support for the Mujahideen became the centerpiece of US foreign policy by 1985 and came to be called the Reagan Doctrine.[52] Under the aggressive new proactive stance toward the Soviet Union, the US provided military and other support to anti-communist resistance movements in Afghanistan, Angola, Nicaragua, and Poland's *Solidarność* trade union.

From 1979, Afghanistan became home to violence and heroin production that was to become the norm over the following thirty-five years. The CIA and US State Department's USAID played a major role in fomenting Islamic hate toward communism that did not vanish when the Soviets left Afghanistan in 1989.

American universities produced books for Afghan children praising the virtues of Jihad and of killing communists. The books were financed by a USAID $50 million grant to the University of Nebraska in the 1980s. USAID was often used as a covert conduit for CIA operations. The textbooks sought to create enthusiasm in Islamic militancy. They called on Afghan children to "pluck out the eyes of the Soviet enemy and cut off his legs." Years later, the same US-produced books were approved by the Taliban for use in madrassas and were widely available in both Afghanistan and Pakistan.[53]

Money from a bizarre coalition of forces poured into the Mujahideen being trained and based across the Afghan border in Pakistan. The USA, Saudi intelligence service or *al-Istakhbarat al-'Ama*, the Kuwaitis, Saddam Hussein's Iraq, Qaddafi's Libya, and Khomeini's Iranians all paid the Salafist Islamic "freedom fighters" of Mujahideen over $1 billion per year during the 1980s.[54]

The Afghanistan conflict from 1979 through the final Soviet troop pullout in February 1989 was the bloodiest and costliest conflict of the Cold War. More than 13,000 Soviet soldiers paid with their lives, and some 40,000 were wounded. Roughly two million Afghans lost their lives during the war, and an additional 500,000 to two million were wounded and maimed.[55]

The ISI of Pakistan's Zia-ul-Haq, working with Osama bin Laden and other groups, had trained more than 100,000 Islamic radical jihadists in every art of modern warfare and terrorist techniques. They worked side by side together with the CIA, Britain's MI6, the Israeli intelligence services, and Saudi intelligence. Over the ensuing near quarter century, each of those "sponsors" would finance and deploy those Mujahideen veterans under the guise of one or another Islamic Jihad organization. One of the more infamous came to be named "Al Qaeda," or the Base, and its nominal head was the Saudi Osama bin Laden. Citing Western intelligence sources, *Jane's Defence Weekly* reported in 2001:

> In 1988, with US knowledge, Bin Laden created Al Qaeda (The Base): a conglomerate of quasi-independent Islamic terrorist cells in countries spread across at least 26 countries, including Algeria, Morocco, Turkey, Egypt, Syria, Uzbekistan, Tajikistan, Burma, Lebanon, Iraq, Saudi Arabia, Kuwait, Indonesia, Kenya, Tanzania, Azerbaijan, Dagestan, Uganda, Ethiopia, Syria, Tunisia, Bahrain, Yemen, Bosnia as well as the West Bank and Gaza. Western intelligence sources claim Al Qaeda even has a cell in Xinjiang in China.[56]

For the Wahhabite Sunni Muslim world, the defeat of the Soviet Union in Afghanistan was greeted as a "victory" for Islam and the Global Caliphate. For Washington, it was seen as a major defeat of America's Cold War communist adversary. Each player in the Mujahideen Great Game—Washington and Jihadist Islamists—looked at the events through completely different lenses.

From their triumph in Afghanistan, the CIA helped bring key cadre of the Mujahideen into Chechnya, Bosnia, and other battles in the post-Soviet Central Asia theatre. For the Jihadists, that was yet another assist on the road to the Global Caliphate that they were quite happy to accept.

Endnotes

1   Patrick Wood, *The Trilateral Commission: Usurping Sovereignty*, August 3, 2007, accessed in http://www.theendrun.com/the-trilateral-commission-usurping -sovereignty.

2   Ibid.

3   Zbigniew Brzezinski, *US history: How Jimmy Carter and I Started the Mujahideen, January 1998*, accessed in http://www.liveleak.com/view?i=a13_1240427874.

4   Iskander Rehman, *Arc of Crisis 2.0?*, March 7, 2013, National Interest, accessed in http://nationalinterest.org/commentary/arc-crisis-20-8194.

5   Andrew Gavin Marshall, *Creating an "Arc of Crisis": The Destabilization of the Middle East and Central Asia The Mumbai Attacks and the "Strategy of Tension,"* Global Research, December 7, 2008, accessed in http://www.globalresearch.ca/creating-an-arc-of-crisis-the-destabilization-of-the-middle-east-and-central-asia.

6   F. William Engdahl, *A Century of War: Anglo-American Oil Politics and the New World Order.* London: Pluto Press, 2004: p. 171.

7   Richard Cottam, Goodbye to America's Shah, Foreign Policy Magazine, March 16, 1979, accessed in http://www.foreignpolicy.com/articles/1979/03/16/goodbye_to_america_s_shah.

8   Peter Dale Scott, *The Road to 9/11: Wealth, Empire, and the Future of America*, University of California Press: 2007: p. 67.

9   F. William Engdahl, op. cit., p. 171.

10   Ian Johnson, *A Mosque in Munich: Nazis, the CIA and the Rise of the Muslim Brotherhood in the West*, Houghton, Mifflin Harcourt, 2010, p. 162.

11   Ibid., p. 133.

12   Robert Dreyfuss, *Devil's Game*, 2005, Metropolitan Books, New York, p. 132.

13   Ibid.

14   Ibid., p. 134.

15   Ibid., p. 162. See also *Muslim World League and World Assembly of Muslim Youth*, Pew Research, September 15, 2010, accessed in http://www.pewforum.org/2010/09/15/muslim-networks-and-movements-in-western-europe-muslim-world-league-and-world-assembly-of-muslim-youth/.

16   Ian Johnson, op. cit., p. 197.

17   Dean Henderson, *Afghan History Suppressed: Part I— Islamists Heroin and the CIA*, February 11, 2013, Veterans Today, accessed in http://www.veteranstoday.com/2013/02/11/afghan-history-suppressed-part-i-islamists-heroin-and-the-cia/.

18   Peter R. Blood, ed., *Afghanistan: A Country Study: DAOUD'S REPUBLIC, JULY 1973- APRIL 1978*, Library of Congress, Washington DC, 2001, accessed in http://countrystudies.us/afghanistan/28.htm.

19 Dean Henderson, op. cit.

20 Robert Gates, *From the Shadows: The Ultimate Insider's Story of Five Presidents and How They Won the Cold War*, New York, Simon & Schuster, 2007, p. 144.

21 Dean Henderson, op. cit.

22 Artemy M. Kalinovsky, *A Long Goodbye: The Soviet Withdrawal from Afghanistan*, 2011, Harvard University Press, pp. 24.

23 Ibid., pp. 25–28.

24 Ibid.

25 Institute for the Study of War, *Hizb i Islami Gulbuddin (HIG)—Overview*, accessed in http://www.understandingwar.org/hizb-i-islami-gulbuddin-hig.

26 Dean Henderson, op. cit.

27 Institute for the Study of War, *Hizb-i-Islami Gulbuddin (HIG),* accessed in http://www.understandingwar.org/hizb-i-islami-gulbuddin-hig.

28 Ibid.

29 Craig Unger, *House of Bush, House of Saud – The Secret Relationship between the World's Two Most Powerful Dynasties*, London, Scribner, 2004, p. 100.

30 Andrew Marshall, *Terror blowback burns CIA—America's spies paid and trained their nation's worst enemies*, The Independent, 1 November 1998, accessed in http://www.independent.co.uk/news/terror-blowback-burns-cia-1182087.html.

31 John Lumkin, *Maktab al-Khidamat*, GlobalSecurity.org, accessed in http://www.globalsecurity.org/security/profiles/maktab_al-khidamat.htm.

32 Ahmed Rashid, *Taliban: Militant Islam, Oil, and Fundamentalism in Central Asia*, New Haven, Yale University Press, 2000, p. 91.

33 Vijay Prashad, *War Against the Planet*, Counterpunch, November 15, 2001, accessed in http://www.counterpunch.org/2001/11/15/war-against-the-planet/.

34 John Lumkin, op. cit.

35 Abdullah Azzam (Shaheed), *Defence of the Muslim Lands; The First Obligation After Iman*, English translation work done by Muslim Brothers in Ribatt, accessed in http://archive.org/stream/Defense_of_the_Muslim_Lands/Defense_of_the_Muslim_Lands_djvu.txt.

36   Wikipedia, *Zia-ul- Haq's Islamization*, accessed in http://en.wikipedia.org/wiki/Zia-ul-Haq%27s_Islamization.

37   Hasan-Askari Rizvi, *Pakistan's Foreign Policy: an Overview 1974-2004.* PILDAT briefing paper for Pakistani parliamentarians, 2004, pp. 19-20.

38   Dean Henderson, *CIA Created Afghan Heroin Trade*, November 10, 2012, accessed in http://beforeitsnews.com/conspiracy-theories/2012/11/cia-created-afghan-heroin-trade-2445926.html.

39   Robert Parry, *Second Thoughts on October Surprise*, June 8, 2013, accessed in http://consortiumnews.com/2013/06/08/second-thoughts-on-october-surprise/.

40   Murray Waas and Craig Unger, *Annals of Government: How the US Armed Iraq—In the Loop: Bush's Secret Mission*, The New Yorker Magazine, November 2, 1992, accessed in http://www.jonathanpollard.org/2002/111402.htm.

41   Ibid.

42   Ibid.

43   Private conversation with the author in January 1985 in Stockholm Sweden with an officer of an anti-narcotics unit of Swedish Customs.

44   Robert Parry, *The Consortium: Bush and a CIA Power Play*, 1996, accessed in http://www.consortiumnews.com/archive/xfile7.html.

45   John Kerry, Senator, *The BCCI Affair: A Report to the Committee on Foreign Relations, United States Senate*, December 1992, 102d Congress 2d Session Senate, accessed in http://www.fas.org/irp/congress/1992_rpt/bcci/.

46   Ibid.

47   Ibid.

48   David Sirota and Jonathan Baskin, *Follow the Money*, Washington Monthly, September 2004, accessed in http://www.washingtonmonthly.com/features/2004/0409.sirota.html.

49   Alfred McCoy, *Drug Fallout*, Progressive magazine, August 1997, accessed in http://www.thirdworldtraveler.com/CIA/CIAdrug_fallout.html.

50   Ibid.

51   Ibid.

52 Charles Krauthammer, *The Reagan Doctrine*, April 01, 1985, TIME, accessed in http://content.time.com/time/magazine/article/0,9171,964873,00. html#ixzz2mEiNO7lX.

53 Washington Blog, *Sleeping With the Devil: How US and Saudi Backing of Al Qaeda Led to 911*, September 5, 2012, accessed in http://www.washingtonsblog. com/2012/09/sleeping-with-the-devil-how-u-s-and-saudi-backing-of-al-qaeda-led-to-911.html.

54 Vijay Prashad, op. cit.

55 Henry S. Bradsher, *Afghan Communism and Soviet Intervention*, (Oxford University Press, 1999), 177–178.

56 Rahul Bedi, *Why? An attempt to explain the unexplainable,* Jane's Defense Weekly, 14 September 2001, accessed in http://www.takeoverworld.info/janes_marriage.htm.

CHAPTER EIGHT

GLOBALIZING JIHAD: FROM AFGHANISTAN TO BOSNIA

"Back in the house, a Mujahideen entered the detainees' room carrying Gojko Vujicic's head on an s-shaped butcher's hook. Blood dripped from the head. The Mujahideen threw Vujicic's head onto Krstan Marinkovic's lap, then took the severed head from one detainee to another, forcing them to 'kiss your brother.'"

—International Criminal Tribunal for the Former
Yugoslavia (ICTY) official judgment at trial of Bosnian
Muslim Army commander in Chief, Rasim Delić.

"The US saw that to avoid falling into a decline similar to that of the Soviet Union, it had to keep pace with potential adversaries of the future. . . . The United States could not accept the idea of Europe as it is today, a Continent that not only can manage quite happily without America, but one which is economically and technologically more powerful."

—Gianfranco Miglio, Italian professor with ties to
Washington on US decision to destroy Yugoslavia in 1989

Destroying Yugoslavia

In November 1989, one of the most dramatic events of the past century took place in Berlin. The Berlin Wall, dividing the Communist-controlled German Democratic Republic in the east of the city from the Federal

Republic of Germany in the western part of Berlin, cracked open. Thousands poured over the wall into the West, dancing and singing. It signaled that the Soviet Union had raised the white flag of surrender in the East-West Cold War. It was not long after their humiliating defeat in Afghanistan.

After more than four decades, the Cold War was over or, at least, so many hoped and believed.

Reality was to prove very much otherwise. For its part, Washington was just warming up to launching what would become an unending series of wars, destabilizations, confrontations, and Color Revolutions, all aimed at extending the power of the USA, the self-proclaimed "Sole Superpower" after the defeat of the Soviet Union. One of the first targets of the Pentagon war machine and US intelligence after the fall of the Berlin Wall was the socialist Federal People's Republic of Yugoslavia.

From its very creation, Yugoslavia was an artificial entity, an ethnically explosive mix of Christian Orthodox Serbs, Roman Catholic Slovenes and Croats, and partly Muslim Bosnia-Herzegovinians among other ethnic groups. It had been pasted together by victorious allies, notably the British and French, after their victory of the First World War in 1918. The victor powers carved out a new state, later named Yugoslavia, by taking Slovenia and Croatia away from the Austro-Hungarian Empire. In 1945, Marshall Josef Tito declared the establishment of the Socialist Republic of Yugoslavia. Yugoslavia then was composed of six nominally equal, federated republics: Croatia, Montenegro, Serbia, Slovenia, Bosnia-Herzegovina, and Macedonia.

With the Soviet Union in shambles, Washington faced an entirely new challenge. Suddenly, the rationale for permanent US military and political control over the nations of the European Union was under existential threat. Europe was beginning to sense its true independent power in the world as leading circles within the EU contemplated life after NATO, where Europeans would no longer have to bow to countless Washington dictates merely because of a real or imagined threat of the Soviets.

In March 1990 the Italian magazine *30 Days* interviewed Gianfranco Miglio, an Italian professor with ties to Washington. Miglio told the journal:

> The US saw that to avoid falling into a decline similar to that of the Soviet Union, it had to keep pace with potential adversaries of the future. They include Japan and the Continent of Europe,

*Until 1989, Yugoslavia was a multiethnic federation of states with
Roman Catholics in Slovenia and Croatia and Orthodox Christian
Serbs and Muslims mainly in Bosnia-Herzegovina.*

united around German economic power. . . .The United States
could not accept the idea of Europe as it is today, a Continent
that not only can manage quite happily without America, but
one which is economically and technologically more powerful.[1]

At that point Washington began secretly planning for a new war in the
heart of Europe. It was to be a war that could and would be used, among
other things, to establish permanent US military bases in Europe. More
importantly, it would be used to justify not only the retaining of NATO,
an organization controlled by Washington, but also actually expanding
NATO into the states of the former Warsaw Pact. NATO would become
the military superstructure of a new "American Century," President George
H.W. Bush's self-described "New World Order."[2]

By the end of the 1980s, Washington had become aware that Europe's
leaders were hard at work drafting new rules of association that later became
incorporated into what was called the Maastricht Treaty. On November

9, 1989, the Berlin Wall came down and the Soviet Union opened to the West. Within months, the Soviet Union itself dissolved and France and Italy began pressing Germany for adoption of what became the Maastricht Treaty. The treaty was the planned cornerstone of what was called by its proponents a "United States of Europe," a future European Union to replace the old European Economic Community.

At the end of the 1980s European elites privately regarded the United States as an empire in terminal collapse. America's industry was technologically outmoded, or obsolete in most vital areas, from steel to automobiles, to machine tools, and to aerospace. Its major banks, such as Citigroup, Chase, and Wells Fargo, were in severe crisis, de facto bankrupt but for covert government and Federal Reserve support.

Leading Europeans viewed America as a declining empire, much as Britain had been before 1914. They were determined to fill the ensuing global power vacuum with their new European Union. The Maastricht Treaty, in addition to the provision to create a European Central Bank for a monetary union, also included a little-discussed pillar for creation of a common European Defense and Security Policy, an independent European "NATO" with a separate command structure run by the EU countries and not by Washington. That European Defense and Security Policy was a pillar that Washington saw as a direct threat to America's global power.[3]

Washington's response was to covertly trigger events in Yugoslavia that would explode in a violent war in Europe. It would shatter the illusion that European wars were a thing of the past, the illusion that no war would ever again divide Europe, and that European countries were able to live together in peace and prosperity. It would be used to insist on the retention of NATO after the reason for its creation—the Soviet Union—had long ceased to exist. The events in and around Yugoslavia would be used to push the extension of NATO to the very steps of Moscow and beyond.

The Administration of George H.W. Bush deployed the International Monetary Fund (IMF) to impose impossible economic conditionalities on Yugoslavia, which, in the late 1980s, was in negotiations over repayment of their large dollar debts. The country would be deliberately brought to financial and economic catastrophe by US interventions. In 1988, the country had a staggering $21 billion in foreign debts, much of it incurred during the 1970s and 1980s to pay for oil imports during the two oil crises of 1973–74 and 1979.

In 1988, as it became clear that the Soviet system was on its last legs, Washington sent in advisers to Yugoslavia from a then-little-known private, non-profit NGO organization, the National Endowment for Democracy, or NED as it was known in Washington circles. That "private" organization, with funds given it by the US Government, began handing out generous doses of US dollars in every corner of Yugoslavia, financing opposition groups, buying up hungry young journalists with dreams of a new life, and financing everyone from trade union opposition to Slobodan Milosevic in Belgrade, to pro-IMF economists such as the G-17, and various human rights NGOs such as the Soros foundations.[4]

Speaking in Washington in 1998, ten years later and one year before NATO began bombing Belgrade, NED director Paul McCarthy boasted, "NED was one of the few Western organizations, along with the Soros Foundation and some European foundations, to make grants in the Federal Republic of Yugoslavia, and to work with local NGO's and independent media throughout the country."[5]

The severe economic "shock therapy" that Washington imposed on Yugoslavia via the IMF, and the interference into internal Yugoslav opposition groups using US-backed NGOs, like NED or Soros' foundations, were part of a classified top secret Reagan Administration policy toward Yugoslavia.

In 1984, Reagan had signed the National Security Decision Directive (NSDD 133), classified as "Secret Sensitive." It was titled *US Policy Toward Yugoslavia*. It advocated "expanded efforts to promote a 'quiet revolution' to overthrow Communist governments and parties" in Yugoslavia, as well as in other Eastern European communist countries, while reintegrating the countries of Eastern Europe into a "market-oriented" economy, a euphemism for US-led globalization and free-market plunder by Western multinationals.[6]

The Washington NGOs and the IMF laid the groundwork for the ensuing economic and political crisis of Yugoslavia that led to the breakup. The breakup was accomplished with heavy outside help from the German Foreign Ministry and German BND intelligence, as well as France and Britain. All the while the USA was orchestrating the key events in the background.

Under IMF demands for privatization of state companies, the Yugoslavian GDP sank in 1990 by 7.5 percent and by another 15 percent in 1991. Industrial production plunged 21 percent. The IMF had as well demanded wholesale privatization of state enterprises. The result was the bankruptcy of more than 1,100 companies by 1990 and more than 20 percent unemployment.

The economic pressure on the various regions of Yugoslavia created an explosive cocktail. Predictably, amid growing economic chaos, each region fought for its own survival against its neighbors. Leaving nothing to chance, the IMF ordered all wages to be frozen at 1989 levels while inflation rose dramatically as a consequence of IMF demands to eliminate state subsidies. That predictably led to a fall in real Yugoslav earnings of 41 percent in the first six months of 1990. By 1991, inflation was over 140 percent.

In this situation, the IMF ordered full convertibility of the dinar and the freeing of interest rates. The IMF then explicitly prevented the Yugoslav government from obtaining credit from its own national bank, crippling the ability of the central government to finance social and other programs. This freeze created a de facto economic secession well before the formal declaration of secession by Croatia and Slovenia in June 1991.[7]

US Congress Lights the Match

All that was needed was a well-placed match to light the fire of war in Yugoslavia.

The Bush Administration lit the match in November 1990 when the US Congress passed the Administration's proposed 1991 Foreign Operations Appropriations Act 101-513. The new US law provided that any part of Yugoslavia failing to declare independence from Yugoslavia within six months of the act would lose all US financial support. The law demanded separate elections in each of the six Yugoslav republics, supervised by the US State Department. It also stipulated that any US or IMF aid must go directly to each republic and not to the central Yugoslav government in Belgrade.[8]

There was one final provision. Only forces that the US State Department defined as "democratic forces" would receive funding. This, in fact, meant an influx of funds to small, right-wing nationalist parties in a financially strangled region that had been suddenly thrown into crisis by the overall Western funding cut-off. The impact was, as expected, devastating.[9]

The US law threw the Yugoslav federal government in Belgrade into crisis. It was unable to pay the enormous interest on its foreign debt or even to arrange the purchase of raw materials for industry. Credit collapsed and recriminations broke out on all sides.

Until that US law, there had been no civil war in Yugoslavia. No republic had seceded, and there was not even any sign of a public dispute between Washington and Yugoslavia. The world was focused, instead, on the war coalition George Bush was organizing against Iraq in the looming war over Kuwait.

The Bush administration had demanded the self-dissolution of the Yugoslav Federation in order to deliberately light the fuse to an explosive new series of Balkan wars. Sir Alfred Sherman, a Balkan expert and a former adviser to British Prime Minister Margaret Thatcher, remarked in 1997, "The war in Bosnia was America's war in every sense of the word. The United States administration helped start it, kept it going, and prevented its early end."[10]

Using groups such as the Soros Foundation of US billionaire hedge fund speculator George Soros, and the National Endowment for Democracy (NED), Washington's financial support was typically channeled into extreme nationalist or former fascist organizations that would guarantee a violent and bloody dismemberment of Yugoslavia.

By February 1991, under pressure from Washington, the Council of Europe dutifully followed the US with its own political demands and explicit economic intervention in the internal affairs of the Yugoslav Federation. Their demand was similar: that Yugoslavia hold multi-party elections or face economic blockade. Right-wing and fascist organizations not seen since the defeat of the Nazi occupation by Tito's anti-fascist partisan movement were suddenly revived and began receiving covert support. These fascist organizations had been maintained in exile by the CIA and British and NATO intelligence in the US, Canada, Germany, and Austria. Now, they became the main conduit for funds and arms into select Yugoslavian republics.[11]

Reacting to this combination of IMF shock therapy and direct Washington destabilization, the Yugoslav president, Serb nationalist Slobodan Milosevic, organized a new Communist Party in November 1990 dedicated to prevent the breakup of the federated Yugoslav Republic. The experience of World War II fueled the Serb mobilization. Then almost a million people—primarily Orthodox Serbs but also Jews, Gypsies, or Romani, and tens of thousands of others—died in Croatian Ustaši-run death camps, the most notorious of which was Jasenovac.[12]

On May 5, 1991, the precise date of the six-month deadline imposed by US Foreign Operations Law 101-513, Croatian separatists staged violent demonstrations and laid siege to a Yugoslav military base in Gospić. The Yugoslav Federal Government, under attack, ordered the army to intervene. The civil war had begun.

Slovenia and Croatia declared independence from the central Yugoslavia state on June 25, 1991, and the German government of Helmut Kohl, led by Foreign Minister Hans-Dietrich Genscher, immediately recognized both as independent states.[13]

As the largest nationality and the one that opposed the breakup of the Yugoslav Federation, the Serbs became the target and the excuse for Western intervention. Western propaganda began portraying Serbs as the new Nazis of Europe. The stage was set for a gruesome series of regional ethnic wars, which would last a decade and result in the deaths of more than 200,000 people.

The CIA stepped into this chaotic and highly volatile situation, along with US military Special Operations Forces, to fuel the wars using its battle-hardened veteran Islamic Mujahideen cadre from the Afghan Soviet war to incite further chaos in Islamic Bosnia-Herzegovina and, later, in Kosovo in order to finally finish off the Yugoslav Republic.

Jihad Comes to Bosnia

The success of the CIA's Mujahideen operation in Afghanistan had created the idea in Washington of actively backing similar Jihads, or Holy Wars, using veterans of the Mujahideen in Afghanistan as the core terrorist or guerrilla force to further weaken or destroy other regimes where a large Muslim population existed.

As early as 1980, Afghan-American Zalmay Khalilzad, a close adviser to President Carter's national Security Adviser, Zbigniew Brzezinski, and one of the architects of the US Mujahideen strategy in Afghanistan, advocated that the US should aggressively deploy political Islam as a weapon not only against Soviet-control in Afghanistan but also directly "behind enemy lines" in Soviet Muslim Central Asia, including Chechnya, Uzbekistan, and beyond.[14]

Khalilzad was an Afghan-born Sunni Muslim who became a Reagan Administration senior State Department official advising on the Soviet war in Afghanistan and the 1980s Iran-Iraq War. From 1990 through 1992, Khalilzad served under President George H.W. Bush in the Defense Department as Deputy Undersecretary for Policy Planning. That was precisely the time when the Bush Administration decided to bring the Mujahideen Jihad model into Yugoslavia and the former Soviet Union itself after the collapse of the Warsaw Pact in 1991.[15]

By 1992, the internal civil war between the various federal states of Yugoslavia had spread to predominantly Muslim Bosnia-Herzegovina, situated between Roman Catholic Croatia and Orthodox Serbia. The war in Bosnia, which lasted until 1995, gave the missing piece of the puzzle of how Khalilzad's Afghan Mujahideen transformed into a global Jihad force, later using the name Al Qaeda.

Izetbegović's Coup

On March 18, 1992, in Lisbon, the EU put forward a plan drafted by Britain's Lord Carrington and Portuguese ambassador José Cutileiro. It was an attempt to prevent a bloody civil war inside Bosnia-Herzegovina between Muslim, Christian Orthodox, and Roman Catholics, calling for partition of the country by religious concentrations. All three leaders in Bosnia-Herzegovina on that day signed—Serb, Croat, and Bosnia-Herzegovinan. Alija Izetbegović signed the agreement on behalf of the Bosnian-Herzegovina Muslims, or Bosniaks as they had been historically known since the Ottoman occupation.

Only days after the agreement was signed, the US Ambassador to Yugoslavia, Warren Zimmermann, flew to Sarajevo to meet with Alija Izetbegović, leader of the Bosnian Muslims. According to Alfred Sherman, Zimmermann gave Izetbegović assurances of US support for a fully independent nation without internal division if he would renege on the Lisbon Agreement. Zimmermann promised Izetbegović all political, diplomatic, and, notably, military aid if he would agree to renege on the Lisbon treaty. Izetbegović did just that.[16]

US Acting Secretary of State and former US Ambassador to Yugoslavia Lawrence Eagleburger had given the instructions to Zimmermann to immediately fly to Sarajevo to persuade Izetbegović to renege. That EU Lisbon agreement, in the minds of many, could have avoided a Bosnian war between Orthodox Christian Serb, Bosnian Muslim, and Croatian Catholic populations living in Bosnia-Herzegovina. That was precisely what Washington wanted to prevent happening. They wanted the Bosnian war for their larger geopolitical strategy in Europe and beyond.[17]

Washington had decided to play the radical Islam strategy once more, and Izetbegović was to be their man. He was a distinguished-looking professor of philosophy and a grey-haired Sunni Muslim affectionately called "Grandpa" by Bosniaks.

Days after meeting Zimmermann, Izetbegović withdrew his signature and renounced the peace plan he had just agreed to in Lisbon, declaring his opposition to any type of ethnic division of Bosnia. Within weeks, a full-blown war developed in Bosnia.[18]

Izetbegović had won a rotating presidency of the Bosnian Federation in 1990 through dubious means, eliminating a far more popular rival, Fikret Abdić. Once President, Izetbegović managed to "suspend due to extraordinary circumstances" the agreed provision that the Bosnian presidency rotate on a yearly basis between Bosnian Croat, Serb, and Muslim candidates. He seized power for himself alone with help from Washington, de facto excluding rotation to Serb and Croatian minorities.[19]

That was the first step on the road to a US-backed Muslim Bosnia-Herzegovina state. It was also a major step in triggering the ethnic civil war in Yugoslavia that raged with such atrocities for almost a decade. At the time, the Bosnia-Herzegovina population was almost equally divided between in three major ethnic-religious groups with one third Bosnian Muslim, a third Serbian Christian Orthodox, and a third Croatian Roman Catholic. Soon, the outside world would be fed the idea that the overwhelming majority of Bosnians were Muslims.

Waffen SS Handschar Revived

Alija Izetbegović was a controversial choice for the Clinton Administration to back as President of Bosnia. During World War II, he had been a member of a Bosnian Muslim youth organization modeled on Egypt's Muslim Brotherhood called *Mladi Muslimani*, or Young Muslims.

The Bosnian Mladi Muslimani—and Izetbegović personally—had been involved during the war in working with the Nazis and the Croatian Ustaše in their campaign to exterminate Jews, orthodox Serbs, and communists in Yugoslavia on behalf of Heinrich Himmler's *Waffen*-SS. When Nazi Germany occupied Yugoslavia in 1941, they set up the puppet state of Croatia, officially the "Independent State of Croatia," which included Bosnia, Herzegovina, and parts of Dalmatia. Hitler installed Ante Pavelić's pro-Nazi Ustaše in power. In Pavelić's fascist Catholic-based Ustaše movement, Hitler found an ideological ally as the Ustaše forces of Pavelić, with the de facto blessing of the Vatican, unleashed a savage genocide in their new country.[20]

Bosnian Muslims recruited by Izetbegović played a decisive part in that genocide against Orthodox Serbs, Jews, and others during the Second World War. Between 1941 and 1945 Bosnia was part of the "Independent State of Croatia" in which Serbs were being persecuted as fiercely as Jews in the Nazi Reich, by the Bosnian Muslim *Waffen*-SS *Handschar* Division organized by Grand Mufti of Jerusalem Amin-el Husseini, the Himmler and Hitler friend, to carry out a savage genocide.[21]

Izetbegović had joined the Mladi Muslimani organization in Sarajevo in March 1943, where he allegedly recruited young Muslims for the SS *Handschar* Division in collaboration with German intelligence services, ABWER and GESTAPO.[22]

During World War II, Izetbegović recruited for the Nazi Muslim SS Handschar Division in fascist Croatia, who used this fez with Nazi Death Skull.

In the spring of 1943, as a leader of the Mladi Muslimani in Sarajevo, Izetbegović personally welcomed Nazi collaborator Amin-el Husseini, the Grand Mufti of Jerusalem, to Sarajevo. In 1946, after the war, Izetbegović was arrested and sentenced to three years in prison for his wartime activities, something the US State Department press officers chose to forget in 1992 when they promoted him as a democratic hero.[23]

In 1970, Izetbegović had authored a manifesto entitled the *Islamic Declaration*, where he laid out his views on relationship between Islam, state, and society. There he wrote, among other things, "There can be no peace or coexistence between the Islamic faith and non- Islamic societies and political institutions. . . Islam clearly excludes the right and possibility of activity of any strange ideology on its own turf. Therefore. . . the state should be an expression and should support the moral concepts of the religion."[24]

Izetbegović was as fanatical a Jihadist as Egypt's Hassan al-Banna and his friends in the Muslim Brotherhood. He advocated a return to the era in the 1800s, when Bosnia was a part of the Islamic Ottoman Empire, ruling through strict Sharia law and subjecting Christian citizens to their total domination.

Propaganda: A Bodyguard of Lies

When Izetbegović's Islamic Declaration was published in Yugoslavia in 1970, the authorities interpreted it as a call for introduction of Sharia law in Bosnia and banned the publication. In 1983, Izetbegović and several other fundamentalist Muslims were put in prison, charged with plotting a coup and disseminating "Islamic propaganda."[25]

During the Bosnian war after 1992, Izetbegović called Muslims who had died in the war *shuhaad*, "martyrs for the faith," indicating it was a holy war, *jihad*, not a struggle for multi-ethnic democracy as Izetbegović's Washington PR firm, Ruder Finn, so skillfully portrayed the Bosnian war to the Western Media.[26]

Ruder Finn did a masterful job at manipulating the propaganda war in Washington and the West. James Harff, director of Ruder Finn's Global Public Affairs section working for Izetbegović, boasted about his success against Serbia. "Nobody understood what was going on in (former) Yugoslavia," he said in an October 1993 interview with French journalist Jacques Merlino. "The great majority of Americans were probably asking themselves in which African country Bosnia was situated."[27]

Ruder Finn took advantage of that ignorance. Their first goal was to persuade influential US Jewish organizations to oppose the Serbs—not an easy task given the history of the Croatian fascist Ustaše and the Bosnian Muslim *Waffen*-SS *Handschar* Division atrocities against Jews during the Second World War.

"The Croatian and Bosnian past was marked by a real and cruel anti-Semitism," said Harff. "Tens of thousands of Jews perished in Croatian camps. So there was every reason for intellectuals and Jewish organizations to be hostile towards the Croats and Bosnians." [28]

Harff used a report in the New York *Newsday* about Serbian prisoner detention camps, called concentration camps, to persuade Jewish groups to demonstrate against the Serbs. Harff boasted,

> This was a tremendous coup. When the Jewish organizations entered the game on the side of the Bosnians, we could promptly equate the Serbs with the Nazis in the public mind. By a single move, we were able to present a simple story of good guys and bad guys which would hereafter play itself. We won by targeting Jewish audience, the right target. Almost immediately there was a clear change of language in the press, with the use of words with high emotional content, such as "ethnic cleansing," "concentration camps," etc., which evoked inmates of Nazi Germany and the gas chambers of Auschwitz. The emotional change was so powerful that nobody could go against it.[29]

With their propaganda machine in Washington effectively demonizing Serbs as Nazis and portraying Bosnian Muslims as the hapless victims of Serb atrocities, real or imagined, the way was clear to blame the Serb forces in Bosnia for every imaginable crime.

Osama and the Bosnian Mujahideen

With Izetbegović, a Jihadist autocrat, as their man in Bosnia-Herzegovina, US intelligence began to secretly redeploy veterans of the Afghan Mujahideen war against the Soviets and other Jihadist volunteers around the world into Bosnia-Herzegovina to fight on the side of Izetbegović's Muslim forces against the Serbs.

Foreign Jihad fighters were brought in by US and other NATO intelligence, largely via Croatia, into Bosnia-Herzegovina. Islamic countries sent trainers and "volunteers" to fight with Muslim forces in Bosnia and established secret training camps there. In addition to Afghanistan, the fighters came from Saudi Arabia, Turkey, Pakistan, Sudan, Iran, and Syria—forming a veritable seed crystal of the emerging Global Jihad.[30]

The US encouraged and covertly facilitated the smuggling of arms to the Muslims via Iran, Turkey, and Eastern Europe, a fact which Washington denied at the time, even in the face of overwhelming evidence. The Clinton

Administration used NATO and UNPROFOR, the United Nations Protection Force, as its policy instruments and blocked all peace moves—of which there were several between 1992 and 1995—until they were good and ready.[31]

Reliable estimates put the number of foreign Islamic Jihadists who fought alongside and within Izetbegović's Bosnian Army against Serbs, in the war that lasted from 1992 to its forced end in 1995, at somewhere between 4,000 and 20,000 fighters, most of them Saudi veterans of Afghanistan, Yemen, Algeria, Egypt, or Pakistan. They were smuggled in mainly through Zagreb in Croatia, the so-called Croatian Pipeline.[32] Croatian President Franjo Tudjman was also arming the Bosnian Croatian minority population and saw an armed Muslim force as a de facto ally in his drive to remove as many Serbs as possible from Croatia's Krajina region, as well as from her Bosnian border regions.[33]

While their numbers were relatively small in comparison with the size of the Bosnian Army, the battle-hardened Mujahideen played a catalytic role in spreading fanatical Jihad radicalism to the regular Army during the war. The Izetbegović regime revamped its entire security and military apparatus to reflect the Mujahideen Islamic revolutionary outlook. It created Mujahideen units throughout the Army; some members of these units were designated *shaheed* ("martyr," or suicide bomber), with special white garb symbolizing a shroud. The foreign Muslim Jihadist fighters were given Bosnian citizenship, allowing the Clinton Administration to claim that very few of the fighters were "foreigners."[34]

During the war, there were three principal Mujahideen units in the Bosnian army, the first two of which were headquartered in the American IFOR/SFOR zone—the 7th Muslim Liberation Brigade of the 3rd Corps, headquartered in Zenica, and the 9th Muslim Liberation Brigade of the 2nd Corps, headquartered in Travnik. And the 4th Muslim Liberation Brigade of the 4th Corps was headquartered in Konjic in the French zone.[35]

In addition to those three Mujahideen units in the Bosnian Army of Izetbegović, there was the elite Bosnian Muslim *Handschar* ("scimitar") Division, a 6,000-strong special unit that gloried a fascist culture, imitating the SS *Handschar* division formed by Bosnian Muslims in 1943 to fight for the Nazis against the Serbs, Jews, and Gypsies. The majority of *Handschar* officers were Albanian, whether from Kosovo, then a Serb province where

Albanians were the majority, or from Albania itself. They were trained and led by veterans from Afghanistan and Pakistan Mujahideen.[36]

Violent Islamic fundamentalism was suddenly in the heart of Europe, and Washington made it all happen. From 1992 to 1995, the Pentagon and CIA covertly assisted the movement of thousands of Mujahideen and other Islamic jihadists from Central Asia, the Arabs, and other Muslim countries into Europe to fight alongside Bosnian Muslims against the Serbs. [37]

As part of the Dutch government's inquiry into the Srebrenica massacre of July 1995, Professor Cees Wiebes of Amsterdam University compiled a report published in April 2002 entitled *Intelligence and the War in Bosnia*.[38]

In the report Wiebes documented the secret alliance between the Pentagon and radical Islamic groups from the Middle East to assist Bosnia's Muslims. By 1993, there was a vast amount of weapons smuggling through Croatia to the Muslims, a violation of a UN Security Council arms embargo to Bosnia. The arms smuggling Wiebes stated, was organized by "clandestine agencies" of the USA, Turkey, and, curiously enough, by the "arch-enemy of the US"—Iran. Wiebes documented that it involved Islamic groups that included Osama bin Laden's Afghan Mujahideen networks and the pro-Iranian Hezbollah.[39]

Arms bought into Bosnia by Iran and Turkey with the financial backing of Saudi Arabia were airlifted from the Middle East to Bosnia under the direct involvement of the Pentagon. Significant aid in the form of Jihadists and money came from Saudi Arabia, Egypt, Syria, Malaysia, Libya, Sudan, and other Islamic countries that enabled Izetbegović's US-trained Bosnian-Herzegovina Army to fight a long war.[40]

A principle financial conduit to buy and smuggle arms to the Muslim forces in Bosnia was the Third World Relief Agency (TWRA) run by a Sudanese doctor and close friend of Bosnia's Izetbegović, Dr. Fatih al-Hasanayn. TWRA established an office in Zagreb that was used as the conduit for Jihadist fighters and arms into Bosnia. An estimated $2.5 billion from Saudi and other Islamic states came into the Bosnian Jihad, much of it through al-Hasanayn's Third World Relief Agency.[41]

Osama bin Laden, then a little-known Saudi Jihadist who had worked with the CIA in Afghanistan through his Afghan Services Bureau, or *Maktab al-Khidamat* (MAK), funneling Arab Sunni Jihadi volunteers and money into Afghanistan's war against the Soviet occupation in the 1980s, now worked closely with TWRA in Bosnia. Bin Laden was reported by

Der Spiegel Belgrade-based journalist, Renate Flottau, to have been visiting in person several times at the office of Izetbegović in Sarajevo at the time of the Bosnian war, where Flottau met the Saudi Jihadist.[42]

Egyptian intelligence at the time identified Osama bin Laden as a key player in the Bosnian Jihad, noting that he carried a Bosnian passport. At the time of the Bosnian "Jihad," bin Laden was in exile in Khartoum, Sudan, where the head of the Sudanese Muslim Brotherhood, Hasan al-Turabi, had ensured a safe haven for the Saudi Afghan veteran. Al-Turabi was also a close associate of fellow Sudanese jihadist Fatih al-Hasanayn and his TWRA.[43]

Through the Zagreb offices of TWRA, the "Croatian Pipeline," arms transactions were carried out, funds collected, and intelligence gathered under its cover. TWRA had additional offices in Sarajevo, Budapest, and Istanbul and had direct personal links with the Bosnian government and Izetbegović personally.

The airfield used to secretly smuggle the arms to the Jihadist forces had been built by the Pentagon near Sarajevo and run by Islamist Izetbegović confidante Hasan Čengić, a fanatical Jihadist who had spent time in the 1980s in prison along with Izetbegović. Čengić, also a member of the TWRA Supervisory Board, was Bosnian Deputy Defense Minister and chief liaison officer for the American military aid program. Based mainly in Vienna during the war, Čengić was in charge of procuring weapons smuggled into Bosnia, including from Iran, with the blessing of the Clinton Administration and US Ambassador to Zagreb Peter Galbraith. At the end of April 1994, the Croatian Prime Minister Valentić and the Bosnian Deputy Prime Minister visited Teheran for consultations with President Ali Akbar Rafsanjani. A tripartite agreement was drawn up for arms supplies and humanitarian assistance to Bosnia.[44]

The longer the war in Bosnia-Herzegovina raged, the better for Washington's attempt to revive the role of a US-led NATO in the Balkans and Europe. The tentacles of a coordinating network for the Global Jihad were emerging from the Bosnia war, and it was getting its nutrition with the assistance of the CIA and Pentagon.

Mujahideen Atrocities in Bosnia-Herzegovina

The Washington propaganda machinery turned out endless faked stories of Serb bombings of civilian villagers and hospitals, attacks on UN so-called "safe zones," as well as fabricated accounts of tens of thousands of rapes of

Muslim women. The *New York Times* falsely claimed there were Serb-run "rape camps." At the same time the Muslim Jihadist mercenaries working alongside Izetbegović's army carried out appalling atrocities against Bosnian Serbs that were entirely blacked out of US and Western media.[45]

In one of the most heinous such incidents, the same Western media, led by *The New York Times*, CNN, and other US media worked closely with the disinformation propagandists of the Clinton Administration. They demonized the Serbian Army for what has come to be known as the "Srebrenica massacre" of innocent Bosnian Muslims in the US "safe zone" of Srebrenica in eastern Bosnia-Herzegovina near to the Serbian state border. In one very egregious case of journalistic conflict of interest, CNN's Sarajevo correspondent, Christiane Amanpour, was sharply criticized for her lopsided pro-Bosnian Muslim bias. She was married to Jamie Rubin, who was Assistant Secretary of State and spokesman for Madeline Albright's State Department during the Clinton administration.[46]

After intense military fighting between Izetbegović's Muslim jihadist forces and Bosnian Serb secessionists in the so-called Republika Srpska, a part of Bosnia-Herzegovina which sought to link up with Serbia by removing the border along the River Drina separating them from Milosevic's Serbian state, Bosniak Muslim forces in the enclave of Srebrenica carried out grave violations of UN "safe zone" conditions and waged countless attacks on Bosnian Serb civilians in surrounding villages.[47]

On July 12, 1992, on the holy day when Orthodox Serbs celebrate Saints Peter and Paul, Muslim forces from Srebrenica raided the Serbian villages of Zalazje, Sase, and Biljača. Sixty-nine civilians and soldiers were killed. Out of twenty-two captured Serbs, only ten bodies were recovered. The attacks began in the summer of 1992 and lasted until early 1993. The Jihadists destroyed fifty-five out of fifty-nine Serbian villages in the larger Srebrenica municipality, resulting in the deaths of 550 villagers. According to the Serbian sources, the number of Serbian victims to the Muslim Jihad in the Srebrenica region exceeded 3,000.[48]

The Bosnian Muslim Jihadists were using the UN Srebrenica "safe haven" as a base for attacks on Serbian civilians. That military aggression under cover of Srebrenica's United Nations protection was in criminal violation of the UN humanitarian rules for "safe haven." The UN was later forced to admit that Bosnian forces were violating the no-fly zone around Srebrenica and were smuggling weapons into the area (ICTY testimony by

David Harland, civil affairs officer and political adviser to the UNPROFOR Commander in Bosnia and Herzegovina).[49]

Naser Orić was in charge of the Bosnian Muslim forces in Srebrenica. French General Philippe Morillon, commander of the UN's UNPROFOR troops in Bosnia from 1992 to 1993, described Orić's role in his testimony before the International Criminal Tribunal for the Former Yugoslavia, the Hague Court:

> Naser Orić engaged in attacks during Orthodox holidays and destroyed villages, massacring all the inhabitants. This created a degree of hatred that was quite extraordinary in the region. . .There were terrible massacres committed by the forces of Naser Orić in all the surrounding villages. . . I think you will find this in other testimony, not just mine. Naser Orić was a warlord who reigned by terror in his area and over the population itself. I think that he realized that those were the rules of this horrific war, that he could not allow himself to take prisoners. According to my recollection, he didn't even look for an excuse. It was simply a statement: One can't be bothered with prisoners.[50]

Izetbegović's Bosnian Muslim Jihadists, most notably Naser Orić and the foreign Mujahideen, were unbelievably savage in their attacks. The Jihadists deliberately carried out their attacks on the Christian Holy Days: St. George's Day, St. Vitus' Day, St. Peter and Paul's Day, and Christmas. Victims, including women, the elderly, and even children, were tortured before being killed. As his family was fleeing the massacre, an eleven-year-old boy named Slobodan Stojanović returned to the village to get his dog. He was later found shot dead, his ear cut off and his stomach cut open in the shape of a cross.[51]

Even pro-Sarajevo accounts conceded that Muslim Jihad forces under Naser Orić in Srebrenica murdered over 1,300 Serbs and "ethnically cleansed" a vast area.[52] Other accounts give far larger numbers of deaths at the hands of Orić's army in Srebrenica. Muslim General Sefer Halilović, testifying at the Hague Tribunal, confirmed there had been at least 5,500 Bosnian Muslim Army soldiers in Srebrenica. More importantly, these fighters had slaughtered more than 3,500 Christians in surrounding villages prior to the fall of Srebrenica, including young children, women, and the elderly.[53]

Even worse, the "safe haven" meant that Bosnian Muslim forces would be able to attack outside of the main area of central Srebrenica, kill Orthodox Serbian Christians, then return to Srebrenica in order to be protected and to reinforce their stronghold, and to rearm.[54]

*A smiling Naser Orić at the Hague War Crimes Trial
knowing the US will keep him free.*

In 2006, at the Hague ICTY, Orić was indicted for the torture and cruel treatment of eleven and the killing of seven Serb men detained in the Srebrenica police station in 1992–1993. He was also accused of having ordered and led numerous guerrilla raids into as many as fifty Serb-populated villages in 1992–1993, particularly in the municipalities of Bratunac and Srebrenica. In the course of combat, Bosnian Serb buildings, dwellings, and other property in predominantly Serb villages were burnt and destroyed, hundreds of Serbs were murdered, and thousands of Serb individuals fled the area. Orić was sentenced to two years in prison for not preventing atrocities against Bosnian Serb prisoners, a most mild sentence that was later dismissed on appeal. He apparently had friends in high places.[55]

When later questioned if he had been aware of these atrocities being committed by Bosnian Muslim Mujahideen forces against Serb civilians, then US Ambassador to Croatia Peter Galbraith, the man who facilitated the illegal and secret arming of Izetbegović's forces, lied. He stated that Washington was aware of a "small numbers of atrocities" being committed by the foreign Mujahideen in Bosnia, but he dismissed the atrocities as being, "in the scheme of things, not a big issue."[56]

The ferocity of the Muslim Mujahideen treatment of Serbs prior to the Srebrenica massacre of Muslim men in July 1993 was not unlike later video scenes from Al Qaeda fighters against Syrian President Assad in 2013, when an Al Qaeda Jihadist was filmed cutting out a Syrian government soldier's heart and savagely eating it in front of the camera for the world to see.[57]

One of such countless instances of Jihadist barbarity against Bosnian Serbs before the Srebrenica massacre was documented in a later court trial against Bosnian Muslim Army Commander in Chief Rasim Delić by the International Criminal Tribunal for the Former Yugoslavia (ICTY).

It came out in trial that Bosnian Muslim soldiers under his command, which Delić claimed were foreign Mujahideen, carried out a summary execution and decapitation of a Serb prisoner named Gojko Vujicic. After the beheading, the Mujahideen displayed Vujicic's severed head to other Serb prisoners. The Hague Court's judgment describes the scene as follows:

> Back in the house, a Mujahideen entered the detainees' room carrying Gojko Vujicic's head on an s-shaped butcher's hook. Blood dripped from the head. The Mujahedin threw Vujicic's head onto Krstan Marinkovic's lap, then took the severed head from one detainee to another, forcing them to "kiss your brother." The Mujahedin then hung Vujicic's head on a hook in the room where it remained for several hours.[58]

All of that was proudly videotaped by the Jihadists. The Mujahideen were clearly not concerned about Geneva Conventions of War and treatment of prisoners.

The savage Mujahideen atrocities committed against Serbs, many of them women and children or the elderly, created a rage and fury for revenge among the Bosnian Serb soldiers fighting to take control of Srebrenica away from the Bosnians. In his Hague testimony, French General Philippe Morillon said of the Bosnian Serbs after Orić's savage attacks, "They were in this hellish circle of revenge. It was more than revenge that animated them all. Not only the men. The women, the entire population was imbued with this. It wasn't the sickness of fear that had infected the entire population of Bosnia-Herzegovina, the fear of being dominated, of being eliminated. It was pure hatred."[59]

Morillon stated that Orić had secretly pulled his Jihad troops out of Srebrenica a week before it fell: "I said that Mladic [Bosnian Serb Army commander—F.W.E.] had entered an ambush in Srebrenica, a trap, in fact. He expected to find resistance, but there was none. He didn't expect the massacre to occur but he completely underestimated the amount of hatred that accrued. I don't believe that he ordered the massacres, but I don't know. That is my personal opinion." The Serbs finally reacted to Orić's provocations. When they took Srebrenica far more easily than they thought they would, they took their revenge on the men they found there. But, unlike Naser Orić and El Mujahid, they let the women, children, and the elderly go to safety before they began shooting the men.[60]

According to the Dutch government inquiry after the massacre, knowledge of the looming attack by Serb forces on an unarmed Srebrenica was known prior to the attack. But US intelligence and military, and German and French intelligence services withheld information regarding the VRS attack. Highly important intercepts revealing prior knowledge of the attack were supposedly not passed on to UNPROFOR and not even to NATO allies, including the United Kingdom and the Netherlands.[61] In short, Washington wanted the Srebrenica massacre as *casus belli* to demonize the Serbs.

Retired Major-General Lewis Mackenzie, a Canadian General who was in command of Srebrenica just prior to the massacre before being replaced by the Dutch, wrote in Canada's largest newspaper, *Globe and Mail*, on July 14, 2005, an op-ed titled "The real story behind Srebrenica: The massacre in the UN 'safe haven' was not a black and white event." Mackenzie stated:

> As the snow cleared in the spring of 1995, it became obvious to Nasar Orić, the man who led the Bosnian Muslim fighters that the Bosnian Serb army was going to attack Srebrenica to stop him from attacking Serb villages. So he and a large number of his fighters slipped out of town. Srebrenica was left undefended with the strategic thought that, if the Serbs attacked an undefended town, surely that would cause NATO and the UN to agree that NATO air strikes against the Serbs were justified. And so the Bosnian Serb army strolled into Srebrenica without opposition.[62]

Orić's calculation proved correct. On August 30, 1995 after the Serb taking of Srebrenica and the one-sided Western demonization of the Serbs as the sole responsible party, the Secretary General of NATO announced the start of Operation Deliberate Force, widespread airstrikes against Bosnian Serb positions, supported by UNPROFOR rapid reaction force artillery attacks.

On September 14, 1995, the NATO air strikes were suspended to allow the implementation of an agreement with Bosnian Serbs for the withdrawal of heavy weapons from around Sarajevo. The Clinton Administration got what they wanted—the pretext for NATO to continue and a permanent 80,000-man NATO occupation force in Bosnia-Herzegovina to enforce "peace." The war formally ended with the signing by all parties of the Dayton Agreement in Paris on December 14, 1995. US Special Forces and global Mujahideen jihadists moved on to the next Jihad against Serbian Yugoslavia—the geopolitically strategic Serb province of Kosovo bordering Albania.

Forging Global Jihad

In his Hague trial defense, General Delić also revealed the previously hidden connection between the foreign Mujahideen Jihadists and what later came to be called Al Qaeda.

Delić claimed under oath that the Mujahideen fighters, known as *El Mujahid*, or "The Holy Warriors," indeed committed the atrocities but that they were not under his control. He insisted that, rather, they were commanded by Sheikh Anwar Shaban, headquartered in the Islamic Center in Milan, a testimony willingly corroborated by ex-El Mujahid fighters in the Hague court.[63]

"Combat reports were sent to the Islamic Cultural Center in Milan. Sheik Anwar Shaban, who founded and ran the Center, was the real authority in the El Mujahid Detachment. The detachment also sent reports to the terrorist organization al-Qaida," his defense counsel stated.[64]

The Hague trial of General Delić brought into the open the direct role of what later came to be called Al Qaeda, the Saudi-Egyptian network of global Jihadists trained by the CIA and Pentagon that grew out of the Muslim Brotherhood organizations in Egypt and Saudi Arabia.

Anwar Shaban was a leader of *Al-Gama'a al-Islamiyya*, the banned Egyptian terrorist offshoot of the Muslim Brotherhood organization linked to the 1981 assassination of Egypt's President Anwar Sadat.

After fleeing Egypt in 1991, Shaban got political asylum in Italy, where he set up the Islamic Center in Milan generously financed by donors from Saudi Arabia and the United Arab Emirates, both dominated by the severe Wahhabite Muslim ideology.

From his Milan center, between 1992 and his death at the hands of the Croatian Army in 1995, Shaban was a key link between what was becoming Al Qaeda—veterans of the Afghan Mujahideen committed to global Jihad—and the Bosnian Muslim El Mujahid fighters. He was in charge of recruiting, financing, and transporting fighters and weapons to Bosnia-Herzegovina.[65]

Shaban was recognized by all as Commander of the El-Mujahid forces in Bosnia.

Sheikh Anwar Shaban, who was also given Bosnian citizenship, under the cover of his Islamic Center, ran a Bosnian Mujahideen training camp some 50 kilometers outside of Milan to train fighters heading to Bosnia. Among his closest associates was the man later identified as Number Two behind Osama bin Laden in Al Qaeda, Egyptian Muslim Brotherhood member Ayman al-Zawahiri, as well as Sheikh Omar Abdul-Rahman. Bosnian intelligence documents later showed that El Mujahid's Sheikh Anwar Shaban was "in close telephone contact with Al-Qaeda operatives and with Osama bin Laden personally."[66]

During the later stage of the Bosnian war, al-Zawahiri went to California's Silicon Valley to raise funds for the Bosnian Jihad. He was hosted in California by Ali Mohamed, a US double agent and veteran of US Army Special Forces. In 1993, according to reports, bin Laden had named al-Zawahiri to be responsible for the Balkans Jihad.[67]

The CIA and Pentagon were building their new weapon of turning Jihad into a global surrogate war-making machine. Their next step was to move their Jihad to Kosovo using a band of heroin traffickers the CIA would reform as the Kosovo Liberation Army, or KLA.

Endnotes

1   Cited in F. William Engdahl, *A Century of War: Anglo-American Oil Politics and the New World Order*, 2010, edition.engdahl, Wiesbaden, p. 221.

2   George H.W. Bush in a speech on September 11, 1990, to a Joint Session of Congress. Bush declared, "Out of these troubled times, our . . . objective—a New World Order—can emerge. . . . Today, that new world is struggling to be born, a world quite different from the one we have known." accessed in http://www.bibliotecapleyades.net/sociopolitica/esp_sociopol_nw072.htm.

3   The views of European elites is taken from several private discussions the author held at the end of the 1980s.

4   F. William Engdahl, op. cit., p. 239.

5   Ibid., p. 239.

6   Sean Gervasi, *Germany, US and the Yugoslav Crisis*, Covert Action, Winter 1992–3 Number 43, accessed in http://www.tmcrew.org/news/nato/germany_usa.htm.

7   Ibid., p. 240.

8   Sara Flounders, *The Bosnian Tragedy: Origins of the breakup—a US law*, International Action Center, 1995, New York, accessed in http://www.iacenter.org/bosnia/origins.htm.

9   Ibid.

10   Alfred Sherman, Chairman, The Lord Byron Foundation for Balkan Studies, *AMERICA'S INTERVENTION IN THE BALKANS*, 1997, Third Annual Conference devoted to US policy in Southeast Europe held in Chicago, March 1997, accessed in http://www.balkanstudies.org/sites/default/files/newsletter/Intervention%20pdf%20Book%5B1%5D.pdf.

11   Ibid.

12   Ibid.

13   Ibid.

14   Zalmay Khalilzad, *The Return of the Great Game: superpower rivalry and domestic turmoil in Afghanistan, Iran, Pakistan, and Turkey*, Discussion paper no. 88, September 1980, The California seminar on International Security and Foreign Policy.

15   Wikipedia, *Zalmay Khalilzad*, accessed in http://en.wikipedia.org/wiki/Zalmay_Khalilzad

16   Alfred Sherman, op. cit., p. 7.

17   Ibid.

18   Wikipedia, *Alija Izetbegović*, accessed in http://en.wikipedia.org/wiki/Alija_ Izetbegovi%C4%87. Also see de Krnjevic-Miskovic, Damjan, *Alija Izetbegovic, 1925-2003*, in the National Interest.

19   Nebojsa Malic, *The Real Izetbegovic: Laying to Rest a Mythical Autocrat*, October 23, 2003, accessed in http://www.antiwar.com/malic/m102303.html.

20   Michael Phayer, *Canonizing Pius XII—Why did the pope help Nazis escape?*, Commonweal, June 23, 2004. See also Mark Aarons John Loftus, *Unholy Trinity: How the Vatican's Nazi Networks Betrayed Western Intelligence to the Soviets*. New York: St. Martin's Press, 1992, p. 112.

21   Neboisa Malic, op. cit.

22   John R. Schindler, *Unholy Terror: Bosnia, al-Qa'ida, and the Rise of Global Jihad*, 2008, Zenith Press, p. 276.

23   Sean Mac Mathúna, *The Role of the SS Handschar division in Yugoslavia's Holocaust*, accessed in http://www.fantompowa.net/Flame/yugoslavia_ collaboration.htm.

24   Alija Izetbegovic, *"The Islamic Declaration" ("Islamska deklaracija")*, 1970, reprinted by BOSNA, Sarajevo, 1990, p. 22.

25   BBC News, Obituary: *Alija Izetbegovic*, October 19, 2003, accessed in http:// news.bbc.co.uk/2/hi/europe/3133038.stm.

26   Washington PR firm, Ruder Finn was hired by the Izetbegovic government to lobby the US Congress and especially Jewish organizations and US media to side with Izetbegovic and the Bosnian Muslims against the Serbs. On 23 June 1992, Izetbegovic's government in Sarajevo signed a contract with Ruder Finn who set up a "Bosnia Crisis Communication Center" in contact with American, British, and French media; media appearance coaching for Bosnian foreign minister Haris Silajdzic; sending press releases to U.S. Congressmen and "Fax Updates" on developments in Bosnia-Herzegovina to the most important world media and parliamentarians; organizing personal contacts between Silajdzic and Al Gore, Margaret Thatcher, and other influential personalities, including 17 U.S. Senators; placing articles on in the editorial pages of the New York Times, the Washington Post, USA Today, the Wall Street Journal, all demonizing the Serbs as the "new Nazis." Izetbegovic understood well the value of propaganda in war. (Wikipedia, *Ruder Finn*).

27   Richard Palmer, *What Really Happened in Bosnia*, theTrumpet.com, 12 July 2011, accessed in http://europenews.dk/en/node/45289.

28   Ibid.

29   Ibid.

30   Anon., *Help from Holy Warriors*, Newsweek, October 5, 1992, pp. 52–53.

31   Alfred Sherman, op. cit., p. 7.

32   Cees Wiebes, *Intelligence and the war in Bosnia 1992–1995: The role of the intelligence and security services*, Netherlands Institute for War Documentation (NIOD), Lit Verlag, Berlin/London, 2002, accessed in English in www.srebrenica.nl., p. 139.

33   John R. Schindler, *Unholy Terror: Bosnia, Al Qa'ida and the Rise of Global Jihad*, p. 182.

34   Congressional Press Release, *Clinton-Approved Iranian Arms Transfers Help Turn Bosnia into Militant Islamic Base*, US Congress, 16 January 1997. Posted at globalresearch.ca 21 September 2001, accessed in http://www.globalresearch.ca/articles/DCH109A.html.

35   Ibid.

36   Ibid.

37   Peter Dale Scott, *The US Al Qaeda Alliance: Bosnia Kosovo and Now Libya. Washington's On-Going Collusion with Terrorists*, July 29, 2011, Global Research, accessed in http://www.globalresearch.ca/the-us-al-qaeda-alliance-bosnia-kosovo-and-now-libya-washington-s-on-going-collusion-with-terrorists.

38   Cees Wiebes, op. cit.

39   Ibid.

40   Ibid.

41   John R. Schindler, *Unholy Terror: Bosnia, Al Qa'ida and the Rise of Global Jihad*, pp. 147–148.

42   Ibid., p. 124.

43   Ibid., pp. 148–150.

44   Cees Wiebes, op. cit., pp. 148–159.

45   Alfred Sherman, op. cit., pp. 24–25.

46   Wikipedia, Christiane Amanpour, accessed in http://en.wikipedia.org/wiki/ Christiane_Amanpour#cite_note-26.

47   Blog, *Bratunac and Srebrenica twin commemorations double standards*, accessed in http://antisrbizam.com/blog/60-bratunac-and-srebrenica-twin-commemorations-double-standards.

48   Ibid.

49   Richard Palmer, op. cit.

50   Ibid.

51   Blog, Bratunac . . ., op. cit.

52   Ibid.

53   Lee Jay Walker, *Ratko Mladic: killing 3500 Christians near Srebrenica and Islamic jihad*, 14 June, 2011, Pakistan Christian Post, accessed in http://europenews. dk/en/node/44247.

54   Ibid.

55   Wikipedia, *Naser Orić*, accessed in http://en.wikipedia.org/wiki/ Naser_Ori%C4%87.

56   John Rosenthal, *The Other Crimes of Bosnia*, BigPeace.com, June 2, 2011; summarizing interview of Galbraith by J.M. Berger, "Exclusive: U.S. Policy on Bosnia Arms Trafficking."

57   YouTube, +21 *1 One of al-Qaeda members in Syria, rips out the heart of a Syrian and eats it*, accessed in http://www.youtube.com/watch?v=nwMAjIxpO8A.

58   Cited in John Rosenthal, *THE OTHER CRIMES OF BOSNIA: WHAT ABOUT THE JIHAD?*, Posted By Ruth King on June 2nd, 2011, accessed in http://bigpeace.com/jrosenthal/2011/06/02/the-other-crimes-of-bosnia/.

59   Richard Palmer, op. cit.

60   Ibid.

61   Cees Wiebes, op. cit., p. 243.

62   Lee Jay Walker, op. cit.

63   Damir Kaletovic and Anes Alic in Sarajevo for ISN, *Al Qaida's Bosnian war move*, ETH Zurich, 03 Oct 2008, accessed in http://www.isn.ethz.ch/Digital-Library/Articles/Detail//?lng=en&id=92320.

64   Ibid.

65   Ibid.

66   John Rosenthal, op. cit.

67   Richard Palmer, op. cit.

CHAPTER NINE

"HOLY WAR" AND HEROIN IN KOSOVO AND THE CAUCASUS

"After bombing Yugoslavia into submission, NATO then stood by and submissively allowed the KLA to murder, pillage and burn. The KLA was given a free hand to do as they wished. Almost all of the non–Albanian population was ethnically cleansed from Kosovo under the watchful eyes of 40,000 NATO troops.

—James Bissett, former Canadian Ambassador to
Yugoslavia and Albania to Canadian newspaper

Jihad and CIA Go to Kosovo

The actual fighting in Bosnia-Herzegovina ended with the signing of the Dayton Accords in Paris on December 14, 1995 that put an end to the three-and-a-half-year long Bosnian War and opened the long-term NATO occupation of the country. NATO, and not the European Union, was in control. Bosnia-Herzegovina, once a multiethnic federal state, was established as a de facto Muslim state, in effect, a client state under control of the IMF and of NATO.

Even before the Bosnian fighting ceased, Washington had shifted its attention to Kosovo, whose Albanian ethnic population was also predominantly Muslim and which had been part of Serbia more or less since the Middle Ages. The second front was being prepared in NATO's war against Serbia. The Clinton Administration had learned around that time of vast oil and gas reserves in the Caspian Sea and wanted to secure a pipeline through the Balkans to control that oil and, above all, keep it from the Russians.[1]

In December 1995, the American Petroleum Institute in Washington, an organization representing the major US oil companies, had issued an estimate that the Caspian Basin, north of Afghanistan, contained "two-thirds of the world's known reserves, or 659 billion barrels."[2] The Caucasus was becoming a US strategic "area of interest," to put it mildly.

A retired Croatian Army Major personally told this author, in Zagreb in 2006, of a private conversation he had had in 1995, just after the abrupt end of the Bosnian war. The Croatian military man asked a senior CIA officer in Zagreb whom he knew from the Bosnian War why it was that the US was so suddenly ending the fighting in Bosnia. The CIA man replied to the effect that, at that point, Washington found it far more important to secure a permanent military base in Kosovo, from where they would be able to control the entire region, including the Middle East and the Caucasus.[3]

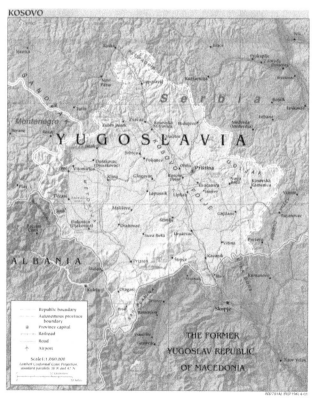

The tiny mountain area of Kosovo was split from Serbia to become a huge NATO base.

The Clinton Administration's Pentagon had farmed out the training of what would come to be called the Kosovo Liberation Army (KLA) to a US private mercenary group made up of former US Special Forces and military. According to former US Army Captain David Hackworth, retired US military officers working for the private US military contractor MPRI (Military Professional Resources Incorporated) not only trained KLA personnel, Sunni Muslim in origin, but even fought alongside them against the Yugoslav government forces.[4]

Former NSA official Wayne Madsen reported that what the US and Western media called the "Kosovo Liberation Army" was, in fact, a grouping of mafia clans in Kosovo who had been known drug traffickers well before working for the US. Madsen noted that covert support to the KLA was established around 1996 in the wake of the NATO Bosnia occupation as a "joint endeavor between the CIA and Germany's *Bundesnachrichtendienst* (BND). The task to create and finance the KLA was initially given to Germany: They used German uniforms, East German weapons, and were financed in part by drug money, according to intelligence analyst John Whitley."[5]

In Kosovo, the Clinton Administration had no interest in backing moderates who were open to a diplomatic solution with Belgrade. The KLA leaders whom Washington chose were accused of assassinating moderate Kosovo Albanians, including some of those who agreed to the Rambouillet peace accords. According to Albanian State Television, the KLA had sentenced the democratically elected president of the Republic of Kosovo, Ibrahim Rugova, to death in absentia. During the Rambouillet peace talks, Washington deliberately froze out Kosovo moderates in favor of the Jihadists of the KLA mafia, who were guaranteed not to go for peace.[6] Washington wanted war, and the KLA Muslims were its warriors.

By 1998, as the KLA matured its killing and sabotage skills under training from Pentagon contractor MPRI, the US and Germany recruited Mujahideen mercenaries from Afghanistan, Saudi Arabia, Bosnia, and elsewhere to train the KLA in guerrilla and diversion tactics. It was financed by Saudi Arabia and Kuwait.[7] One of the leaders of an elite KLA unit during the Kosovo conflict was Mohammed al-Zawahiri, brother of Egyptian Jihadist and Afghan and Bosnia veteran Ayman al-Zawahiri, Osama bin Laden's lieutenant at that time.

From Terrorists to Heroin-Pushing "Freedom Fighters"

During the war, the KLA jihadists collaborated with the NATO troops, and they were designated by NATO as "freedom fighters."

In May 1999, in the midst of the NATO "humanitarian" bombing of Yugoslavia—by then reduced to only Serbia and Montenegro—*The Washington Times* newspaper published documentation that Clinton Administration officials were well aware that their Kosovo allies, the KLA, were trafficking in heroin. The paper reported from the documents it had obtained that

> Drug agents in five countries, including the United States, believe the KLA has aligned itself with an extensive organized crime network centered in Albania that smuggles heroin and some cocaine to buyers throughout Western Europe and, to a lesser extent, the United States. The documents tie members of the Albanian Mafia to a drug smuggling cartel based in Kosovo's provincial capital, Pristina. The cartel is manned by ethnic Albanians who are members of the Kosovo National Front, whose armed wing is the KLA. The documents show **it is one of the most powerful heroin smuggling organizations in the world** (emphasis added—F.W.E.). . . . Movement of drugs over a collection of land and sea routes from Turkey through Bulgaria, Greece and Yugoslavia to Western Europe and elsewhere is so frequent and massive that intelligence officials have dubbed the circuit the "Balkan Route."[8]

The shocking report was ignored by mainstream media, as well as by the Clinton Administration.

In 1998, a year before the illegal NATO bombing of Yugoslavia to "prevent ethnic cleansing" of the Kosovo population by Serbia, the US State Department had even listed the KLA as an international terrorist organization, saying it had bankrolled its operations with proceeds from the international heroin trade and from loans from known Mujahideen terrorists, including Osama bin Laden. "They were terrorists in 1998 and now, because of politics, they're freedom fighters," said one top US drug official, who asked not to be identified.[9] Obviously, not all of the Washington bureaucracy was as enthusiastic about the KLA as Clinton and his inner circle were.

A US Government Drug Enforcement Administration report on the KLA and its heroin traffic noted at the time that a majority of heroin seized in Europe was transported over the Balkan Route. The DEA report said drug smuggling organizations composed of Kosovo's ethnic Albanians were considered "second only to Turkish gangs as the predominant heroin smugglers along the Balkan Route." Furthermore, the report noted, "Kosovo traffickers were noted for their use of violence and for their involvement in international weapons trafficking."[10]

Leading KLA members were trained in camps run by Osama bin Laden and his number two man, Egyptian former Muslim Brotherhood member, Ayman al-Zawahiri. The heroin that the KLA smuggled into the West came from Afghanistan, where bin Laden and the Mujahideen were still entrenched and working with Hekmatyar's heroin gang after the 1989 expulsion of the Soviets. Annually, the KLA-mafia Kosovo networks ran some $2 billion a year in heroin from Afghanistan to the West.[11] The CIA was getting multiple payoffs—first from its war in Afghanistan financed by heroin proceeds, secondly by shifting those Mujahideen fighters to the Balkans to merge with the KLA heroin distribution networks in Europe.

KLA fighters were ruthless. Even Human Rights Watch, a Washington NGO backing Kosovo and the KLA, documented that "The KLA was responsible for serious abuses. . . including abductions and murders of Serbs and ethnic Albanians considered collaborators with the state. . . attacks on Serbs, Roma, and other non-Albanians, as well as ethnic Albanian political rivals. . . widespread and systematic burning and looting of homes belonging to Serbs, Roma, and other minorities and the destruction of Orthodox churches and monasteries."[12]

In short, the US knew exactly who they were backing with the KLA. James Bissett, Canadian Ambassador to Yugoslavia and Albania, wrote in 2001 that, "as early as 1998, the Central Intelligence Agency assisted by the British Special Air Service were arming and training Kosovo Liberation Army members in Albania to foment armed rebellion in Kosovo. . . . The hope was that with Kosovo in flames NATO could intervene."[13] And intervene it did, massively violating both its own NATO Charter and the United Nations Charter in the process. Clinton "democracy" made its own rules of international law, which reduced to the age old adage "might makes right."

Ethnic Cleansing, but of Serbs . . .

With the jihadist-trained Muslim KLA fighters training their sights on Serb targets for assassination, the US was hoping to provoke Milosevic's army into a major response in order to justify a new NATO bombing of Yugoslavia. In February 1996, the KLA, ready to test its new terror skills given by the Saudi Mujahideen and US advisers, made a series of attacks against police stations and Yugoslav government officers in Kosovo, then part of Yugoslavia.

Agim Çeku, the military commander of the KLA, was a veteran of the Krajina Croatian ethnic cleansing, which drove an estimated 350,000 ethnic Serbs from their homes into predominantly Serb parts of Yugoslavia. The same Pentagon contractor, MPRI, who trained Çeku's KLA, had trained the Croatian Army for what was called Operation Storm and Strike.[14] The Pentagon and CIA role in the KLA operation was massive.

The KLA Jihadist Mafiosi (UÇK in Albanian) got a logo befitting a Habsburg Austro-Hungarian monarch.

The US-directed KLA kidnapping of Serb Yugoslav security forces resulted in a significant increase in Yugoslav government casualties. That, in turn, led to the hoped-for major Yugoslavian reprisals. By early March 1996, these terror and counterterror operations led Serb inhabitants of numerous Kosovo villages to flee to other villages, cities, or the hills for refuge from KLA brutality. The "KLA provocations, as personally witnessed in ambushes of security patrols which inflicted fatal and other casualties, were clear violations of the previous October's agreement [and United Nations

Security Council Resolution 1199]," noted Roland Keith, then a field office director of the OSCE's Kosovo Verification Mission.[15]

A report from the US Committee for Refugees spoke of, "Kosovo Liberation Army. . . attacks aimed at trying to 'cleanse' Kosovo of its ethnic Serb population." The UN High Commissioner for Refugees estimated that 55,000 refugees, most Kosovo Serbs, had fled their Kosovo homes to Montenegro and Central Serbia. "Over 90 mixed villages in Kosovo have now been emptied of Serb inhabitants and other Serbs continue leaving, either to be displaced in other parts of Kosovo or fleeing into central Serbia." The NATO North Atlantic Council stated that KLA was "the main initiator of the violence" and that it had "launched what appears to be a deliberate campaign of provocation."[16]

By 1998, the KLA escalated its attacks on Belgrade Serb government officials in Kosovo. By that time, the KLA had a mere 500 trained fighters. Then as the USA, Germany, and Great Britain sent arms shipments and provided training to the KLA, they built it up into a major guerrilla army, with as many as 30,000 members at the peak.[17]

German intelligence, in coordination with Washington, played a major role in building the KLA into a fighting force. In 1996, the British weekly *The European* carried an article by a French expert stating, "German civil and military intelligence services have been involved in training and equipping the rebels with the aim of cementing German influence in the Balkan area. . .The birth of the KLA in 1996 coincided with the appointment of Hansjoerg Geiger as the new head of the BND (German secret service). . .The BND men were in charge of selecting recruits for the KLA command structure from the 500,000 Kosovars in Albania."[18]

The US and German intervention using the KLA Jihadists turned a small conflict into a major crisis. As a pretext, NATO relied on the crisis it itself had created in order to justify waging a war of aggression against Yugoslavia.

By 1999, the Clinton Administration was ready to push a reluctant NATO to launch what would be only the second air strike in NATO history, the first being that in Bosnia-Herzegovina four years earlier. The 1999 NATO strikes were done in violation of the UN Charter, of the UN Security Council wishes, and of the NATO Charter itself that only permits military action in event of a strike against a NATO member country.

Using the invented pretext that Milosevic's Serb Army was engaging in massive ethnic cleansing of Kosovo Albanian Muslims and that they threatened a "humanitarian catastrophe," President Bill Clinton ordered air strikes against civilian as well as government targets across Serbia in what it called Operation Noble Anvil, with no regard to the UN or to other uneasy NATO members. Nothing about that anvil was noble.

Astonishing to many, Clinton's near-unilateral decision to bomb Belgrade, a decision that had earlier been strongly opposed by the Helmut Kohl government in Germany, found support from a newly elected "Red-Green" coalition in Germany of Social Democrat Chancellor Gerhard Schroeder and Green Party Foreign Minister Joschka Fischer. Fischer, remarkably to those who knew German party politics, had managed to arm-twist his traditionally anti-war Green party into backing the illegal NATO bombing, giving Clinton a badly needed NATO foreign ally.[19]

Clinton brazenly lied to the American people, claiming that the events of the Serbs in Kosovo were comparable to the Holocaust. CNN reported, "Accusing Serbia of 'ethnic cleansing' in Kosovo similar to the genocide of Jews in World War II, an impassioned President Clinton sought Tuesday to rally public support for his decision to send US forces into combat against Yugoslavia, a prospect that seemed increasingly likely with the breakdown of a diplomatic peace effort."[20]

Clinton's State Department claimed Serbian troops had committed genocide. In May 1996, US Defense Secretary William S. Cohen suggested that there might be up to 100,000 Albanian fatalities. However, five months after the end of NATO bombing, only 2,108 bodies were ever found—tragic but hardly genocide in terms of a theater of war.[21]

The US-led bombing strikes lasted from March 24, 1999, to June 10, 1999. Belgrade was devastated including with bombs containing radioactive depleted uranium. On the understanding that the United Nations would enforce order in Kosovo were Milosevic to remove Yugoslav troops, Milosevic withdrew, and the decade long war in Yugoslavia ended.

By then, Washington had what it wanted: Kosovo as a new US military bastion in the Balkans, a de facto defeated Serbian resistance to the US Balkanization, and the destruction of the Yugoslav Third Way guided economy model.

Aftermath in Kosovo

Two years after the war, James Bissett, former Canadian Ambassador to Yugoslavia and Albania, wrote,

> After bombing Yugoslavia into submission, NATO then stood by and submissively allowed the KLA to murder, pillage and burn. The KLA was given a free hand to do as they wished. Almost all of the non-Albanian population was ethnically cleansed from Kosovo under the watchful eyes of 40,000 NATO troops. Moreover, in defiance of United Nations resolution 1244 which brought an end to the fighting, NATO adamantly refused to disarm the KLA fighters. Instead, NATO converted this ragtag band of terrorists into the Kosovo Protection Force—allegedly to maintain peace and order in Kosovo.[22]

The former leaders of the KLA, now calling themselves the Government of Kosovo, also thrived in their old heroin smuggling, with clear support of the CIA and US Government, which had arranged for the KLA leaders to take over political control of a new Kosovo government. In 2000, *Mother Jones* magazine reported that after the NATO bombing in support of the KLA, Afghan heroin, much of it distributed by Kosovar Albanians, now accounted for almost 20 percent of the heroin seized in America—nearly double the percentage four years earlier. In Europe, the estimate was "Kosovo Albanians control 40% of Europe's heroin."[23]

"Jihadistan"

The outcome of the war also left the Saudi-backed al-Qaeda's jihadists far more strongly entrenched in the Balkans than they ever had been. In the words of Profesr John Schindler, Bosnia, "the most pro-Western society in the *umma* [Muslim world] was converted into a *Jihadistan* through domestic deceit, violent conflict, and misguided international intervention."[24]

Saudi Arabia, a major financier of the Mujahideen in the Balkans, began a major effort building mosques in former Yugoslavia, some 150 new glossy mosques all over tiny Bosnia and now in Kosovo, to spread the strict fanatical Saudi Wahabist Islam in a region where Muslims had been, by tradition, moderate and peaceful. In Sarajevo, the capitol of Bosnia, they built a grandiose $30 million King Fahd mosque. Saudi mosques, which began appearing all over Bosnia-Herzegovina and Kosovo, were complete with Saudi fanatical Wahhabite Imams who preached the fundamentalist Jihad ideology. As a US-backed Prime Minister, Hashim Thaçi encouraged the Saudi connection, especially Saudi money.[25]

Kosovo warlord Hashim Thaçi in Saudi Arabia to meet King Abdullah to solicit money.

More than a decade after the war ended, Kosovo journalists found a Saudi-based Wahhabi group exercising alarming financial influence over the highest Kosovo Islamic leadership. Kosovo's chief Muslim cleric, Naim Ternava, was accused of accepting backing from Wahhabi elements in Saudi Arabia.

The Kosovar investigative journalists showed that Ternava's religious administration approved payments for local mosques by Al Waqf Al Islami (AWAI—The Islamic Foundation), based in Jeddah.[26] Saudi Arabia was one of the first countries, in addition to the United States, to recognize the self-proclaimed Republic of Kosovo, run by mafia gangster boss Prime Minister Hashim Thaçi, the former political leader of the KLA.

After the war, Kosovo unemployment was running at a depression level of 45 percent. It was ripe for being bought or so fundamentalist Saudis reckoned. "What I saw during the past 10 years was a strong infiltration of Saudi money," said Flaka Surroi, owner of Kosovo's independent Koha Media. "They brought in the mosques, they brought in their dogma and ideology at the same time. They identified the poorest people in the communities, they offered them a steady salary every month just so they take over the ideology and start wearing the veil."[27]

KLA Foxes Guard the Henhouse

In elections in Kosovo in 2007, Thaçi declared his party victor despite the fact that only 45 percent turned out to vote and that his party got of that only 34 percent of the vote, meaning he had de facto a mere 15 percent popular support. It had been agreed with Washington beforehand that he would take over. Democracy was not as important to the US in Kosovo as was power. NATO had already slated the KLA "provisional government" (PGK) to run civilian state institutions. Following NATO's military occupation of Kosovo, the KLA took over municipal governments and public services, including schools and hospitals.

With the withdrawal of Yugoslav troops and police, the KLA immediately took control of Kosovo's police stations, something tantamount to asking Al Capone's men to take charge of the Chicago police during Prohibition. Under the formal authority of the United Nations, the Organization for Security and Cooperation in Europe (OSCE) had the task of training and installing a 4,000-strong police force with a mandate to "protect civilians" under the jurisdiction of the KLA-controlled "Ministry of Public Order." The KLA-controlled police force was also responsible for the massacres of civilians organized in the immediate wake of NATO's military occupation of Kosovo.[28]

President of the US George W. Bush shakes hands with Kosovo President Fatmir Sejdiu (center) and Kosovo Prime Minister Hashim Thaçi (left) during a meeting in the White House on July 21, 2008, after Kosovo declared independence.

Washington de facto installed the former KLA as the government of Kosovo with Thaçi as its "boss." Thaçi became the leader of the so-called "Democratic Party of Kosovo" and Prime Minister of Kosovo after January 2008.

The KLA's former military head, Agim Çeku, became Prime Minister of Kosovo after the war. The move caused some controversy in Serbia, where he was regarded as a war criminal for his role leading the Croatian Army in "Operation Storm," the ethnic cleansing of the Serb villages in Croatia.

On February 17, 2008, without any public discussion or legal basis, Thaçi declared Kosovo independent from Serbia, over the objections not only of Russia and Serbia but of many other EU states. Thaçi then became Prime Minister of the newly independent "state." Soon, Thaçi began regular trips as Prime Minister of the Republic of Kosovo to Saudi Arabia, one of the first nations to recognize the Kosovo rump state, in order to cash in on Saudi petrodollars. Thaçi and the Saudis became "soul brothers," and the fanatical Wahhabite ideology began to spread to Kosovo as a result.[29]

Some people outside Kosovo were not entirely comfortable with Thaçi. A report to the Council of Europe issued in December 2010 stated that Hashim Thaçi was the leader of the "Drenica Group" in charge of trafficking human organs taken from Serbian prisoners, as well as heroin and arms. Washington paid no mind. Thaçi was their man in Kosovo.[30]

Washington's argument for extending NATO eastward had advanced significantly in the process of the Yugoslav war. Hungary, Poland, and the Czech Republic became prospective NATO partners, something inconceivable just five years earlier.

The Bosnian War of 1992–1995 was the crucible for growing a Global Islamic Jihad movement, one which the CIA and Pentagon covertly backed through Saudi Arabia and other proxies, in order to advance their agenda in the post-Cold War world.

Thousands of tons of bombs later, and after an estimated $40 billion of destruction to the economy and infrastructure of Serbia, the Pentagon began the construction of one of the largest US military bases anywhere in the world: Camp Bond Steel near Gnjilane in southeast Kosovo. It was a vast fortress housing up to 7,000 soldiers, an airfield, and a state-of-the-art telecommunications center that gave the United States a commanding and clearly permanent military presence in the strategic Balkans within air reach of the increasingly strategic Caspian Sea.

In June 1999, no sooner was the bombing of Serbia over than the US government announced it was funding a feasibility study for an AMBO pipeline by a US-registered Albanian Macedonian Bulgarian Oil Corporation (AMBO). The project was backed by the US government. Washington proposed to run it from the Bulgarian Black Sea port of Burgas via the Republic of Macedonia to the Albanian Adriatic port of Vlorë. The 912-kilometer pipeline was to bypass the Turkish Straits, as well as Russia, in transportation of Caspian oil to the West.

CIA's Jihadists secure US oil control

The next step in Washington's new Eurasian strategy was to make certain the oil in the Caspian and Caucasus regions belonged to the Anglo-American oil majors and not the Russians, as during the Cold War.

Referring to imposition of NATO control over Serbia and Kosovo a senior US government official Joseph Grandmaison declared, "The prospect that the US government would guarantee security in the region and also provide financial guarantees, now makes it (AMBO) a much more attractive proposition." The AMBO engineering feasibility study had been undertaken by Halliburton Corporation's Brown & Root when Dick Cheney was head of Halliburton.[31]

With Camp Bond Steel as a firm base in the Balkans after the Yugoslav wars, Washington and their Jihadists turned their attention to Russia and the former states of the Soviet Union with predominant Muslim populations. Chechnya, a significantly Muslim part of Russia through which a vital Russian oil pipeline from the Caspian oil fields ran, became the next target of Washington's Jihad network as the US moved in to control the vast oilfields of Azerbaijan and Kazakhstan, two former Soviet states.[32]

As the Bosnian and Kosovo wars were being wound down by NATO, US intelligence services found another target for their Mujahideen Holy Warriors—the Caucasus, the mountainous area of the former Soviet Union bordering Turkey, Iran, and, now, the newly-proclaimed Russian Federation.

During the Clinton Administration in the mid-to-late 1990s, geophysical tests by Halliburton and the major US and British oil companies confirmed vast untapped oil and gas reserves in the Caspian Basin in the Caspian Sea between Azerbaijan, Russia, Kazakhstan, Iran, and Turkmenistan. Less than a decade before, the reserves had all been a part of the Soviet Union.

Geopolitical map of the Caucasus Region (2008)

When the Soviet Union dissolved in 1991, the US deployed Mujahideen to grab the vast oil assets of Azerbaijan and the Caspian Sea in the Caucasus.

No more. US and British major oil companies—Amoco and BP—immediately moved in to fill the vacuum.

Western geophysical estimates by Halliburton, Dick Cheney's firm, and others put the possible oil reserves of the Caspian Basin at around 200 billion barrels of oil, comparable to a new Saudi Arabia, as well as natural gas reserves estimated by the US Department of Energy to be comparable to those of North America.[33] The market value of the combined oil and gas resources at the then oil and gas prices of around $20 a barrel was estimated at $5 trillion. The Clinton Administration shifted focus from Russia to the states of the Caspian.[34]

In 1995, the US-Azerbaijan Chamber of Commerce was created to lobby the Clinton Administration for a strong US intervention into the Caspian Sea region, including the Caucasus. The Chamber was no collection of lightweights. It included some of the most influential figures in Washington, including then CEO of Halliburton Corp. Dick

Cheney, the man later to drive the George W. Bush Administration into the wars in Iraq and Afghanistan. The Chamber was chaired by former Secretary of State and Texas power broker James Baker III. It included such Washington influential people as Zbigniew Brzezinski, Henry Kissinger, and General Brent Scowcroft. They were power brokers no US President could ignore lightly. Soon, Clinton's focus turned from Yugoslavia and the Balkans to the Caucasus and a new war for control of oil and gas in the Caspian Basin.

The Caucasus Pipeline War

In 1998, just as he was preparing to bomb Kosovo, Clinton appointed two key people to develop a US energy strategy for the Caucasus and Caspian: Richard Morningstar and Morningstar's old college pal, Matt Bryza.

From 1997 to 1998, Bryza was advisor to Ambassador Richard Morningstar, coordinating US efforts in the Caucasus and Central Asia. Morningstar was appointed by the Clinton administration as the Special Advisor to the President and the Secretary of State for Caspian Basin Energy Diplomacy in 1998, where he was one of the chief architects of US Caspian strategic energy plans. The idea was to develop pipelines independent of Russia from the Caspian Sea through the South Caucasus to Europe.

Morningstar and Bryza played a key role in bringing to life the main project of the US-Azerbaijan Chamber of Commerce: to build what came to be known as the Baku–Tbilisi–Ceyhan (BTC) oil pipeline, "the world's most political pipeline," bringing Baku oil from Azerbaijan through Georgia to Turkey and the Mediterranean. Both had intimate ties to Dick Cheney and to Richard Perle, an Assistant Defense Secretary under Reagan, and an early backer as of using Mujahideen Jihadists to attack the Soviets in Afghanistan.[35]

To prepare the political stage for a US-British-controlled oil pipeline in the backyard of Russia required some help. The CIA and Pentagon turned to their recent Mujahideen allies, who had done so well for them in Bosnia and Kosovo.[36]

Osama bin Laden, who had been orchestrating Washington's growing Global Jihad from his US-approved safe haven in Khartoum in Muslim Brotherhood-controlled Sudan, began in 1995 turning his attention and his Mujahideen cadre to a sensitive, largely Muslim part of the Russian Federation in the Caucasus—Chechnya.[37]

Chechnya had traditionally been a predominantly Sufi Muslim society, where religion was private and personal not political and evangelical. The infiltration of the US-sponsored Mujahideen operatives linked to Osama bin Laden from the early 1990s transformed the character of the Chechen resistance movement, spreading al-Qaeda's hardline Wahhabite Islamist ideology. US intelligence ties had been established in the early 1990s in Azerbaijan under General Richard Secord's Mega Oil operation. From there, Mujahideen activities had quickly extended into Dagestan and Chechnya, turning Baku into a shipping point for Afghan heroin to the Chechen Mujahideen mafia.[38]

The only existing oil pipeline from Baku in the Caspian was Russian, and it ran through Chechnya's capital, Grozny. It was a 100,000 barrel/day pipeline from the Soviet era that took Azeri oil north via Machatschkala, the capital of Russia's Dagestan province, and across 146 kilometers of Chechen territory to the Black Sea Russian port of Novorossiysk. The pipeline was a major competition and obstacle to the alternative route of Bryza and Morningstar and the British and US oil majors.[39]

Bin Laden brought in an old Jihad crony, Ibn al-Khattab, to become the Commander, or Emir, of Jihadist Mujahideen in Chechnya together with Chechen warlord Shamil Basayev.

Osama bin Laden was brought into contact with Chechen Islamic Jihadist Ibn al Khattab (above) to start the US-backed Chechen war against Moscow after 1995.

Ibn al-Khattab had been born in Saudi Arabia and had fought with bin Laden's Mujahideen in Afghanistan in the 1980s, as well as in the US-steered war in Bosnia.[40] The Saudi government gave significant financial support to Ibn al-Khattab's Chechen Jihad against Moscow, and to his organization called the Islamic International Brigade, in coordination with Washington. His Islamic International Brigade in the Caucasus consisted of an estimated 1,500 Jihadists recruited from Chechnya, Dagestan, Arabs, Turks, and other foreign Muslims.

Saudi sheikhs declared the Chechen resistance a legitimate Jihad, or Holy War, and private Saudi donors sent money to Khattab and his Chechen colleagues. Mujahideen wounded in Chechnya were sent to Saudi Arabia for medical treatment. Former US FBI agent Ali Soufan stated that "the United States had been on the side of Muslims in Afghanistan, Bosnia, and Chechnya."[41] In fact, they had financed, transported, and armed them.

The CIA airlifted the Afghan-based Mujahideen into the Caucasus, where they were smuggled across the Georgian border into Chechnya. Another main Chechen Jihadist terror training base was in NATO-member country Turkey. At the time, Saudi intelligence and the CIA were in intimate collaboration regarding the use of Mujahideen and Osama bin Laden's Holy Warrior terrorists.[42]

In 1991, the leaders of Central Asia were approached by major US and British oil companies during ongoing negotiations between Kazakhstan and the US oil company Chevron. George H.W. Bush, by then US President, actively backed the plans of US oil companies to exploit and, above all, control the resources of the Caspian region, as well as to build a pipeline not controlled by Moscow that could bring the oil and gas production to the West.[43]

In that same year, 1991, Richard Secord, Heinie Aderholt, and Ed Dearborn—veterans of US covert intelligence operations in Laos and, later, of Oliver North's illegal guns-for-drugs operations with the Nicaraguan Contras—came to Baku under the cover of an oil company named MEGA Oil. George H.W. Bush backed the idea of a project to build a US-controlled oil pipeline stretching from Azerbaijan across the Caucasus to Turkey.

MEGA never found oil, but its airlifts of Mujahideen into the Caucasus to create terror and chaos along the route of the Russian oil pipeline in Chechnya and Dagestan helped to bring Azerbaijan and its oil firmly into the US sphere with the construction of the Baku–Tbilisi–Ceyhan (BTC) pipeline from Baku through Georgia to Ceyhan in Turkey.[44]

MEGA operatives in Azerbaijan engaged in military training. They reportedly passed "brown bags filled with cash" to members of the Azeri government and, above all, set up an airline based on the model of Air America, which soon was picking up hundreds of Mujahideen mercenaries in Afghanistan and flying them secretly into the Caucasus.

Gulbuddin Hekmatyar, Mujahideen warlord, controlling Afghan heroin traffic in 1988 with CIA Deputy Director Richard Kerr.

Gulbuddin Hekmatyar, who at that time was still allied with bin Laden, recruited Afghan mercenaries to fight against Russia and its Armenian allies in Azerbaijan and Chechnya. Hekmatyar, naturally, used the new Caucasus link to flood Western countries with his Afghan heroin, all with full US knowledge. The heroin went through Baku into Chechnya, Russia, on to Europe and even North America.[45]

Demonizing Putin

At the same time the CIA and Pentagon were pouring Jihadists into Russia's Chechnya, they set up a propaganda arm in Washington to make the case for Chechen independence from the "brutal" Russian occupation. It was run as part of a US intelligence organization named Freedom House and was called the American Committee for Peace in Chechnya (ACPC).

Its members were some of the bloodiest war hawks in the United States of the time: Richard Perle, a notorious neoconservative who was a Pentagon adviser; Elliott Abrams of Iran-Contra scandal fame; Kenneth Adelman, former US ambassador to the UN, who egged on the 2003 invasion of Iraq by predicting it would be "a cakewalk"; Frank Gaffney of the neoconservative militarist Centre for Security Policy; Bruce Jackson, former US military intelligence officer and one-time vice-president of Lockheed Martin, now president of the US Committee on NATO; and James Woolsey, former CIA director.[46]

In short, the peace they advocated was Russian surrender.

The ACPC launched a highly successful international media campaign to demonize Russia. With a war-weary Russian population increasingly against a new military war in Chechnya after the Afghan debacle, Boris Yeltsin's government declared a ceasefire with the Chechens in 1996 and signed a peace treaty a year later in 1997.

Russian military deaths were estimated to be as high as 14,000. Chechen militants killed as many as 15,000. Some 100,000 civilians were killed, with possibly over 200,000 injured and more than 500,000 people displaced by the new US-instigated war. The Russian Baku oil pipeline route was off the table, just as Washington wanted. The way was clear for BP and ExxonMobil to go ahead with their risky alternative route through Georgia.

By that time Washington had begun to develop a new strategy in addition to using the predominantly Arab Jihadists of Osama bin Laden and the Mujahideen.

Senior CIA Islam experts began to turn to Turkey, also, like Saudi Arabia, a Sunni Muslim country but with one advantage over the Arabs: the Turkish Ottoman Empire had stretched originally as far as China and across Central Asia. Washington began to actively build a Turk option for waging Jihad across Central Asia and, ultimately, to China in order to control Eurasia. A barely educated, reclusive Turkish Imam named Fethullah Gülen would be their vehicle.

Endnotes

1   F. William Engdahl, op. cit.

2   American Petroleum Institute, December, 1995, *Caspian Sea Said to Contain Two Thirds of Worlds Known Oil Reserves*, accessed

in http://www.historycommons.org/timeline.jsp?timeline=complete_911_timeline&startpos=700#amidlate90sturkishfronts.

3   Conversation of the author in Croatia in 2006 with "Major A.," a senior Croatian officer involved in procurement of weapons for the Croatian Army in the early 1990s.

4   Peter Dale Scott, *The US Al Qaeda Alliance: Bosnia, Kosovo and Now Libya. Washington's On-Going Collusion with Terrorists*, Global Research, July 29, 2011, accessed in http://www.globalresearch.ca/the-us-al-qaeda-alliance-bosnia-kosovo-and-now-libya-washington-s-on-going-collusion-with-terrorists.

5   Wayne Madsen, *US and Germany Trained and Developed the KLA*, The Progressive, August, 1999, accessed in http://www.projectcensored.org/22-us-and-germany-trained-and-developed-the-kla/.

6   Wayne Madsen, *The US Connections To The KLA*, 18 September, 2012, accessed in http://serbianfbreporter.wordpress.com/2012/09/18/the-u-s-connections-to-the-kla/.

7   Wayne Madsen, *US and Germany Trained . . .* , op. cit.

8   Jerry Seper, *KLA Finances Fight with Heroin Sales: Terror Group Is Linked to Crime Network*, The Washington Times (Washington, DC), May 3, 1999, accessed in http://www.sarantakos.com/kosovo/ks18kla.html.

9   Ibid.

10   Ibid.

11   Peter Dale Scott, op. cit.

12   Human Rights Watch, *Under Orders: War Comes in Kosovo*, accessed in http://www.hrw.org/reports/2001/kosovo/undword.htm.

13   James Bissett, WE CREATED A MONSTER, Toronto Star, July 31, 2001, accessed in http://web.archive.org/web/20080510052014/http:/www.deltax.net/bissett/a-monster.htm.

14   Wayne Madsen, op. cit.

15   Roland Keith, *Failure of Diplomacy, Returning OSCE Human Rights Monitor Offers A View From the Ground in Kosovo*, The Democrat, May 1999.

16   Cited in *Kosovo Liberation Army*, accessed in http://en.wikipedia.org/wiki/Kosovo_Liberation_Army.

17   Gregory Elich, *War Criminals Real and Imagined*, Centre for Research on Globalisation, globalresearch.ca, 18 November 2001, accessed in http://global-research.ca/articles/ELI111A.html.

18   Roger Fallgot, *How Germany Backed KLA*, The European, 21–27 September 2008, pp. 21–27.

19   In an interesting note that is difficult to verify, this author was told by a very reliable source inside the higher levels of the German SPD socialist party of Schroeder that, shortly before the October 1998 German elections that replaced Kohl with a Schroeder-Fischer coalition, the two were called to the Clinton White House for a private discussion of the upcoming German elections. Reportedly, Clinton offered substantial support in money and other things to ensure the victory of Schroeder-Fischer on the quid pro quo proviso, among others, that a Schroeder government backed the US in Kosovo. In the event, Fischer brought his Green party behind the NATO bombing and Schroeder sent German troops to Kosovo.

20   Stephen Erlanger, *Early Count Hints at Fewer Kosovo Deaths*, The New York Times, November 11, 1999, p. A6.

21   Ibid.

22   James Bissett, op. cit.

23   Peter Klebnikov, *Heroin Heroes*, Mother Jones, January/February 2000. Clinton, at the same time, mounted a vigorous campaign against Colombian heroin, conveniently increasing the demand for Afghan heroin.

24   John Schindler, *Unholy Terror: Bosnia, Al-Qa'ida, and the Rise of Global Jihad*, Zenith Press, 2007, p. 324.

25   Sylvia Poggioli, Radical Islam Uses Balkan Poor To Wield Influence, NPR, October 25, 2010, accessed in http://www.npr.org/templates/story/story.php?storyId=130801242.

26   Stephen Schwartz, *How Radical Islam Infiltrates Kosovo*, August 30, 2012, Weekly Standard, accessed in http://www.weeklystandard.com/blogs/how-radical-islam-infiltrates-kosovo_651173.html.

27   Sylvia Poggioli, op. cit.

28   Michel Chossudovsky, "Kosovo 'Freedom Fighters' Financed by Organized Crime," Covert Action Quarterly, Spring-Summer 1999 accessed in http://www.projectcensored.org/22-us-and-germany-trained-and-developed-the-kla/.

29   Roberta Fedele, *Kosovo courts Saudi investments,* Saudi Gazette, June 17, 2012, accessed in http://www.saudigazette.com.sa/index.cfm?method=home. regcon&contentid=20120617127191.

30   Paul Lawis, *Kosovo PM is head of human organ and arms ring Council of Europe reports*, London Guardian, 14 December, 2010.

31   F. William Engdahl, op. cit. p. 241.

32   Wayne Madsen, *Washington's «Civil Society» and CIA Financing of Chechen and Other Caucasus Regional Terrorists*, Strategic Culture Foundation, 29 April, 2013, accessed in http://www.strategic-culture.org/news/2013/04/29/ washington-civil-society-cia-financing-chechen-other-regional-terrorists.html.

33   Fiona Hill and Regine Spector, *The Caspian Basin and Asian Energy Markets*, The Brookings Institution, Washington, September 2001, accessed in http:// www.brookings.edu/research/papers/2001/09/globaleconomics-hill.

34   Joe Barnes, *Unlocking the Assets: Energy and the Future of Central Asia and the Caucasus—National Interests in the Caspian Basin*, James Baker III Institute for Public Policy, April, 1998, accessed in http://bakerinstitute.org/media/ files/Research/95010710/u-s-interests-in-the-caspian-basin-getting-beyond-the-hype.pdf.

35   Sibel Edmonds, *Obama Appoints a Not-Too-Long-Ago-Hatched Neocon Larva*, 27 July, 2010, accessed in http://www.boilingfrogspost.com/2010/07/27/ obama-appoints-a-not-too-long-ago-hatched-neocon-larva/.

36   Ibid.

37   Peter Dale Scott, *The Falsified War on Terror . . .* , op. cit.

38   Nafeez Mosaddeq Ahmed, Our terrorists, New Internationalist, October 1, 2009, accessed in http://newint.org/features/2009/10/01/blowback-extended-version/#sthash.uCpcnKXP.dpuf.

39   Thomas I. Steinberg, *Warum Tschetschenien?*, Junge Welt, Berlin, September 25, 2004, accessed in http://www.steinbergrecherche.com/tschetschenien.htm.

40   Wikipedia, Ibn al Khattab, accessed in http://en.wikipedia.org/wiki/ Ibn_al-Khattab.

41   Peter Dale Scott, *The Falsified War . . .* , op. cit.

42 Sibel Edmonds, *US NATO Chechen Militia Joint Operations Base*, Boiling Frogs Post, November 22, 2011, accessed in http://www.boilingfrogspost.com/2011/11/22/bfp-exclusive-us-nato-chechen-militia-joint-operations-base/.

43 Peter Dale Scott, *USA and Al Qaeda Relations . . .* , op. cit.

44 Ibid.

45 Ibid.

46 Sibel Edmonds, *US NATO Chechyn . . .* , op. cit.

CHAPTER TEN

CIA BACKS A "NEW OTTOMAN CALIPHATE" IN EURASIA

"You must move in the arteries of the system without anyone noticing your existence until you reach all the power centers. . . . You must wait for the time when you are complete and conditions are ripe, until we can shoulder the entire world and carry it. . . . You must wait until such time as you have gotten all the state power . . . in Turkey. . . . Until that time, any step taken would be too early—like breaking an egg without waiting the full forty days for it to hatch."

—Imam Fetullah Gülen, CIA-asset in a
sermon to followers in Turkey

"Because of the large amount of money that Gülen's movement uses to finance his projects, there are claims that he has secret agreements with Saudi Arabia, Iran, and Turkic governments. There are suspicions that the CIA is a co-payer in financing these projects."

—US State Department in a hearing opposing
Gülen's application for US residency

Fethullah Gülen's Spider Net

As they were deploying Osama bin Laden's Arab Mujahideen "holy warriors" into Chechnya and the Caucasus during the 1990s—in order to secure oil pipeline routes for the Anglo-American oil companies independent of Russian control—the CIA, working with a network of self-styled "neoconservatives" in Washington, began to build their most ambitious political Islam project ever.

It was called the Fethullah Gülen Movement, also known in Turkish as *Cemaat,* or "The Society." Their focus was *Hizmet,* or what they defined as the "duty of Service" to the Islamic community. Curiously enough, the Turkish movement was based out of Saylorsburg, Pennsylvania, in the scenic foothills of the Pocono Mountains. There, its key figure, the reclusive Fethullah Gülen, was busy building a global network of Islam schools, businesses, and foundations, all with untraceable funds.[1] His Gülen Movement, or *Cemaat,* had no main address, no mailbox, no official organizational registration, no central bank account, nothing. His followers never demonstrated for Sharia or Jihad—their operations were all hidden from view.

In 2008, US Government court filings estimated the global value of Gülen's empire at anywhere between $25 and $50 billion. No one could prove how large it was as there were no independent audits. In a US Court testimony during the hearing on Gülen's petition for a special US Green Card permanent residence status, one loyal *Cemaat* journalist described the nominal extent of Gülen's empire:

> The projects sponsored by Gülen-inspired followers today number in the thousands, span international borders and are costly in terms of human and financial capital. These initiatives include over 2000 schools and seven universities in more than ninety countries in five continents, two modern hospitals, the *Zaman* newspaper (now in both a Turkish and English edition), a television channel (*Samanyolu*), a radio channel (Burc FM), CHA (a major Turkish news agency), *Aksiyon* (a leading weekly news magazine), national and international Gülen conferences, Ramadan interfaith dinners, interfaith dialog trips to Turkey from countries around the globe and the many programs sponsored by the Journalists and Writers Foundation. In addition, the Isik insurance company and Bank Asya, an Islamic bank, are affiliated with the Gülen community.[2]

Bank Asya was listed among the Top 500 Banks in the world by London's *Banker* magazine. It had joint-venture banking across Muslim Africa, from Senegal to Mali in a strategic cooperation agreement with the Islamic

Development Bank's Senegal-based Tamweel Africa Holding SA.[3] *Zaman*, which also owned the English-language *Today's Zaman*, was the largest daily paper in Turkey. The journalist's description of the Gülen holdings named in the US Court document was very carefully formulated, especially with the statement "projects sponsored by Gülen-inspired followers," which left actual ownership conveniently vague and completely untraceable.

By the late 1990s, Gülen's movement had attracted the alarm and attention of an anti-NATO wing of the Turkish military and of the Ankara government.

After leading a series of brilliant military campaigns in the 1920s to win the Independence War that he initiated against an invasion by foreign and allied forces of British, Greek, Italian, French, and other victors of World War I, Ataturk had established the modern Turkish state. He then launched a series of political, economic, and cultural reforms aimed at transforming the religiously-based Ottoman Caliphate into a modern, secular, and democratic nation-state. He built thousands of new schools, made primary education free and compulsory, and gave women equal civil and political rights, and reduced the burden of taxation on peasants.

Gülen and his movement aimed at nothing less than to roll-back the remains of that modern, secular Kemalism in Turkey, and return to the Caliphate of yore. In one of his writings to members, he declared, "With the patience of a spider we lay our net until people get caught in it."[4]

In 1998, Gülen defected to the US shortly before a treasonous speech he had made to his followers at a private gathering was made public. He had been recorded calling on his supporters to "work patiently and to creep silently into the institutions in order to seize power in the state," treason by the Ataturk constitution of Turkey.

"Confronting the World" from Pennsylvania

In 1999, Turkish television aired footage of Gülen delivering a sermon to a crowd of followers in which he revealed his aspirations for an Islamist Turkey ruled by Sharia (Islamic law), as well as the specific methods that should be used to attain that goal. In the secret sermon, Gülen said,

> You must move in the arteries of the system without anyone noticing your existence until you reach all the power centers . . . until the conditions are ripe, they [the followers] must continue

like this. . . You must wait for the time when you are complete and conditions are ripe, until we can shoulder the entire world and carry it. . . You must wait until such time as you have gotten all the state power, until you have brought to your side all the power of the constitutional institutions in Turkey. . . Until that time, any step taken would be too early—like breaking an egg without waiting the full forty days for it to hatch. It would be like killing the chick inside. The work to be done is in confronting the world. Now, I have expressed my feelings and thoughts to you all—in confidence. . . trusting your loyalty and secrecy.[5]

Shortly after Gülen fled to Pennsylvania, Turkish prosecutors demanded a ten-year sentence against him for having "founded an organization that sought to destroy the secular apparatus of state and establish a theocratic state."

Gülen never left the United States after that time, curiously enough, even though the Islamist Erdoğan courts later cleared him in 2006 of all charges.[6] His refusal to return, even after being cleared by a then friendly Erdoğan Islamist AKP government, heightened the conviction among opponents in Turkey about his close CIA ties.

Gülen was charged in 2000 by the then secular Turkish courts of having committed treason. Claiming diabetes as a medical reason, Fethullah Gülen had managed to escape to a permanent exile in the United States, with the help of some very powerful CIA and State Department friends, before his indictment was handed down.[7] Some suspected he was forewarned.

Outwardly, Gülen cultivated an appealing profile on his official website as a purveyor of a "modern," peaceful Sufi form of Islam, one adapted to today's world. It wasn't the 16th century harsh Islam of the Wahhabite Bedouins of the Saudi Arabian desert. Under a benign-looking portrait of a pensive, almost philosophical Gülen stood the slogan, "Understanding and Respect." Self-promoting articles with titles such as "Islamic scholar Gülen's poems turned into songs for international album," were typical, all praising the sublime wisdom of Gülen, giving an aura of Sufi tranquility, peace, and love.[8]

In a 2008 profile, *The New York Times* described Gülen's organization, by then firmly entrenched across the United States with more than one hundred state-financed Charter Schools: "The Gulen movement... does not seek to subvert modern secular states, but encourages practicing Muslims to use to the full the opportunities they offer. It is best understood as the Islamic equivalent of Christian movements appealing to business and the professions."[9] A better press promotion was hard to imagine. Similar articles or coverage of Gülen with uncritical praise emerged from the mainstream Western media ranging from the London *Economist* to CNN.

Gülen's ultra-professional website claimed that the Gülen Movement, "funds all of its activities by donations from members of the community from the general public and does not accept any help support from governments in any form. This approach has helped the Movement stay away from corruption and politics."[10]

Because of the movement's large and extensive business holdings, Gülen's *Hizmet* had been described as having "characteristics of a cult or of an Islamic Opus Dei." The comparison was perhaps more than to the point, in many respects.[11]

CIA Gives Wolf Sheep's Clothing

Unlike the CIA's Mujahideen Jihadists, like Hekmatyar in Afghanistan or Naser Orić in Bosnia, the CIA decided to give Fethullah Gülen a radically different image. No blood-curdling, head-severing, human-heart-eating Jihadist, Fethullah Gülen was presented to the world as a man of "peace, love and brotherhood," even managing to grab a photo op with Pope John Paul II, which Gülen featured prominently on his website.

Gülen and the late Pope John Paul II in Rome in 1998, posing as a man of peace and ecumenical harmony.

The Gülen organization in the US hired one of Washington's highest-paid Public Relations image experts, George W. Bush's former campaign director, Karen Hughes, to massage his "moderate" Islam image.[12] "Why is this Imam different from all other Imams?" was the essential message.

In reality, he was no different in goals from Hassan al-Banna or the Grand Mufti of Jerusalem or Said Ramadan or other Muslim Brotherhood leaders of the past eighty or more years whose strategy was to establish a new Islamic Caliphate under strict Islamic Sharia law. But, unlike the projects of al-Banna and the Egyptian Brotherhood, the Gülen project centered on the creation of a New Ottoman Caliphate, retracing the vast Eurasian domain of the former Ottoman Turkic Caliphates. Gülen, the Turkish wolf, simply had a better tailor to cut and form the sheep's clothing.

Notably, when Gülen fled Turkey to avoid prosecution for treason in 1998, he chose not to go to any of perhaps a dozen Islamic countries which could have offered him asylum. He chose, instead, the United States. He did so with the help of the CIA.

In the aftermath of September 11, 2001, and the ensuing climate of closer scrutiny of Islamic groups in the United States, the US Government's Department of Homeland Security and the US State Department both opposed Gülen's application for what was called a "preference visa as an alien of extraordinary ability in the field of education."

They presented a detailed Court argument demonstrating that the fifth-grade dropout, Fethullah Gülen, should not be granted a preference visa. They argued that his background,

> contains overwhelming evidence that plaintiff is not an expert in the field of education, is not an educator, and is certainly not one of a small percentage of experts in the field of education who have risen to the very top of that field. Further, the record contains overwhelming evidence that plaintiff is primarily the leader of a large and influential religious and political movement with immense commercial holdings. The record further showed that much of the acclaim that plaintiff claimed to have achieved had been sponsored and financed by plaintiff's own movement.[13]

Until an open clash in 2013, Fetullah Gülen (left) was the éminence grise behind Recep Erdoğan's AK Party; Gülen is widely branded in Turkey as a CIA asset.

However, over the objections of the FBI, of the US State Department, and of the US Department of Homeland Security, three former CIA operatives intervened and managed to secure a Green Card and permanent US residency for Gülen. In their court argument opposing the Visa, US State Department attorneys had notably argued, "Because of the large amount of money that Gülen's movement uses to finance his projects, there are claims that he has secret agreements with Saudi Arabia, Iran, and Turkic governments. There are suspicions that the CIA is a co-payer in financing these projects."[14]

Gülen's CIA "Friends"

The three CIA people supporting Gülen's Green Card application were former US Ambassador to Turkey George Fidas, Morton Abramowitz, and Graham E. Fuller. They headed a list of twenty-nine persons who signed statements backing Gülen's US Visa appeal.[15]

George Fidas had worked thirty-one years at the CIA dealing, among other things, with the Balkans, and had held a very senior position under the CIA Deputy Director on retiring. When he left the CIA, he joined the highly secretive faculty of the US Joint Military Intelligence College.[16]

Morton Abramowitz was reportedly also with the CIA, if "informally."[17] He had been named US Ambassador to Turkey in 1989 by President George H.W. Bush. Sibel Edmonds, former FBI Turkish translator and "whistleblower," named Abramowitz, along with Graham E. Fuller, as part of a dark cabal within the US Government that she discovered were using networks out of Turkey to advance a criminal, "deep state" agenda across the Turkic world, from Istanbul into China. The network that she documented included significant involvement in heroin trafficking out of Afghanistan.[18]

On retiring from the State Department, Abramowitz served on the board of the US Congress-financed National Endowment for Democracy (NED) and was a cofounder, along with George Soros, of the International Crisis Group. Both the NED and International Crisis Group were implicated in various US "Color Revolutions" since the 1990s collapse of the Soviet Union, from *Otpor* in Serbia to the 2004 Orange Revolution in Ukraine, to the 2009 Green Revolution in Iran, to the 2011 Lotus Revolution in Tahrir Square in Egypt.[19]

Journalist Diane Johnstone described Abramowitz' International Crisis Group as, "a high-level think tank supported by financier George Soros. . .devised primarily to provide policy guidance to governments involved in the NATO-led reshaping of the Balkans." Johnstone added, "its leading figures include top US policymaker Morton Abramowitz, the *eminence grise* of NATO's new 'humanitarian intervention' policy and sponsor of Kosovo Albanian [KLA—F.W.E.] separatists."[20]

The Board members and "advisers" to Abramowitz' International Crisis Group included the former US National Security Adviser and architect of the Afghan Mujahideen strategy of the 1980s, Zbigniew Brzezinski; Prince Turki al-Faisal, former head of Saudi Intelligence and former Ambassador of Saudi Arabia to the US; General Wesley Clark, former US NATO Supreme Allied Commander who ran the USA's illegal bombing of Serbia in 1999; and former NATO Secretary-General, Javier Solana.[21]

As head of Saudi Intelligence in the early 1980s, Prince Turki al-Faisal had played a central role working with Pakistan's ISI intelligence and the CIA to create the Afghan Mujahideen. It was Turki who personally sent Osama bin Laden, a Saudi from an extremely wealthy family close to the Saudi monarchy, into Pakistan near the Afghan border some weeks before the December 1979 Soviet invasion. Bin Laden's mission was to establish the Maktab al-Khidamat (MAK) to help finance, recruit, and train Mujahideen fighters in Afghanistan to fight the Soviets. Prince Turki had been informed beforehand by US intelligence of the imminent Soviet invasion to come at the end of 1979.[22]

Abramowitz and his International Crisis Group cohorts were not really a group that could be accused of excessive love of democracy or human rights. Their name belied their actual intent—fostering international crises to advance a covert deep state Washington agenda.

Abramowitz and Graham E. Fuller, both with extensive experience and knowledge inside Turkish political Islam, were also well acquainted with each other. Abramowitz even wrote the forward to one of Fuller's books on the Turkish Kurdish question.[23]

Graham E. Fuller, the third CIA "friend" of Fethullah Gülen, was also no low-level CIA numbers analyst. He had been immersed in the CIA's activities in steering Mujahideen and other political Islamic organizations since the 1980s. He spent 20 years as CIA operations officer stationed in Turkey, Lebanon, Saudi Arabia, Yemen, and Afghanistan and was one of the CIA's early advocates of using the Muslim Brotherhood and similar Islamist organizations to advance US foreign policy.[24]

In 1982, Graham Fuller had been appointed the National Intelligence Officer for Near East and South Asia at CIA. There he was responsibe for Afghanistan, where he had served as CIA Station Chief, for Central Asia, and for Turkey. In 1986, under Ronald Reagan, Fuller became the Vice-Chairman of the National Intelligence Council, with overall responsibility for national level strategic forecasting.[25]

Fuller, author of *The Future of Political Islam*, was also the key CIA figure to convince the Reagan Administration to tip the balance in the eight-year long Iran-Iraq war by using Israel to illegally channel weapons to Iran in what became the Iran-Contra Affair.[26]

In 1988, as the Afghan Mujahideen war was winding down, Fuller "retired" from the CIA with a last rank as a very senior Deputy Director of the CIA's National Council on Intelligence, to go over to the RAND Corporation, presumably to avoid embarrassment around his role in the Iran-Contra scandal for then Presidential candidate George H.W. Bush, Fuller's former boss at CIA.[27]

RAND was a Pentagon- and CIA-linked neoconservative Washington think tank. Indications are that Fuller's work at RAND was instrumental in developing the CIA strategy for building the Gülen Movement as a geopolitical force to penetrate former Soviet Central Asia. Among his RAND papers, Fuller wrote studies on Islamic fundamentalism in Turkey, Sudan, Afghanistan, Pakistan, and Algeria, the "survivability" of Iraq, and the "New Geopolitics of Central Asia" after the fall of the USSR, where Fethullah Gülen's cadre were sent to establish Gülen schools and Madrassas.

In 1999, while at RAND, Fuller advocated using Muslim forces to further US interests in Central Asia against both China and Russia. He stated, "The policy of guiding the evolution of Islam and of helping them against our adversaries worked marvelously well in Afghanistan against the Russians. The same doctrines can still be used to destabilize what remains of Russian power, and especially to counter the Chinese influence in Central Asia."[28]

Clearly, by all evidence, Fuller and his associates in and around a certain faction in the US intelligence community intended their man, Fethullah Gülen, to play a major role, perhaps *the* major role, in their operations to "destabilize what remains of Russian power, and especially to counter the Chinese influence in Central Asia."[29]

Since the 1990s the Caucasus, including Chechnya, were a major preoccupation of CIA insurgency and terror operations using Jihadist Muslims.

CIA career man Graham E. Fuller was a key backer of Fetullah Gülen and architect of the CIA Islam strategy since Afghanistan's Mujahideen.

Embarrassing ties between Graham Fuller and that network of CIA-backed Caucasus Jihadists came to light in the aftermath of the April 2013 "Boston bombers" attack. The two accused "bomber" brothers, Tamerlan and Dzhokhar Tsarnaev, had an uncle born in Chechnya named Ruslan

Tsarnaev. Ruslan was married in the 1990s until their divorce in 1999 to Samantha A. Fuller, the daughter of Graham E. Fuller.[30]

Fuller even admitted that "Uncle Ruslan" had lived in Fuller's home in the suburban Washington area and that Fuller went several times to the Caucasus and Kyrgyzstan in Central Asia just as the CIA was heating up the Chechen Islamic terror against Moscow, allegedly to "visit" his daughter and son-in-law.[31]

Ruslan Tsarnaev, who changed his name to Ruslan Tsarni, had worked in the past for companies tied to Dick Cheney's Halliburton, as well as working as a "consultant" in Kazakhstan on the Caspian Sea in the 1990s with the State Department's USAID, which has been widely identified as a CIA front.[32]

Graham Fuller and Fethullah Gülen apparently enjoyed a kind of mutual admiration society. In 2008, just around the time he wrote a letter of recommendation to the US Government asking to give Gülen the special US residence visa, Fuller wrote a book titled *The New Turkish Republic: Turkey as a Pivotal State in the Muslim World*. At the center of the book was a paean of praise for Gülen and his "moderate" Islamic Gülen Movement in Turkey:

> Gülen's charismatic personality makes him the number one Islamic figure of Turkey. The Gülen Movement has the largest and most powerful infrastructure and financial resources of any movement in the country. . . . The movement has also become international by virtue of its far-flung system of schools. . . in more than a dozen countries including the Muslim countries of the former Soviet Union, Russia, France and the United States.[33]

CIA and Gülen in Central Asia

Once safely entrenched in his remote, guarded compound in rural Pennsylvania, Graham Fuller's Turkish friend, Fethullah Gülen, and Gülen's global political Islam *Cemaat* spread across the Caucasus and into the heart of Central Asia all the way to Xinjiang Province in western China, doing precisely what Fuller had called for in his 1999 statement: "destabilize what remains of Russian power, and especially to counter the Chinese influence in Central Asia."[34]

Gülen's organization had been active in that destabilizing with help from the CIA almost the moment the Soviet Union collapsed in 1991, when the nominally Muslim Central Asian former Soviet republics declared their independence from Moscow.

Gülen was named by one former FBI authoritative source as "one of the main CIA operation figures in Central Asia and the Caucasus."[35]

By the mid-1990s, more than seventy-five Gülen schools had spread to Kazakhstan, Tajikistan, Azerbaijan, Turkmenistan, Kyrgyzstan, Uzbekistan, and even to Dagestan and Tatarstan in Russia amid the chaos of the post-Soviet Boris Yeltsin era. The schools all followed the same "elite school" model, offering high-quality education in the native language, Russian, as well as Turkish and English, and selecting pupils only from "best" families, whose sons would clearly become future leaders of those countries.

Similar to the Roman Catholic Jesuits, Gülen's elite pupils in Central Asia were required to live in male-only boarding schools, collective living centers where strict discipline, absolute obedience, enforced Koran readings, five-time daily prayers, and constant studying of the writings of Gülen were demanded. The students were indoctrinated with the "message of the community (*Cemaat*)," a constant indoctrination which one former Gülen disciple likened to the Scientology sect.[36] The Gülen Movement concentrated their main recruitment energy on young Muslim males, knowing that they were credulous and, therefore, easy to indoctrinate.

Gülen school pupils were required to wear uniforms. The mission of the Gülen schools was, nominally, to reestablish Islam but a version of Islam according to the Gülen Movement. It was a well-thought-out strategy of penetration of the former Soviet Union and beyond to China's Muslim Turkic Xinjiang Uyghur Autonomous Region, the heart of China's oil and energy economy.[37]

The Islamist cadre—Gülen-associated Turkish businessmen, students, teachers—were sent into the former states of the Soviet Union almost the moment of the dissolution of the Soviet Union with their well-prepared strategy.

As one Central Asia field researcher described the Gülen operation,

> The method was always the same: businessmen from a particular city in Turkey, for example Bursa, will decide to concentrate their efforts on a particular Central Asian city, for example

Tashkent. Gülen-tied investment will then become important in Tashkent, and a kind of "twinning" between the two cities resulted. Gülen group members—kind of missionaries—were sent by the movement with the aim of making contact with important companies, bureaucrats and personalities in order to profile local needs. They then would invite some of these important personalities to Turkey. The Gülen hosts would greet them and show them the Gülen private schools and foundations of the Gülen "community" or *Cemaat* without ever mentioning the connection to the Islamist Gülen Movement.[38]

Gülen's cadre flooded the Central Asian republics with their literature and even established local editions of Gülen's *Zaman* newspaper in Bishkek, Ashgabat, and Almaty.[39] A new Ottoman Caliphate was coming into view for Gülen and his backers in Washington.

CIA Provides the "English Teachers"

In the early 1990s, as the Gülen schools proliferated across countries of the former Soviet Union, as well as inside Russia, many, if not all, of his schools operated as bases for CIA agents to infiltrate and penetrate those regions.

In 2011, Osman Nuri Gündeş, former head of Foreign Intelligence for the Turkish MIT, the "Turkish CIA," and chief intelligence adviser in the mid-1990s to Prime Minister Tansu Çiller, published a bombshell book that was only released in Turkish. In the book, Gündeş, then 85 and retired, revealed that, during the 1990s, the Gülen schools then growing up across Eurasia were providing a base for hundreds of CIA agents under cover of being "native-speaking English teachers."[40]

According to Gündeş, the Gülen movement "sheltered 130 CIA agents" at its schools in Kyrgyzstan and Uzbekistan alone. More revealing, all the American "English teachers" had been issued US Diplomatic passports, hardly standard fare for normal English teachers.

Gündeş' book further detailed that one Gülen man owned eighteen Gülen schools in Uzbekistan in which seventy CIA operatives "taught English" under a project code-named "Friendship Bridge." The CIA "teachers," he added, submitted reports to an arm of the Pentagon. At the same time, Gündeş claimed, sixty American CIA operatives posing as English teachers at Gülen schools there also carried US Diplomatic passports.[41]

Gündeş claimed that first contacts of Gülen with the CIA went back to the 1980s, when the then unknown Gülen associated himself with fierce right-wing anti-communist circles in Turkey backed by the joint CIA and NATO "Gladio" network. The same Gladio network, codenamed *Counter-Guerrilla* by the US intelligence services, was responsible for a series of far-right terrorist attacks in Turkey and facilitated a bloody US-backed 1980 military coup. Counter-Guerrilla death squads were responsible for the 3,500 unsolved murders in the Southeast region of the country during the 1970s and 1980s.[42] Fethullah Gülen's past was definitely not "peace and love."

Gülen, back then, began his own anti-communist organization in the city of Erzurum, working with Radio Free Europe in a CIA propaganda project against the Soviet-Union, the city where previous CIA Istanbul station chief Paul Henze was working. Henze was a key figure in the Turkish coup in 1980. By 1981 Gülen had also come to the attention of Richard Perle, US Assistant Secretary of Defense for International Security Policy in the new Reagan administration. Gülen's main contact in the CIA, however, was Morton Abramowitz, stationed in Turkey as a CIA employee before he came there as US ambassador in the late 1980s.[43]

It was not long before Russian and other Central Asian intelligence services reacted to the Gülen presence. The Russian government banned all Gülen schools and the activities of his Nur sect in Russia. Over 20 Turkish followers of Gülen were deported from Russia in 2002 to 2004. In 1999, Uzbekistan closed all Gülen's Madrassas and arrested eight journalists who were graduates of Gülen schools, finding them guilty of setting up an illegal religious group and of involvement in an extremist organization. In Turkmenistan, government authorities placed Gülen's schools under close scrutiny and ordered them to scrap the teaching of the history of religion from curriculums.[44] But the Gülen-CIA penetration of Central Asia using Islam did not cease. It expanded, if more cautiously.

Gülen Builds His "Spider Web" in Turkey

The Gülen Movement made major incursions into the Turkish state institutions at the same time it was setting up CIA "schools" and Madrassas across Central Asia. Gülenists inside Turkey had already begun their patient "spider web" of institutional power back in the 1980s. Taking more than a page from the handbook of Ignatius Loyola and Francis Xavier of the

Society of Jesus in the 1500s, Gülen concentrated on establishing a major foothold in the education of the future Turkish elites.

One analyst described the enormous religious transformation of the once secular Kemalist Turkey after some thirty years of Gülen activity:

> Turkey had over 85,000 active mosques, one for every 350 citizens—compared to one hospital for every 60,000 citizens—the highest number per capita in the world and, with 90,000 imams, more imams than doctors or teachers. It had thousands of madrasa-like *Imam-Hatip* schools and about four thousand more official state-run Qur'an courses, not counting the unofficial *Qur'an* schools, which may expand the total number tenfold. Spending by the governmental Directorate of Religious Affairs (*Diyanet İşleri Başkanlığı*) had grown five-fold, from 553 trillion Turkish lira in 2002 (approximately US$325 million) to 2.7 quadrillion lira during the first four-and-a-half years of the AKP government; it had a larger budget than eight other ministries combined.[45]

Gülen's senior aide, Nurettin Veren, described the impressive education network of the Gülen Movement in Turkey. According to Veren in 2009, some 75 percent of Turkey's two million preparatory school students were enrolled in Gülen institutions. Gülen controlled thousands of top tier secondary schools, colleges, and student dormitories throughout Turkey, as well as private universities, the largest being Fatih University in Istanbul.[46]

Gülen followers targeted youth in the eighth through twelfth grades, the crucial adolescent years. Then they mentored and indoctrinated them. They then educated them in the Fethullah schools and prepared them for future careers in legal, political, and educational professions in order to create the ruling future Islamist Turkish state. Taking their orders from Fethullah Gülen, wealthy followers continued to open schools and indoctrination centers at such a rate that Turkish columnist Emre Aköz called it "the education jihad."[47]

Veren went on to describe what had emerged from the focus on educating this new Islamist elite: "These schools are like shop windows. Recruitment and Islamization activities are carried out through night classes. . . . Children whom we educated in Turkey are now in the highest positions. There are governors, judges, military officers. There are ministers in the government. They consult Gülen before doing anything."[48]

Using the new power of the then popular pro-Gülen AK Party (AKP) of Prime Minister Recep Tayyip Erdoğan, Gülen got the Islamist government to change textbooks, emphasize religion courses, and transfer thousands of certified Imams from their positions in the Directorate of Religious Affairs to positions as teachers and administrators in Turkey's public schools, making the line between Islam and the State difficult, if not altogether gone. Abdullah Gül, Turkey's first Islamist President and a Gülen sympathizer, appointed a Gülen-affiliated professor, Yusuf Ziya Özcan, to head Turkey's Council of Higher Education (*Yükseköğretim Kurulu, YÖK*) and used his presidential prerogative to appoint Gülen sympathizers to university presidencies.[49]

They concentrated especially on controlling the national police and the courts. In 2009, former US Ambassador to Turkey James Jeffrey told a journalist, "It's impossible to prove that members of the Gülen Movement control the police, but we have met no one who disputes the fact."[50] If you can arrest your political opponents and try them with "friendly judges," you can do most anything. That, at least, seemed to be the aim of Gülen's people.

Turkey was in the process of a slow motion transformation into what one commentator termed an Islamic fascist state. When the AKP came to power in 2002, they collaborated with Gülen *Cemaat* members already in the judiciary to strip the military of its political power, weakening the military's traditional role as guardians of the Ataturk Constitution.

According to Gareth Jenkins of Johns Hopkins University, who studied the Gülen Movement's rise to power in Turkey, "The Gülenists were basically given free [rein] in the police and the judiciary. So even though they already had a foothold in the police it's really taken off since the AK Party came to power." The Gülenists and Erdoğan's machine in the AKP, initially collaborated to eliminate the key opposition figures from the secular elite, including from the military, academia, journalists, and leftist activists. They were imprisoned, often with no legal rights, accused of plotting to overthrow Turkey's government.[51]

By the beginning of the new millennium, the Gülen Movement was weaving its spider web into every layer of the secular Turkish state. The successful election of Recep Tayyip Erdoğan as Prime Minister, whose AK Party won a parliamentary majority in 2002, was reportedly due to a deal struck between the politically ambitious Erdoğan and the equally ambitious, if more discreet, Fethullah Gülen. In return for urging his many followers to vote for Erdoğan and the AKP, Gülen was assured official "protection" for his movement in Turkey. According to one US diplomat with knowledge, in 2004, almost one-fifth of the AKP members of Turkish Parliament were Gülen followers who took their "orders" from Gülen and not Erdogan. That included, significantly, the Justice and Culture ministers.[52]

It was an uneasy pact between two cunning players, as events in 2013 would later reveal, when Gülen and Washington began to demonize Erdoğan for deviating from Washington's script with Iran, Syria, and other strategic matters.[53]

Heroin, NATO, and Gülen's Spider Webs

Significantly, while the CIA-sponsored Gülen Movement was spreading its tentacles through its schools and Madrassas from Turkey, where they all but controlled the national police, and across into Central Asia, the CIA and NATO were busy creating new heroin labs and transit routes out of Afghanistan across Central Asia.[54] Such a "religious" movement, with schools everywhere, would provide a perfect cover for heroin trafficking.

In 2010, the United Nations Office on Drugs and Crime released a report describing major Afghanistan heroin routes into the West. "Heroin crosses from the Azerbaijan-e Khavari province of Iran into Turkey and traverses Turkey's Hakkari or Van districts [on the borders respectively to Iraq and Iran-F.W.E.]. An estimated 95 metric tons of heroin were shipped across Turkey's borders every year," said the UN report. In addition, the UN report went on, "the Armenia-occupied Upper (Nagorno) Garabagh region of Azerbaijan and Georgia's breakaway republic of Abkhazia, represent hubs of heroin trafficking in the Caucasus and the entire region."[55]

When the known major heroin drug routes out of Afghanistan to the West were mapped and an overlay map of the creation of major NATO or US military airfields was superimposed, along with a map of the major CIA or US-backed Jihadist operations—whether Saudi-backed Al Qaeda or CIA's Gülen Movement—from Afghanistan's Mujahideen to Kyrgyzstan, to Kosovo, to Chechnya, and to Dagestan, a coherent picture emerged that, as seasoned researcher Sibel Edmonds described it, was the heart of a drugs-jihadist-NATO insurgency across Eurasia. She described the key points as follows:

1-After the US invasion of Afghanistan and under US-NATO control, heroin production and sales boom. 2- Azerbaijan has become one of the most strategically important heroin transit hubs since the beginning of Gladio Operation B, and since it has joined and come under NATO. 3- Just like Turkey, nations with airfields under US command, such as Kyrgyzstan's Manas Airbase and Azerbaijan's NATO Air Fields, have become the most important transit-Transportation hubs for heroin.[56]

The CIA's Gülen Movement straddled all key points in that drug and destabilization nexus across Eurasia. Then, shortly after the beginning of the newly-elected Bush-Cheney Administration, the relations between the CIA and Prince Turki's Al Qaeda network of Mujahideen operatives, including Osama bin Laden, would undergo a dramatic transformation. It began on September 11, 2001.

Endnotes

1   Guardian, *Turkey up from the depths*, The Guardian, 27 December 2013, accessed in http://www.theguardian.com/commentisfree/2013/dec/27/turkey-murky-depths.

2   Cited in Fethullah Gulen v. Michael Chertoff, *Secretary, U.S. Dept. of Homeland Security, et al.*, Case 2:07-cv-02148-SD, U.S. District Court for the Eastern District of Pennsylvania.

3   Wikipedia, *Bank Asya*, accessed in http://en.wikipedia.org/wiki/Bank_Asya.

4   Maximilian Popp, *Islam: Der Pate 1.Teil*, Der Spiegel, 06. August 2012, accessed in http://www.spiegel.de/spiegel/islam-das-treiben-des-tuerkischen-predigers-fethullah-guelen-a-850649.html.

5   Rachel Sharon-Krespin, *Fethullah Gülen's Grand Ambition-Turkey's Islamist Danger*, Middle East Quarterly, Winter 2009, pp. 55–66.

6   AP, *Gulen acquitted of trying to overthrow secular government*, AP, May 6, 2006, accessed in http://wwrn.org/articles/21432/?&place=turkey&section=church-state.

7   Sibel Edmonds, *Turkish Intel Chief Exposes CIA Operations via Islamic Group in Central Asia*, January 6, 2011, accessed in http://www.boilingfrogspost.com/2011/01/06/turkish-intel-chief-exposes-cia-operations-via-islamic-group-in-central-asia/.

8   Official website, *Fethullah Gülen*, accessed in http://www.fethullah-gulen.org/.

9   TURKEY: *Fethullah Gulen profile*, The New York Times, January 8, 2008, accessed in http://www.nytimes.com/2008/01/18/world/europe/18iht-190x-an-Turkishpreacherprofile.9324128.html?_r=1&.

10 *Gülen Movement*, accessed in http://www.fethullah-gulen.org/.

11 Guardian, *Turkey: up from the depths*, The Guardian, 27 December 2013, accessed in http://www.theguardian.com/commentisfree/2013/dec/27/turkey-murky-depths.

12 Sibel Edmonds, *Turkish Imam Fethullah Gulen Nabs George Bush PR Queen*, Boiling Frogs Post, April 5, 2011, accessed in http://www.boilingfrogspost.com/2011/04/05/turkish-imam-fethullah-gulen-nabs-george-bush-pr-queen/.

13 Fethullah Gulen v. Michael Chertoff, op. cit.

14 Mizgîn, *Gülen, the CIA and the American Deep State*, Rastibini Blogspot, June 29, 2008, accessed in http://rastibini.blogspot.de/2008/06/glen-cia-and-american-deep-state.html.

15 Sibel Edmonds, *Boston Terror CIAs Graham Fuller and NATO CIA Operation Gladio B Caucasus and Central Asia*, Boiling Frogs Post, April 27, 2013, accessed in http://www.boilingfrogspost.com/2013/04/27/bfp-breaking-news-boston-terror-cias-graham-fuller-nato-cia-operation-gladio-b-caucasus-central-asia/.

16 *George Fidas Bio*, accessed in http://www.wcl.american.edu/org/nsls/EMININT/bios/Fidas.htm.

17 Sibel Edmonds, *Boston Terror CIA's Graham . . .*, op. cit.

18 Ibid.

19 Michael Barker, *Taking the Risk Out of Civil Society: Harnessing Social movements and Regulating Revolutions*, Australasian Political Studies Association Conference, University of Newcastle 25–27 September 2006, accessed in http://www.newcastle.edu.au/school/ept/politics/apsa/PapersFV/IntRel_IPE/Barker,%20Michael.pdf.

20 Diane Johnstone, *How it is Done: Taking over the Trepca Mines*, The Emperor's New Clothes, February 28, 2000, accessed in http://emperors-clothes.com/articles/Johnstone/howitis2.htm.

21 International Crisis Group website, accessed in http://www.crisisgroup.org/en/about/board.aspx.

22 Craig Unger, *House of Bush, House of Saud—The Secret Relationship between the World's Two Most Powerful Dynasties*, London, Scribner, 2004, p. 100.

23 Mizgîn, op. cit.

24 Center for Grassroots Oversight, *Profile: Graham Fuller*, The Center for Grassroots Oversight, accessed in http://www.historycommons.org/entity.jsp?entity=graham_fuller.

25 Sibel Edmonds, *Boston Terror, CIA's Graham Fuller . . .*, op. cit.

26 Center for Grassroots Oversight, op. cit.

27 Wikipedia, *Graham E. Fuller*.

28 Richard Labeviere, *Dollars for Terror: The United States and Islam*, Algora Publishing, 2000, p. 6.

29 Sibel Edmonds, *Graham Fuller: Edmonds' State Secrets Privilege, FBI Gladio-B Target, Handler-Sponsor of Turkey's Imam Gulen*, Boiling Frogs Post, April 27, 2013, accessed in http://www.boilingfrogspost.com/2013/04/27/bfp-breaking-news-boston-terror-cias-graham-fuller-nato-cia-operation-gladio-b-caucasus-central-asia/#sthash.BVO1WENE.dpuf.

30 F. William Engdahl, *Graham Fuller, Uncle Ruslan, the CIA and the Boston Bombings: Part I*, Voltaire Network, 20 May 2013, accessed in http://www.voltairenet.org/article178524.html?var_mode=calcul.

31 Emine Dilek, *The Tale of Uncle Tsarnaev CIA Chief Graham Fuller and a Turkish Islamist Who Lives in USA*, April 27, 2013, accessed in http://www.progressivepress.net/the-tale-of-uncle-tsarnaev-cia-chief-graham-fuller-and-a-turkish-islamist-who-lives-in-usa/.

32 F. William Engdahl, *Graham Fuller . . .*, op. cit.

33 Graham E. Fuller, *The New Turkish Republic: Turkey as a Pivotal State in the Muslim World*, United States Institute of Peace Press, Washington D.C., 2008, p. 56.

34   Richard Labeviere, op. cit.

35   Sibel Edmonds, *Boston Terror, CIA's Graham Fuller . . .*, op. cit.

36   Maximilian Popp, *Mächtiges Gülen-Netzwerk: Der Pate*, Der Spiegel, 11 January 2014, accessed in http://www.spiegel.de/politik/ausland/tuerkei-anhaenger-von-prediger-fethullah-guelen-im-kampf-mit-erdogan-a-942236.html.

37   Farangis Najibullah, *Turkish Schools Coming Under Increasing Scrutiny In Central Asia*, April 25, 2009, accessed in http://www.eurasianet.org/departments/insight/articles/pp042609.shtml.

38   Bayram Balci, *Fethullah Gülen's Missionary Schools in Central Asia and their Role in the Spreading of Turkism and Islam*, Religion, State & Society, Vol. 31, No. 2, 2003, accessed in https://wikileaks.org/gifiles/attach/9/9724_Balci%20central%20Asia%20schools.pdf.

39   Ibid.

40   Sibel Edmonds, *Additional Omitted Points in CIA-Gulen coverage & A Note from "The Insider,"* Boiling Frogs Post, January 11, 2011, accessed in http://www.boilingfrogspost.com/2011/01/11/additional-omitted-points-in-cia-gulen-coverage-a-note-from-%E2%80%98the-insider%E2%80%99/.

41   Ibid.

42   Ibid.

43   "Insider from Turkey," *Fethullah Gülen & the Origin of the Turkish Deep State*, reprinted by Sibel Edmonds, accessed in http://www.boilingfrogspost.com/2011/01/11/additional-omitted-points-in-cia-gulen-coverage-a-note-from-%E2%80%98the-insider%E2%80%99/.

44   Sibel Edmonds, *Turkish Intel Chief Exposes CIA Operations via Islamic Group in Central Asia*, January 6, 2011, accessed in http://www.boilingfrogspost.com/2011/01/06/turkish-intel-chief-exposes-cia-operations-via-islamic-group-in-central-asia/.

45   Rachel Sharon-Krespin, *Fethullah Gülen's Grand Ambition—Turkey's Islamist Danger*, Middle East Quarterly, Winter 2009, pp. 55–66, accessed in http://www.meforum.org/2045/fethullah-gulens-grand-ambition.

46   Ibid.

47   Ibid.

48   Ibid.

49   Ibid.

50   Maximilian Popp, *Islam Der Pate 2 Teil: "Mit der Geduld einer Spinne legen wir unser Netz"*, Der Spiegel, 6 August, 2012, accessed in http://www.spiegel.de/spiegel/islam-das-treiben-des-tuerkischen-predigers-fethullah-guelen-a-850649.html.

51   Jacob Resneck, *Imam Fethullah Gulen Accused of Attempting Coup against Turkish Prime Minister Erdogan*, Religion News Service, January 17, 2014, accessed in http://www.huffingtonpost.com/2014/01/17/fethullah-gulen-corruptio_n_4619428.html#slide=1816963.

52   Maximilian Popp, *Islam Der Pate: 3. Teil: Wer sich mit Gülen anlegt, wird vernichtet*, Der Spiegel, 6 August, 2012, accessed in http://www.spiegel.de/spiegel/islam-das-treiben-des-tuerkischen-predigers-fethullah-guelen-a-850649-3.html.

53   Ibid.

54   Sibel Edmonds, *Connecting the Dots: Afghan Heroin, NATO Azerbaijan Hub and Cargo Business*, 7 March 2013, accessed in http://www.boilingfrogspost.com/2013/03/07/connecting-the-dots-afghan-heroin-nato-azerbaijan-hub-cargo-business/.

55   Azeri News, *Azerbaijan major transit link for drug trafficking: UN*, 24 June 2010, accessed in http://www.azernews.az/region/21639.html.

56   Sibel Edmonds, *Connecting the Dots . . .* , op. cit.

CHAPTER ELEVEN

THE CIA's JIHAD
COMES TO RUSSIA

"What is more important in world history? The Taliban or the collapse of the Soviet empire? Some agitated Moslems or the liberation of Central Europe and the end of the cold war?"

—Zbigniew Brzezinski on US role with
Mujahideen in the Afghan War of the 1980s

"The policy of guiding the evolution of Islam and of helping them against our adversaries worked marvelously well in Afghanistan against the Red Army. The same doctrines can still be used to destabilize what remains of Russian power."

—Graham E. Fuller, former Deputy Director of
the CIA National Council on Intelligence

Cold War That Never Ended

The fall of the Berlin wall in November 1989 and the subsequent dissolution of the Soviet Union in December 1991 did not mark the end of more than four decades of Cold War with the West. It merely marked the beginning of a highly dangerous new phase of Pentagon aggression against a severely weakened Russia desperate to stabilize and open to the West.

For the powerful military–industrial complex that had dominated the US political process in Washington since the creation of NATO in 1949, the extraordinarily weakened state of Russia—the collapse of the Soviet

Union and dissolution of the military Warsaw Pact and the collapse of the entire Soviet economic structures with it—presented a golden opportunity to destroy their former adversary, Russia, as a functioning nation.

If they could succeed in destroying Russia, they believed that they could eliminate the only remaining serious obstacle to what the Pentagon called Full Spectrum Dominance—total control of land, oceans, skies, space, outer space, and even cyberspace. One sole Superpower could dictate to the entire world as it saw fit. This, at least, was the mad dream of certain very powerful "American Oligarchs."

Zbigniew Brzezinski, himself a political strategist who owed his career to David Rockefeller—unquestionably the most influential of the American Oligarchs at the time—as earlier noted, was a principal architect of the Afghan *Mujahideen*, or "Holy Warriors," strategy against the Soviet Red Army during the 1980s. Brzezinski's strategy was actually drafted in 1977 well before Moscow was at all decided that a military presence in Afghanistan was strategically urgent or even necessary.

Brzezinski triumphantly described the CIA's secret war that used Muslim Jihad warriors in Afghanistan as one of his greatest triumphs: "That secret operation was an excellent idea. It had the effect of drawing the Russians into the Afghan trap, and you want me to regret it? The day that the Soviets officially crossed the border, I wrote to President Carter, essentially, 'We now have the opportunity of giving to the USSR its Vietnam War.'"[1]

One of Brzezinski's first official acts as Jimmy Carter's National Security Adviser in 1977 was to establish the Nationalities Working Group at the NSC. It was dedicated to the idea of weakening the Soviet Union by inflaming ethnic tensions among subject Soviet peoples. Brzezinski's prime target was the Islamic populations in and bordering the Soviet Union which was Moscow's Achilles heel, as he saw it.[2]

Brzezinski's plan, according to Dilip Hiro, a longtime Middle East scholar, was "to export a composite ideology of nationalism and Islam to the Muslim-majority Central Asian states and Soviet Republics with a view to destroying the Soviet order."[3]

In his memoirs, CIA Director Robert Gates confirmed Brzezinski's account. Gates revealed publicly, for the first time, that covert US military aid to build up the anti-Soviet Mujahideen Jihadists, along with Saudi money and Pakistani ISI intelligence, began a full six months *before* the December 1979 Soviet military occupation of Afghanistan. The US covert buildup was done deliberately with the intent of forcing Moscow to intervene in what US intelligence estimated would be a quagmire for the Soviet army, just as Vietnam had been for the US military a decade before.[4]

To a major extent the Soviet Union was brought to economic and political collapse by the ten-year long CIA war in Afghanistan that drained the Soviet and Warsaw Pact economies, then closely integrated, and demoralized the spirit of the Soviet population. At the very same time, the CIA was funneling funds into Poland's *Solidarność* trade union organization, with the backing of Polish-born Pope John Paul II. CIA funds also flowed across the Eastern European Warsaw Pact countries, including in Hungary, Czechoslovakia, and the German Democratic Republic, to hit Moscow with a two-front hidden war—one in the east in remote Afghanistan and the second on their western borders, especially Poland.[5]

Afghanistan in 1979 was the first major conflict where the CIA used Jihad fighters—Muslims trained to carry out terrorist acts or even become suicide fighters willing to "die for the glory of Allah" by killing Soviet communist "infidels." It was code-named "Operation Cyclone."[6]

President Ronald Reagan was a great supporter of the Afghan Mujahideen, pictured here at the White House.

It wasn't to be the last time the CIA used fanatical Islamic Jihadists as a lethal weapon. However it was also to have global, unintended consequences that the CIA never imagined. In the late 1980s, Pakistani Prime Minister Benazir Bhutto, alarmed about the growing strength of the Islamist movement, told President George H.W. Bush, "You are creating a Frankenstein."[7]

Operation Cyclone was the largest USA covert action program since World War II, with estimates the US Government spent up to $6 billion or more, a staggering sum in those days.

Uzbeki Korans

When he took office in January 1980, Ronald Reagan's CIA Director, Bill Casey, was not satisfied merely to send Jihad fighters, or Mujahideen, to do battle with the Red Army in Afghanistan. To foster even more unrest across the Soviet Union itself, Casey organized a covert CIA program to make a special translation of the Muslim Koran, their holy book, from Arabic into the Uzbek language. Until then most if not all Korans used by Muslims worldwide had to be mastered in the original Arabic, a bit like requiring Christians to read the Bible in original Hebrew or Greek.

Casey's goal was to spread anti-communist ideas among the ethnic Turkic Muslim peoples of Central Asia, and the CIA's Korans were to be an instrument, along with their special interpretation texts. The translations were based on the extreme Wahhabite Arabic version from Saudi Arabia.[8]

Casey believed that the Soviet ethnic populations presented a marvelous potential CIA recruiting ground among Muslims bitter over Stalin deportations and other severities they had suffered under the Soviet system. Muslim minorities made up a seventh of Russia's population. Muslims constituted the nationalities in the North Caucasus residing between the Black Sea and the Caspian Sea: Circassians, Balkars, Chechens, Ingush, Kabardin, Karachay, and numerous Dagestani peoples. Also, populations of Tatars and Bashkirs, the vast majority of whom were Muslims, lived in the middle of the Volga Basin. There were over 5,000 registered religious Muslim organizations—divided into Sunni, Shia, Sufi, and Ahmadi groups.

In October 1984, as the CIA's covert Mujahideen guerilla force was spreading Jihad terror and violence across Afghanistan, Casey made a secret visit to Pakistan to discuss an escalation of the war. Pakistani ISI General Akhtar Abdur Rahman took Casey to the Afghan border to secret ISI Mujahideen training camps to inspect the Mujahideen. During the visit Casey shocked his Pakistani hosts by proposing that they spread the war directly into not just Afghanistan but also into the Soviet Union itself.

The CIA chief told his Pakistani colleagues of a US intelligence plan to smuggle translations of the Koran into predominately Muslim Central Asian regions of the USSR beginning in Uzbekistan, where a majority were historically Muslim. In addition, Pakistani-trained Mujahideen Jihadist terrorists would infiltrate the porous Soviet borders to make scattered strikes against military installations, factories, and storage depots inside Soviet territory. Casey reportedly told the Pakistanis, "We can do a lot of damage to the Soviet Union."[9]

He was right.

The Koran translations were done on orders from the CIA with money funneled through USAID, nominally a State Department foreign aid program that was often used to disguise CIA-financed projects. The translations were done at the University of Nebraska's Center for Afghanistan Studies in Omaha. [10]

As a part of the Center's CIA projects, they prepared school textbooks for Afghan and other Central Asian Muslim children riddled with pictures or drawings of guns, bullets, and mines explicitly promoting Jihad violence against Soviet soldiers. The following was a typical example in a children's math textbook: "If out of 10 atheists, 5 are killed by 1 Muslim, 5 would be left." Besides the Jihadist graphics and examples, the books contained Islamic tenets and verses from the Koran. [11]

By 1985, someone high up in the Reagan Administration ordered a stop to the Mujahideen incursions inside Soviet territory, as being too risky. In Afghanistan, the CIA textbooks remained and were later adopted by the Taliban who found them so useful to spread their fundamentalism years after the end of the Afghan war. But the seeds were obviously planted in the minds of Washington intelligence circles of using Islamic Jihadists to wreak havoc in the region following the collapse of the Soviet Union.[12]

CIA's Chechen Wars

Not long after their Mujahideen had devastated Afghanistan and caused the departure of the Soviet Army in 1989, the CIA began to look at possible places in the collapsing Soviet Union where their trained "Afghan Arabs" could be redeployed to further destabilize Russian influence over the post-Soviet Eurasian space.

They were called Afghan Arabs because many of them had been recruited from ultraconservative Wahhabite Sunni Muslims from Saudi Arabia, the Arab Emirates, Kuwait, and elsewhere in the Arab world where the ultra-strict Wahhabite Islam was practiced. They were brought to the Jihad in Afghanistan by a Saudi CIA recruit who had been sent to Afghanistan as mentioned in a previous chapter. His name was Osama bin Laden, and he was in charge of something called Maktab al-Khidamat (MAK), which helped finance, recruit, and train Mujahideen fighters.

As the CIA and Pentagon saw it, their Mujahideen fighters had defeated what was arguably the world's most formidable military, the Soviet Red Army, using methods of irregular or guerrilla warfare and a lot of CIA and Saudi money. Washington decided to redeploy their Jihadi terrorists to bring chaos and further destabilize all of Central Asia, even into the Russian Federation itself, which was then in a deep and traumatic crisis during the chaos and economic collapse of the Yeltsin era.

In the early 1990s, Dick Cheney's company, Halliburton, had surveyed the offshore oil potentials of Azerbaijan, Kazakhstan, and the entire Caspian Basin. They estimated the region to be "another Saudi Arabia" worth several trillion dollars on today's market, a prize worth killing for and certainly one the US and UK were determined to keep from Russian control by all means. The first target of Cheney's friends in Washington was to stage a coup in Azerbaijan against elected president Abulfaz Elchibey.

The key lobby backing the US and UK grab of the Caspian Oil was the US-Azerbaijan Chamber of Commerce. The Chamber included some of the most powerful figures in Washington, including then CEO of Halliburton Corp. Dick Cheney. It was chaired by the former Secretary of State and Texas power-broker James Baker III. It included Zbigniew Brzezinski, Henry Kissinger, and General Brent Scowcroft. They were power-brokers no US President could ignore lightly.

The US-Azerbaijan Chamber of Commerce was created for one major project: to build what came to be known as the Baku–Tbilisi–Ceyhan (BTC) oil pipeline, "the world's most political pipeline," bringing Baku oil from Azerbaijan through Georgia to Turkey and the Mediterranean.[13]

At that time, the only existing oil pipeline from Baku in the Caspian was a Russian pipeline from the Soviet era, and it ran through the Chechen capital, Grozny. It was a 100,000 barrel/day pipeline that took Azeri oil north via Machatschkala, the capital of Russia's Dagestan province, and across 146 kilometers of Chechen territory to the Black Sea Russian port of Novorossiysk. The pipeline was the major competition and major obstacle to the very costly alternative route of Washington and the British and US oil majors.[14]

The CIA was given the mandate to destroy that Russian Chechen pipeline and create such chaos in the Caucasus that no Western or Russian company would consider using the Grozny Russian oil pipeline.

Graham E. Fuller, the man who played a major role in the career of CIA asset Fethullah Gülen, and a former Deputy Director of the CIA National Council on Intelligence who was one of the architects of the Mujahideen strategy of using Jihad against Washington foes, in the early 1990s described the CIA Washington strategy in the Caucasus: "The policy of guiding the evolution of Islam and of helping them against our adversaries worked marvelously well in Afghanistan against the Red Army. The same doctrines can still be used to destabilize what remains of Russian power."[6]

The CIA used a dirty tricks veteran, General Richard Secord, for the operation. Secord created a CIA front company, MEGA Oil. Secord had been convicted in the 1980s for his central role in the CIA's Iran-Contra illegal arms and drugs operations.[15]

In 1991, the Bush Administration wanted an oil pipeline from Azerbaijan, routed across the Caucasus, to Turkey. That year, Richard Secord, former Deputy Assistant Secretary of Defense, landed in Baku and set up a front company, MEGA Oil. He was a veteran of the CIA covert opium operations in Laos. In Azerbaijan, he setup an airline to secretly fly hundreds of al-Qaeda Mujahideen from Afghanistan into Azerbaijan. By 1993, MEGA Oil had recruited and armed 2,000 Mujahideen, converting Baku into a base for Caucasus regional *jihadi* operations.[16]

Their first deployment was to support the Azeri army in their bitter fight over the future of Nagorno-Karabakh with Armenia.[17]

According to Jeffrey Silverman, an American investigative journalist in Tbilisi who covered the events at the time, the Mujahideen mercenaries fought alongside Chechen Jihadists and Azeri army regulars. Among the Afghan Mujahideen fighters whom Secord flew in was the notorious Afghan commander and heroin warlord Gulbuddin Hekmatyar. The Armenians were stopped with backdoor help from Washington, preventing Azerbaijan from being split and its oil pipeline route from being blocked.[18]

General Richard Secord's covert Mujahideen operation in the Caucasus also contributed to the military coup that toppled elected president Abulfaz Elchibey that year and installed a more pliable US puppet, Heydar Aliyev. A secret Turkish intelligence report leaked to the *Sunday Times* of London confirmed that "two petrol giants, BP and Amoco, British and American respectively, which together form the AIOC (Azerbaijan International Oil Consortium), are behind the *coup d'état*."[19]

From 1992 to 1995, the Pentagon flew thousands of al-Qaeda Mujahideen from Central Asia into former Yugoslavia to fight alongside Bosnian Muslims against the Serbs. The Mujahideen were "accompanied by US Special Forces equipped with high-tech communications equipment," according to intelligence sources.

Saudi Intelligence head Turki al-Faisal arranged that his agent, Osama bin Laden, the wealthy Saudi Jihadist he had sent to Afghanistan at the start of the Afghan war in the early 1980s, would use his Afghan organization Maktab al-Khidamat (MAK) to recruit "Afghan Arabs" for what was rapidly becoming a global Jihad. Bin Laden's mercenaries were used as shock troops by the Pentagon to coordinate and support Muslim offensives in Chechnya and, later, Bosnia.[20]

Bin Laden brought in an old Jihad crony, a fellow Saudi national named Ibn al-Khattab, to become the Commander, or Emir, of Jihadist Mujahideen in Chechnya together with Chechen warlord Shamil Basayev. No matter that al-Khattab, a Saudi Arab spoke little Chechen, let alone, Russian. He knew what Russian soldiers looked like.

Chechnya then was traditionally a predominantly Sufi society, a mild apolitical branch of Islam. Yet the increasing infiltration of the well-financed and well-trained US-sponsored Mujahideen Jihadists recruited by Osama bin Laden transformed the character of the Chechen resistance movement. They spread al-Qaeda's hardline Islamist ideology across the Caucasus. Under Secord's guidance, Mujahideen terrorist operations had quickly extended into Dagestan and Chechnya, turning Baku into a shipping point for Afghan heroin to the Chechen mafia.[21]

From the mid-1990s, bin Laden paid Chechen guerrilla leaders Shamil Basayev and Omar ibn al-Khattab the handsome sum of several million dollars per month, a King's fortune in economically desolate Chechnya in the 1990s, thereby sidelining the moderate Chechen majority.[21] US intelligence remained deeply involved in the Chechen conflict until the end of the 1990s. According to Yossef Bodansky, then Director of the US Congressional Task Force on Terrorism and Unconventional Warfare, Washington was actively involved in "yet another anti-Russian jihad, seeking to support and empower the most virulent anti-Western Islamist forces."[22]

Bodansky revealed the entire CIA Caucasus strategy in detail in his report, stating that US Government officials participated in,

> "a formal meeting in Azerbaijan in December 1999 in which specific programs for the training and equipping of Mujahideen from the Caucasus, Central/South Asia and the Arab world were discussed and agreed upon, culminating in Washington's tacit encouragement of both Muslim allies (mainly Turkey, Jordan and Saudi Arabia) and US 'private security companies'... to assist the Chechens and their Islamist allies to surge in the spring of 2000 and sustain the ensuing *jihad* for a long time... Islamist *jihad* in the Caucasus as a way to deprive Russia of a viable pipeline route through spiraling violence and terrorism."[23]

The most intense phase of the Chechen wars wound down around the year 2000 only after heavy Russian military action defeated the Islamists.

It was a pyrrhic victory, costing a massive toll in human life and destruction of entire cities. The exact death toll from the CIA-instigated Chechen conflict is unknown. Unofficial estimates ranged from 25,000 to 50,000 dead or missing, mostly civilians. Russian casualties were over 5,200 officially and near 11,000 according to the Committee of Soldiers' Mothers.

The Anglo-American oil majors and the CIA's operatives were happy. They had what they wanted: their Baku–Tbilisi–Ceyhan oil pipeline, bypassing Russia's Grozny pipeline.

The Chechen Jihadists, under the Islamic command of Shamil Basayev, continued guerrilla attacks in and outside Chechnya. The CIA had refocused into the Caucasus.[24]

Basayev's Saudi Connection

Basayev's own career was worth noting in the history of the CIA's Global Jihad. In 1992, he was sent to Azerbaijan to lead a Jihad battalion alongside Azeri forces in their war against Armenia in the enclave of Nagorno-Karabakh. There, Basayev met a Saudi Jihadist named Ibn al-Khattab.[25]

From Azerbaijan, Ibn al-Khattab brought the Chechen Jihadist Basayev to Afghanistan to meet al-Khattab's ally and fellow-Saudi Jihadist, Osama bin Laden, who was then still engaged in leading the Saudi–CIA–Pakistani

ISI operations in Afghanistan that had waged ten years of successful war against the soviet Army there. Ibn al-Khattab's role was to recruit Chechen Muslims willing to wage Jihad against Russian forces in Chechnya on behalf of the covert CIA strategy of destabilizing post-Soviet Russia and her control over Caspian energy.[26]

During the Azerbaijan-Armenian war over Nagorno-Karabakh, where Basayev's Chechen and the Afghan fighters waged Jihad until 1994, air flights from Kabul in Afghanistan to Baku in Azerbaijan carried Afghan Jihad Mujahideen fighters. Return flights took Chechens to training camps near Kunduz and Taloqan.[27] This was the Jihad air traffic transport operation of the CIA and General Secord's MEGA Oil airlines.

Once back in Chechnya, Basayev, along with al-Khattab, created something called the International Islamic Brigade (IIB) with Saudi Intelligence money, approved by the CIA and, according to reliable reports, coordinated through the liaison of Saudi Washington Ambassador and Bush family intimate Prince Bandar bin Sultan. In fact, Prince Bandar, Saudi Washington Ambassador for more than two decades, was so intimate with the Bush family that President George W. Bush, fond of nicknames for those he liked, referred to the Saudi Ambassador as "Bandar Bush," a kind of honorary family member.[28]

Basayev and al-Khattab imported the Saudi fanatical Wahhabite strain of Sunni Islam into Chechnya. In Chechnya, Ibn al-Khattab commanded what were called the "Arab Mujahideen in Chechnya," his own private army of Arabs, Turks, and other foreign fighters. He was also commissioned to set up paramilitary training camps in the Caucasus Mountains of Chechnya that trained Chechens and Muslims from the North Caucasian Russian republics and Central Asia.[29]

Previously, as noted, Islam in Chechnya and Northern Caucasus had been a traditional mix of moderate Islam together with pacific Sufism. Now, especially among targeted unemployed Chechen youth, Wahhabism and extreme Salafism spread rapidly in a context of expanding the Jihad to wage global Holy War against "infidels," especially those infidels not liked by Washington.

In 2010, the UN Security Council published the following report on al-Khattab and Basayev's International Islamic Brigade:

Red-bearded Jihadist known as Omar al Chechen
from the Russia Caucasus wars is a key leader in
the Muhajireen Brigade, a jihadist group that fights
alongside the Al Nusrah Front terrorists in Syria

Islamic International Brigade (IIB) was listed on 4 March 2003. . . as being associated with Al-Qaida, Usama bin Laden or the Taliban for "participating in the financing, planning, facilitating, preparing or perpetrating of acts or activities by, in conjunction with, under the name of, on behalf or in support of" Al-Qaida. . . The Islamic International Brigade (IIB) was founded and led by Shamil Salmanovich Basayev (deceased) and is linked to the Riyadus-Salikhin Reconnaissance and Sabotage Battalion of Chechen Martyrs (RSRSBCM). . . and the Special Purpose Islamic Regiment (SPIR). . .

On the evening of 23 October 2002, members of IIB, RSRSBCM and SPIR operated jointly to seize over 800 hostages at Moscow's Podshipnikov Zavod (Dubrovka) Theater.

In October 1999, emissaries of Basayev and Al-Khattab traveled to Usama bin Laden's home base in the Afghan province of Kandahar, where Bin Laden agreed to provide substantial military assistance and financial aid, including by making arrangements to send to Chechnya several hundred fighters to fight against Russian troops and perpetrate acts of terrorism. Later that year, Bin Laden sent substantial amounts of money to Basayev, Movsar Barayev (leader of SPIR) and Al-Khattab, which was to be used exclusively for training gunmen, recruiting mercenaries and buying ammunition.[30]

The Afghan-Caucasus Al Qaeda "terrorist railway," financed by Saudi intelligence, had two goals. One was to spread fanatical Wahhabite Jihad, or Holy War, into the Central Asian region of the former Soviet Union. The second parallel goal was the CIA's agenda of destabilizing a fragile post-Soviet Russian Federation. The Islamic International Brigade was successful in creating huge security problems across Russia and not merely in Chechnya or Dagestan.

The Chechen-Saudi Islamic International Brigade (IIB) terror attack in the Moscow Theatre in October 2002 was followed in September 2004 by their most gruesome and, ultimately, most deadly single terror action: the hostage seizure in Beslan.

Beslan

On September 1, 2004, armed Jihadist terrorists from Basayev and al-Khattab's IIB took more than 1,100 people as hostages in a siege situation, including 777 children, and forced them into School Number One (SNO) in Beslan in North Ossetia, the autonomous republic in the North Caucasus of the Russian Federation near to the Georgia border.

On the third day of the hostage crisis, as explosions were heard inside the school, FSB and other elite Russian troops stormed the building. In the end, at least 334 hostages were killed, including 186 children, with a significant number of people injured and reported missing. It became clear afterward that the Russian forces had handled the intervention badly.

The Washington propaganda machine, from Radio Free Europe to *The New York Times* and CNN, wasted no time demonizing Putin and Russia for their bad handling of the Beslan crisis rather than to focus on the links of Basayev to Al Qaeda and Saudi intelligence. That would have brought the world's attention to the intimate relations between the family of then US President George W. Bush and the Saudi billionaire bin Laden family.

On September 1, 2001, just ten days before the day of the World Trade Center and Pentagon attacks, Saudi Intelligence head US-educated Prince Turki bin Faisal Al Saud, who had directed Saudi Intelligence since 1977, including through the entire Osama bin Laden Mujahideen operation in Afghanistan and into the Caucasus, abruptly and inexplicably resigned. He resigned just days after having accepted a new term as intelligence head from his King. He gave no explanation but was quickly reposted to London.

The record of the bin Laden-Bush family intimate ties was buried, in fact entirely deleted on "national security" (sic!) grounds in the official US Commission Report on 9/11. The Saudi background of fourteen of the nineteen alleged 9/11 terrorists in New York and Washington was also redacted and deleted from the US Government's final 9/11 Commission report, which was finally released only in July 2004 by the Bush Administration, almost three years after the events.[31]

Basayev claimed credit for having sent the terrorists to Beslan. His demands had included the complete independence of Chechnya from Russia, something that would have given Washington and the Pentagon an enormous strategic dagger in the southern underbelly of the Russian Federation.

By late 2004, in the aftermath of the tragic Beslan drama, President Vladimir Putin reportedly ordered a secret search and destroy mission by Russian intelligence to hunt and kill key leaders of the Caucasus Mujahideen of Basayev. Al-Khattab had been killed in 2002. The Russian security forces soon discovered that most of the Chechen Afghan Arab terrorists had fled. They had gotten safe haven in Turkey, a NATO member; in Azerbaijan, by then almost a NATO Member; or in Germany, a NATO Member; or in Dubai—one of the closest US Allies in the Arab States, and Qatar-another very close US ally. In other words, the Chechen terrorists were given NATO safe haven.[32]

Washington Shifts Battlegrounds

The use of Afghan Arabs to train Chechen Jihadists in the Caucasus after the collapse of the Soviet Union was only one flank of the CIA's drive to sow chaos and conflict across the Caucasus aimed at Moscow.

The British and American oil majors, led by BP, with the US and UK governments backing them, had formed the Baku–Tbilisi–Ceyhan Pipeline Company (BTC Co.) in London on August 1, 2002. The British-American oil pipeline, almost 1,800 kilometers long from Azerbaijan's Azeri–Chirag–Guneshli oil field in the Caspian Sea to Ceyhan in Turkey on the Mediterranean Sea, required a very secure land route.

With Armenia drawing closer to Russia after the Nagorno-Karabakh war, the Caucasus Republic of Georgia was chosen for the route. That, however, meant the need of a Tbilisi government absolutely beholden to Washington.

The Washington choice was Mikheil Saakashvili, a US-educated Georgian clan boss who Washington more or less correctly calculated would sell his grandmother's gold teeth if the price were right.

Washington in 2003 then turned its energies to organizing the Rose Revolution in Georgia that brought Saakashvili in as pro-NATO Georgian President. US NGOs—such as the CIA-linked Freedom House, the US Congress-funded National Endowment for Democracy, and the George Soros Open Society Foundations—financed or trained key opposition leaders and students modeled on the CIA's successful *Otpor* regime change coup in Serbia against Milosevic in 2000.

After the CIA and the US State Department, with US Ambassador to Georgia, Richard M. Miles orchestrating the events, succeeded in installing Saakashvili in Tbilisi as its man in 2003, Washington immediately turned its attention to Ukraine and what they decided to name the Orange Revolution to install Viktor Yushchenko as their pro-NATO president. They used the same operatives in Ukraine's "Orange Revolution" a few months later as they had used in Georgia, including head of Georgia's Parliamentary Committee on Defense and Security, Givi Targamadze, and former members of the Georgian Liberty Institute, as well as members of Georgia's US-financed youth group, *Kmara*, trained and financed by Washington-controlled NGOs.[33]

The CIA "Color Revolutions" to install pro-NATO regimes along Russia's immediate borders, coupled with the use of Mujahideen and of Chechen Islamic Jihadists, created a strategic crisis for the chaotic Russia of Boris Yeltsin.

Soon after taking office in 1999, Russia's new President, Vladimir Putin, a nationalist with a long career in Russian intelligence, including in Germany, faced the daunting task of trying to undo, or at least limit, the damage that the criminal cronies of Yeltsin and their American business partners had done to Russia as a functioning state and nation.

The Washington Color Revolutions in Georgia and Ukraine and the use of Chechen Jihad terrorists to destroy the Russian Grozny pipeline infrastructure were only one, albeit major, part of a geopolitical Grand Chessboard, as Brzezinski termed it in his 1997 book by the same name.

Under the false flag of Washington's War on Terror, in March 2003, the Bush-Cheney Administration launched a full-scale war to occupy Saddam Hussein's Iraq, then location of the world's second largest oil reserves and a close Cold War ally of the Soviet Union. It was also based on a barrage of lies and misrepresentations, as are most wars of aggression in world history.

Endnotes

1   Zbigniew Brzezinski, *The Brzezinski Interview with Le Nouvel Observateur* (1998), translated from the French by William Blum and David N. Gibbs, accessed in http://dgibbs.faculty.arizona.edu/brzezinski_interview.

2   Can Erimtan, *The War in Afghanistan The legacy of Zbigniew Brzezinski and the Volatile Situation in Pakistan*, Today's Zaman, October 07, 2010, accessed in http://www.todayszaman.com/tz-web/news-223646-109-centerthe-war-in-afghanistan-the-legacy-of-zbigniew-brzezinski-and-the-volatile-situation-in-pakistan-bribyi-brcan-erimtancenter.html.

3   Dilip Hiro, quoted in Phil Gasper, *Afghanistan, the CIA, bin Laden, and the Taliban*, International Socialist Review, November–December 2001.

4   Zbigniew Brzezinski, op. cit.

5   Carl Bernstein, *The Holy Alliance*, TIME, February 24, 1992, accessed in http://www.carlbernstein.com/magazine_holy_alliance.php.

6   Peter Bergen, *Holy War Inc.*, Free Press, (2001), p. 68.

7   Mark Hosenball, *War on Terror: The Road To September 11*, Newsweek, October 1, 2001, accessed in http://www.newsweek.com/war-terror-road-september-11-151771.

8   Center for Afghanistan Studies, *University of Nebraska at Omaha-Center for Afghanistan Studies*, accessed in http://supportdanielboyd.wordpress.com/usa-printed-textbooks-support-jihad-in-afghanistan-and-pakistan/.

9   Steve Coll, *Anatomy of a Victory: CIA's Covert Afghan War*, Washington Post, July 19, 1992, accessed in http://emperors-clothes.com/docs/anatomy2.htm.

10   University of Nebraska, University of Nebraska at Omaha Center for Afghanistan Studies, http://www.unomaha.edu/~world/cas/. *Background*, accessed in http://supportdanielboyd.wordpress.com/usa-printed-textbooks-support-jihad-in-afghanistan-and-pakistan/.

11   University of Nebraska, University of Nebraska at Omaha Center for Afghanistan Studies, http://www.unomaha.edu/~world/cas/.

Background, accessed in http://supportdanielboyd.wordpress.com/usa-printed-textbooks-support-jihad-in-afghanistan-and-pakistan/.

12   Mohamad Yousaf, quoted in, *1984–March 1985: US and Pakistan Begin Training Afghans to Attack Inside Soviet Union*, accessed in http://www.historycommons.org/context.jsp?item=a1084caseyvisit.

13   Sibel Edmonds, *Obama Appoints a Not-Too-Long-Ago-Hatched Neocon Larva*, 27 July, 2010, accessed in http://www.boilingfrogspost.com/2010/07/27/obama-appoints-a-not-too-long-ago-hatched-neocon-larva/.

14   Thomas I. Steinberg, *Warum Tschetschenien?*, Junge Welt, Berlin, September 25, 2004, accessed in http://www.steinbergrecherche.com/tschetschenien.htm.

15   Nafeez Mosaddeq Ahmed, *Our terrorists*, New Internationalist Magazine, Issue # 426, accessed in http://newint.org/features/2009/10/01/blowback-extended-version/.

16   Ibid.

17   Peter Dale Scott, *The Road to 911—Wealth Empire and the Future of America* (Berkley: University of California Press, 2007) pp. 163–165.

18   Jeffrey Silverman, VT Tbilisi bureau chief, *personal email to the author*, 16 January, 2014.

19   "*BP Linked to the Overthrow of Azerbaijan Government*," Drillbits and Trailings (17 April 2000, vol. 5, no. 6).

20   Cees Wiebes (2003), *Intelligence and the War in Bosnia 1992–1995: The role of the intelligence and security services* (New Jersey: Transaction Publishers, Rutgers State University, 2003).

21   Nafeez Mosaddeq Ahmed, Our terrorists, New Internationalist, October 1, 2009, accessed in http://newint.org/features/2009/10/01/blowback-extended-version/#sthash.uCpcnKXP.dpuf.

22   Yossef Bodanksy, *The Great Game for Oil'*, Defense & Foreign Affairs Strategic Policy, (June/July 2000).

23   Ibid.

24   Richard Sakwa, ed. (2005), "*Western views of the Chechen Conflict*." Chechnya: From Past to Future. Anthem Press. p. 235.

25   M. Khatchig, *Terror in Karabakh: Chechen Warlord Shamil Basayev's Tenure in Azerbaijan*, ARMENIAN WEEKLY ONLINE, accessed in http://www.armenianweekly.com.

26   Ibid.

27   Ibid.

28   Robert Baer, *The Fall of the House of Saud*, The Atlantic, May 2003.

29   Wikipedia, *Ibn al-Khattab*, accessed in http://en.wikipedia.org/wiki/Ibn_al-Khattab.

30   United Nations Security Council Committee, *QE.I.99.03. ISLAMIC INTERNATIONAL BRIGADE (IIB), pursuant to resolutions 1267 (1999) and 1989 (2011) concerning Al-Qaida and associated individuals and entities*, 2010, accessed in http://www.un.org/sc/committees/1267/NSQE09903E.shtml.

31   BBC, *9/11 probe clears Saudi Arabia*, June 17, 2004, accessed in http://news.bbc.co.uk/2/hi/middle_east/3815179.stm.

32   Sibel Edmonds, *US NATO Chechen Militia Joint Operations Base*, November 22, 2011, accessed in http://www.boilingfrogspost.com/2011/11/22/bfp-exclusive-us-nato-chechen-militia-joint-operations-base/.

33   F. William Engdahl, *Full Spectrum Dominance: Totalitarian Democracy in the New World Order*, Wiesbaden, 2010, edition.engdahl, pp. 45–49.

CHAPTER TWELVE

A "HOLY WAR" AGAINST CHINA

"The policy of guiding the evolution of Islam and of helping them against our adversaries worked marvelously well in Afghanistan against the Russians. The same doctrines can still be used to destabilize what remains of Russian power, and especially to counter the Chinese influence in Central Asia."[1]

—Graham E. Fuller, 1999, key CIA
architect of US Islam strategy

Stirring Up Some Uyghur Muslims

In early 1979, months before the Soviet occupation of Afghanistan, US National Security Adviser Zbigniew Brzezinski drafted a top secret Presidential Order as noted earlier. It was signed by President Jimmy Carter. The order authorized the CIA to train fundamentalist Saudi and other Muslims to wage a Holy War, or Jihad against the Soviet communist "infidels," non-believers in the strict Islamic faith of Sunni conservative Islam. The resulting Mujahideen terror war against Soviet soldiers in Afghanistan was the largest covert action in CIA history, lasting almost nine years before the Soviets retreated out of Afghanistan and, soon after, called an end to the Cold War.[2]

Brzezinski's strategy, which he called the "Arc of Crisis" strategy, was basically to set aflame the Muslim populations of Soviet Central Asia in order to destabilize the Soviet Union at a time of growing Russian economic crisis internally.

In 1998, almost ten years later and well after the collapse of the Soviet Union, in a triumphant interview in the French magazine *Le Nouvel Observateur*, Brzezinski defended his deployment of fundamentalist Islamic radical terrorists in Pakistan and Afghanistan. He revealed, for the first time, in that interview (deliberately excluded from US editions of the magazine) that whereas the Soviet army invaded Afghanistan on December 24, 1979, some six months earlier, on July 3, 1979, President Carter had signed the first top secret directive, code-named Operation Cyclone, for secret US aid to the opponents of the pro-Soviet regime in Kabul. It was done on Brzezinski's advice, correctly calculating that the secret support of radical political Islamic fighters carrying the Sword of Islam would induce the Soviets to invade. Washington wanted the Soviets to undergo their own "Vietnam" defeat in Afghanistan.

Asked by *Le Nouvel Observateur* if he had regrets for having armed and trained future Islamic terrorists, he snapped, "What is most important to the history of the world? . . . Some stirred-up Moslems or the liberation of Central Europe . . . ?"[3]

Since that time, some thirty-five years ago, the US Pentagon and CIA, or definite hawkish factions within, had used radical political Islam—"some stirred up Muslims"—around the world, in order to destabilize countries that stood in the way of the Sole Superpower—the USA—and what President George H.W. Bush in his September 11, 1991, speech called the "New World Order," an American-run totalitarian order.

That covert use of political Islam or "Jihad" Islam by Western, especially US, intelligence were largely either overlooked by US allies and other countries or not understood for the danger it posed.

CIA and Xinjiang's Uyghur Islamist Unrest

One of the major architects of Brzezinski's Islamic Arc of Crisis strategy in 1979 and after was a career senior CIA Middle East specialist, Graham E. Fuller, a specialist in "Islamic extremism," also known as political Islamic Jihadism. In 1999, Fuller wrote a policy paper for the RAND Corporation, a Pentagon-linked think tank, in which he stated, "The policy of guiding the evolution of Islam and of helping them against our adversaries worked marvelously well in Afghanistan against the Russians. The same doctrines can still be used to destabilize what remains of Russian power, and **especially to counter the Chinese influence in Central Asia** [author's emphasis—F.W.E.]."[4]

Fuller's proposal had become fundamental US secret strategic policy by the late 1990s. Washington's policy of "weaponizing" and training radical Islamists and establishing thousands of radical Islamist schools and madrassas across the Middle East, Africa, and Central Asia, complete with CIA-translated radical school books and Koran interpretations that fanned hatred of "infidels" or non-Sunni Muslims, was to be directed at the emerging economic colossus of China and also against a then weaker Russian foe.

With the chaos after the collapse of the Soviet Union in the beginning of the 1990s, the CIA rushed into the newly independent Central Asian republics to immediately establish their presence, using as their proxy the veterans of the Afghan Mujahideen wars. They flew Mujahideen Jihadists into Azerbaijan to get control of the government for US and British oil companies.[5] They brought Mujahideen into Chechnya and the former Soviet Caucasus to wreak terror and chaos there to block a Russian-Azeri oil pipeline and weaken a struggling Russia in the Yeltsin era.

Less known, they also brought their Mujahideen Holy War veterans into Uzbekistan, Kyrgyzstan, and even inside the borders of China's largely Muslim Xinjiang Province. Graham Fuller's plan was being secretly implemented against China.

The 2009 Urumqi Riots

Fuller's plan became bluntly obvious for the Beijing government in 2009, when Uyghur Islamist radicals began a wave of terror and attacks against Han Chinese in Xinjiang supported by CIA and CIA-financed front organizations.

Xinjiang Uyghur Autonomous Region, a strategic province at the heart of China's energy economy and crossroads for vital energy pipelines from Kazakhstan, was also the world's fourth largest concentration of ethnic Turkic Muslim peoples with approximately eight million Uyghurs, Kazaks, and Kyrgyz in Xinjiang.

That made Xinjiang a prime target for a carefully planned activation of a pan-Turkic destabilization strategy developed by the CIA's Graham Fuller and others in Washington. Their aim was to foster the idea of a "New Ottoman (Turkic) Caliphate," or pan-Turkic theocracy, recalling the oppressive Ottoman Caliphate that collapsed after the First World War. The CIA's target Turkic countries or provinces, in addition to Xinjiang and Turkey, were the Azeri populations of Iran and Azerbaijan, Uzbekistan, Kazakhstan, Turkmenistan, and Kyrgyzstan.

Riots and unrest in Urumqi exploded with deadly violence on July 5, 2009. The propaganda voice of Uyghur Muslims behind the riots was the World Uyghur Congress (WUC), a strange exile group in Washington, DC, headed by wealthy Xinjiang political operative Rebiya Kadeer, whose husband, Sidiq Rouzi, left China for the United States to work for the US Government radio stations Radio Free Asia and Voice of America, both known CIA front organizations.

Working together with the WUC was another exiled Uyghur, Erkin Alptekin. Alptekin was founder and Honorary President of another strange group, the Unrepresented Nations and Peoples Organization (UNPO). Just seven weeks before the riots were triggered by the World Uyghur Congress call to protest, a US NGO financed by the US government and a reported front for the CIA, namely the National Endowment for Democracy (NED), held a conference in Washington titled *East Turkestan: 60 Years under Communist Chinese Rule*. The conference was cosponsored by Alptekin's Unrepresented Nations and Peoples Organization. In brief, the Uyghur exile movement had become a CIA asset.[6]

Erkin Alptekin founded UNPO while working for the US Information Agency's official propaganda organization, Radio Free Europe/Radio Liberty, as Director of their Uygur Division and Assistant Director of the Nationalities Services. Radio Liberty had been a propaganda instrument of the CIA and the US State Department since the beginning of the Cold War.

The World Uyghur Congress played a key role to "trigger" the July 2009 riots. Their website wrote about an alleged violent attack on June 26 in China's southern Guangdong Province at a toy factory, where the WUC alleged that Han Chinese workers attacked and beat to death two Uyghur workers for allegedly raping or sexually molesting two Han Chinese women workers in the factory. On July 1, the Munich office of the WUC issued a worldwide call for protest demonstrations against Chinese embassies and consulates for the alleged Guangdong attack, despite the fact they admitted the details of the incident were unsubstantiated and filled with allegations and dubious reports.[7]

According to a press release they issued, it was that June 26 alleged attack that gave the WUC the grounds to issue their worldwide call to action.

On July 5, a Sunday in Xinjiang, the WUC in Washington claimed that Han Chinese armed soldiers seized any Uyghur they found on the streets, and, according to official Chinese news reports, widespread riots and burning of cars along the streets of Urumqi broke out, resulting over the following three days in over 140 deaths.[8]

China's official Xinhua News Agency said that protesters from the Uyghur Muslim ethnic minority group began attacking ethnic Han pedestrians, burning vehicles, and attacking buses with batons and rocks. "They took to the street . . . carrying knives, wooden batons, bricks and stones," they cited an eyewitness as saying. The French AFP news agency quoted Alim Seytoff, general secretary of the Uyghur American Association in Washington, as saying that, according to his information, police had begun shooting "indiscriminately" at protesting crowds.[9]

There are two different versions of the same events: The Chinese government and pictures of the riots indicated it was Uyghur riots and attacks on Han Chinese residents that resulted in deaths and destruction. French official reports put the blame on Chinese police "shooting indiscriminately." Significantly, the French AFP report relied on the NED-funded Uyghur American Association of Rebiya Kadeer for its information.

The riots in Xinjiang, triggered by Washington-based Uyghur organizations, broke out only days after the meeting took place in Yekaterinburg, Russia, of the member nations of the Shanghai Cooperation Organization, as well as Iran's official observer guest, President Ahmadinejad. There was a clear connection. Washington was not at all happy to see the nations of Eurasia cooperate.

A New "Turkic" Empire?

The CIA's main tool to spread Islamist ideology in all the key Central Asian regions, including in Xinjiang, after the Cold War was a reclusive Turkish former Imam named Fethullah Gülen.

The CIA's Graham E. Fuller was a main "sponsor" of Gülen. Fuller and former CIA agent and US Ambassador to Turkey Morton Abramowitz enabled Gülen to obtain permanent residence in Pennsylvania in the 1990s, over the objections of the US State Department, FBI, and Department of Homeland Security.[10] The lawyers from the State Department at that court hearing even claimed Gülen had ties to and was financed by the CIA as reason for denying him US residency.[11] Gülen's organization, like most of the political Jihadist organizations backed by the CIA since the Mujahideen in the 1980s, was also alleged to finance its vast empire by dealing in the distribution of Afghanistan heroin.[12]

*The CIA's Gülen Movement has a network covering the
entire New Silk Road of China into Xinjiang.*

Gülen, a vital asset of the CIA's neoconservative faction that was out
to wreak chaos across China and Central Asia to Russia, Iran, and beyond,
reportedly was tied to Turkish heroin mafias smuggling Afghan heroin to
the West.[13]

Sibel Edmonds was a former FBI Turkish-language translator who was
silenced by the US Justice Department from going public with her uncov-
ering of a deep network of money laundering, illegal drugs, and weapons
dealings, including nuclear weapons. She charged that the network she
discovered from translating secret FBI wiretapped conversations involved
Gülen-affiliated Turkish police, business networks, criminal rogue CIA
agents, the State Department, and US Defense Department neoconservative networks at high levels in Washington. According to Edmonds, who
brought a US Ohio Court case to force disclosure of this criminal network,
Gülen by 2013 had established

> more than 300 madrassas in Central Asia and what he calls
> universities that have a front that is called Moderate Islam, but
> he is closely involved in training mujahideen-like militia Islam
> who are brought from Pakistan and Afghanistan into Central
> Asia where his madrassas operate, and his organization's net-
> work is estimated to be around $25 billion.

It is supported by certain US authorities here because of the operations in Central Asia, but what they have been doing since late 1990s is actually radical Islam and militarizing these very, very young, from the age 14, 15, by commandoes they use, and this is both commandoes from Turkish military, commandoes from Pakistani ISI in Central Asia and Azerbaijan. After that they bring them to Turkey, and from Turkey they send them through Europe, to European and elsewhere.[14]

The Gülen Movement founded madrassas in the 1990s, mostly in the newly independent Turkic republics of Central Asia and Russia. Gülen's Central Asian madrassas were used as training schools for al Qaeda and served as a front for undercover CIA and US State Department officials operating in the region.[15]

One of Gülen's protégé's was Anwar Yusuf Turani, the person who started the East Turkistan Independence Movement from his exile in Washington, DC. In 2004, Turani set up the "East Turkistan Government in Exile" and was "elected" Prime Minister.[16] It was not clear who exactly "elected" Turani. Washington was clearly happy to give him a platform for his anti-Beijing activities in Xinjiang.

Significantly, according to a report in a Turkish investigative magazine, *Turk Pulse*, Turani's organization's "activities for the government in exile are based on a report entitled 'The Xinjiang Project.' That was written by Graham E. Fuller in 1998 for the Rand Corporation and revised in 2003 under the title 'The Xinjiang Problem.'"[17]

In a 1999 interview, Anwar Yusuf Turani claimed that he received financial support from wealthy patrons in Saudi Arabia, home of the ultra-conservative Wahhabite Sunni form of Islam that provided the core of Osama bin Laden's Jihadist Afghanistan Mujahideen terrorist guerrillas in the 1980s.[18] Saudi intelligence cooperated with the CIA in those global Islamist Jihad operations.

ETIM and CIA Jihad in Xinjiang

Another CIA-sponsored Islamist movement involved in terror acts and activities in Xinjiang was the East Turkestan Islamic Movement (ETIM), otherwise known as the Turkestan Islamic Party.

Turkestan Islamic Party Seal—a Koran surrounded by two Scimitars.

In the late 1990s, Hasan Mahsum, also known as Abu-Muhammad al-Turkestani, founder of the East Turkestan Islamic Movement, moved ETIM's headquarters to Kabul, taking shelter under Taliban-controlled Afghanistan. In Afghanistan, ETIM leaders met with Osama bin Laden and other leaders of the CIA-trained Al Qaeda, the Taliban, and the Islamic Movement of Uzbekistan to coordinate actions across Central Asia.[19]

In his own study of Xinjiang, the CIA's Graham E. Fuller noted that Saudi Arabian groups had disseminated extremist Wahhabi religious literature and possibly small arms through sympathizers in Xinjiang, and that young Turkic Muslims had been recruited to study at madrasas in Pakistan, Afghanistan and Saudi Arabia. He adds that Uyghurs from Xinjiang also fought alongside Osama bin Laden's Al Qaeda in Afghanistan in the 1980s.

Fuller noted, "Uyghurs are indeed in touch with Muslim groups outside Xinjiang, some of them have been radicalized into broader jihadist politics in the process, a handful were earlier involved in guerrilla or terrorist training in Afghanistan, and some are in touch with international Muslim mujahideen struggling for Muslim causes of independence worldwide."[20]

The goal of the various Islamist Jihad groups the CIA covertly backed, beginning the time of the Afghan Mujahideen in the 1980s, was to spread a cancer of radical Islamic terror and fanaticism to displace the tradition of moderate, peaceful Islam across Central Asia and into Xinjiang, as the earlier cited statement from the CIA's Graham E. Fuller indicated.

ETIM Joins with IMU

The Islamic Movement of Uzbekistan (IMU), allies of the East Turkestan Islamic Movement, were tied with Al Qaeda of Osama bin Laden. In the period after 1997, the IMU moved into Afghanistan to wage Jihad against the Kabul Government on behalf of the Taliban. They also incorporated Uyghurs from Xinjiang in their battles, giving them vital combat training to return to Xinjiang to wage Jihad inside China.[21]

After the chaotic collapse of Soviet rule in the early 1990s, the initial focus of the Islamic Movement of Uzbekistan was grabbing control of the vital Fergana Valley spread across eastern Uzbekistan, Kyrgyzstan, and Tajikistan. Returning Afghan war veteran and Uzbek paratrooper Jumaboi Khojayev, radicalized by his contact with Osama bin Laden's Saudi Jihad Islamist fighters, joined with Tohir Yuldashev to form a radical Salafist Islamist group in Namangan which they called *Adolat* ("Justice"). They seized control of the civil government in Namangan and quickly imposed Sharia Law, which was ruthlessly enforced by Adolat's vigilantes.

Adolat was initially tolerated by the newly installed President Karimov. When Adolat demanded that Karimov impose Sharia throughout Uzbekistan in 1992, Karimov moved to outlaw Adolat and reestablish central control over the Fergana Valley region—traditionally one of the most militant Islamic regions in Central Asia. The IMU received large sums of money from patrons in Saudi Arabia, reportedly close to then chief of Saudi Intelligence Prince Turki al-Faisal.[22] The triangle of CIA and Saudi intelligence financing Jihadist Islamic groups was to appear again and again.

Fethullah Gülen's madrassas and Islamist schools were all over Uzbekistan at the same time, many harboring dozens of CIA agents posing as "English teachers."[23] It was Graham Fuller's strategy being implemented across Central Asia. Both Russia and China were the ultimate targets.

Significantly, there was a large Uyghur exile Muslim population with offices in Istanbul, where Fethullah Gülen's *Hizmat*, or movement, was deeply entrenched within the government of Islamist Recep Erdoğan. According to the Turkish journal *TurkPulse*, "One of the main tools Washington is using in this affair in order to get Turkey involved in the Xinjiang affair are some Turkish Americans, primarily Fetullah Gulen."[24] The Uyghurs in Turkey were actively engaged in promoting East Turkestan autonomy and separatism.[25]

It was no accident the Osama bin Laden-linked Islamic Movement of Uzbekistan moved into the Fergana Valley. The valley was also a center for Afghanistan heroin traffic. The massive opium production in Afghanistan passed uninterrupted through the Fergana Valley to Russia. The IMU was a product as well of the Saudi-funded and Britain-centered Wahhabi jihadists of Hizb ut-Tahrir (HuT).[26] According to Graham Fuller, Hizb ut-Tahrir, in 2004, was the strongest Islamist opposition fundamentalist movement across Central Asia and had made inroads into Xinjiang. It was headquartered in London, where the British intelligence services reportedly managed them on behalf of the CIA.[27]

The International Crisis Group, an NGO reportedly with very close ties to the US State Department and US intelligence services, issued the following "prediction" about the future of Xinjiang Islamist terrorists:

> There is a risk that Central Asian jihadis currently fighting beside the Taliban may take their struggle back home after 2014. This would pose major difficulties for both Central Asia and China. Economic intervention alone might not suffice. The planned 2014 withdrawal of U.S. and NATO troops from Afghanistan is of special concern: Chinese separatist organizations have trained in Afghanistan as well as Pakistan, and stability—or lack thereof—will have, Beijing feels, direct bearing on Islamist insurgency in China's border areas.[28]

Relevant to the above statement was the fact that the International Crisis Group was founded by Morton Abramowitz, the former CIA agent and later Ambassador to Turkey, who was a close associate of Fethullah Gülen. In fact, Abramowitz, along with Graham Fuller, enabled Gülen, in 2008, to gain permanent US residency and avoid being deported back to Turkey. Abramowitz's friend Fethullah Gülen was working to make the "risk that Central Asian jihadis currently fighting beside the Taliban may take their struggle back home after 2014" become a reality.

The Uyghur Muslim riots—incited by Rebiya Kadeer's World Uyghur Congress, Anwar Yusuf Turani's East Turkistan Independence Movement, and the Turkestan Islamic Party—were all deployed to maximize destabilization and unrest throughout China's vital energy hub in Xinjiang. But the focus of Graham Fuller's friends at the CIA and State Department went far beyond the borders of Xinjiang. Over time, they deployed political Islam cults in Pakistan to disrupt major Chinese-financed infrastructure, in Myanmar to disrupt the vital China-Myanmar energy infrastructure, and across the Middle East and Africa, from Sudan to Libya to Syria, to be in a position to choke off, at will, China's vital oil and gas lifelines.

"New Silk Road" of Eurasia

In September 2013, Chinese President Xi Jinping made a major tour of Central Asian countries to implement Chinese plans to build a New Silk Road across Central Asia.

The plans included more natural gas for Chinese industry from Turkmenistan, requiring construction of a new branch line for the Central Asia-China gas pipeline, which will also include Tajikistan and Kyrgyzstan. Xi Jinping spoke of building an "economic belt along the Silk Road," a trans-Eurasian project spanning from the Pacific Ocean to the Baltic Sea. It would, he said in a speech in Astana in Kazakhstan, create an economic belt inhabited by "close to 3 billion people and [would represent] the biggest market in the world with unparalleled potential."[29]

In his Turkmenistan visit on the same tour, Xi secured the transnational Turkmenistan-China gas pipeline that would go along the route from Turkmenistan to Uzbekistan–Tajikistan–Kyrgyzstan on to China. Beijing's only problem was that the Central Asia-China gas pipeline and other pipelines, power lines, and transport networks all ran through the Xinjiang Uyghur Autonomous Region. Xinjing was targeted by Washington in an ongoing destabilization campaign using Graham Fuller's friends and their Islamic Jihadist terror bands as their proxies.

As such strategic economic moves by China, wonderful and positive moves that could lift the largest part of the world's population into a more prosperous economic life, went forward, certain powerful interest groups in the West—banking, industrial, military, and political—came to view Beijing, only a decade or so earlier the "great friend" of America, now the new emerging Great Enemy. An Asia Pivot military shift was announced by President Obama to refocus US military activities on that growing Chinese influence.

A central part of their strategy to derail China and its growing Eurasian presence would be the increased deployment of Islamic fundamentalism of the Gülen, Al Qaeda, and Muslim Brotherhood kind against China, Russia, and all Eurasia, the one space that Zbigniew Brzezinski in his famous book *The Grand Chessboard* called the only possible challenge to America's future hegemony and dominance.

To understand how that had evolved to the situation of such a threat today it is important to go into the historical roots of political Islam and its emergence after the First World War and after.

Endnotes

1   Richard Labeviere, *Dollars for Terror: The United States and Islam*, Algora Publishing, 2000, p. 6.

2   Zbigniew Brzezinski, *Ex-National Security Chief Brzezinski admits: Afghan Islamism Was Made in Washington*, interview in "Le Nouvel Observateur," Paris, January 15–21, 1998, p. 76, translated by Bill Blum, accessed in http://www.freerepublic.com/focus/f-news/542984/posts. Notably, according to the American author Bill Blum, "There are at least two editions of *'Le Nouvel Observateur.'* With apparently the sole exception of the Library of Congress, the version sent to the United States is shorter than the French version. The Brzezinski interview was not included in the shorter version."

3   Ibid.

4   Richard Labeviere, op. cit.

5   Christoph Germann, *The New Great Game Roundup No. 12*, accessed in http://christophgermann.blogspot.de/2013/07/the-new-great-game-round-up-12.html.

6   F. William Engdahl, *Washington is Playing a Deeper Game with China*, Global Research.ca, July 11, 2009, accessed in http://www.globalresearch.ca/washington-is-playing-a-deeper-game-with-china/14327.

7   Ibid.

8   Ibid.

9   Ibid.

10 Sibel Edmonds, *Boston Terror CIAs Graham Fuller and NATO CIA Operation Gladio B Caucasus and Central Asia*, Boiling Frogs Post, April 27, 2013, accessed in http://www.boilingfrogspost.com/2013/04/27/bfp-breaking-news-boston-terror-cias-graham-fuller-nato-cia-operation-gladio-b-caucasus-central-asia/.

11 Mizgîn, *Gülen, the CIA and the American Deep State*, Rastibini Blogspot, June 29, 2008, accessed in http://rastibini.blogspot.de/2008/06/glen-cia-and-american-deep-state.html.

12   David Livingstone, *Uighur Nationalism Turkey and the CIA*, July 31, 2009, accessed in http://www.terrorism-illuminati.com/node/176#.UvjvNLQtqZQ.

13   Ibid.

14   Sibel Edmonds, *BEFORE THE OHIO ELECTIONS COMMISSION: DEPOSITION IN THE MATTER OF JEAN SCHMIDT, Plaintiff, vs. DAVID KRIKORIAN, Defendant*, Case No. 2009E-003, August 8, 2009, accessed in http://christophgermann.blogspot.de/2013/05/chinas-central-asia-problem.html.

15   Gillian Norman-Jilinda, *Beijing Olympics False Flag Attack*, 8 August 2008, accessed in http://rense.com/general82/bej.htm.

16   Website, *The Government-in-Exile of East Turkestan Republic*, accessed in http://www.eastturkistangovernmentinexile.us/anwar_biography.html.

17   Gillian Norman-Jilinda, op. cit.

18   Dru C. Gladney, and S. Frederick Starr, *Xinjiang: China's Muslim Borderland*, Armonk, New York, 2004, Central Asia-Caucasus Institute, pp. 388–389.

19   Wikipedia, *East Turkestan Islamic Movement*, accessed in http://en.wikipedia.org/wiki/East_Turkestan_Islamic_Movement.

20   Graham E. Fuller and S. Frederick Starr, *The Xinjiang Problem*, Central Asia-Caucasus Institute at Paul H. Nitze School of Advanced International Studies, The Johns Hopkins University, pp. 29–37.

21   Wikipedia, *Islamic Movement of Uzbekistan*, accessed in http://en.wikipedia.org/wiki/Islamic_Movement_of_Uzbekistan.

22   Ramtanu Maitra, *Drug Infested Ferghana Valley Target of the Axis of Three Devils*, 01 August 2010, accessed in http://www.vijayvaani.com/ArticleDisplay.aspx?aid=1341.

23   Sibel Edmonds, *Additional Omitted Points in CIA-Gulen coverage & A Note from "The Insider,"* Boiling Frogs Post, January 11, 2011, accessed in http://www.boilingfrogspost.com/2011/01/11/additional-omitted-points-in-cia-gulen-coverage-a-note-from-%E2%80%98the-insider%E2%80%99/.

24   David Livingstone, op. cit.

25   Graham E. Fuller, op. cit., p. 46.

26   Ramtanu Maitra, op. cit.

27   Graham E. Fuller, op. cit., p. 338.

28   Christoph Germann, *China's Central Asia Problem,* May 29, 2013, accessed in http://christophgermann.blogspot.de/2013/05/chinas-central-asia-problem.html.

29   Wu Jiao and Zhang Yunbi, *Xi proposes a new Silk Road with Central Asia,* China Daily, September 8, 2013, accessed in http://usa.chinadaily.com.cn/china/2013-09/08/content_16952304.htm.

CHAPTER THIRTEEN

A War on Terror: Using Religion to Make War

"Religion is regarded by the common people as true, by the wise as false, and by rulers as useful."

—Seneca (ca. 4 BC–AD 65)

"I prefer to reign over a country in ruins than over one which is damned."

—Ferdinand II, Catholic Habsburg Holy Roman
Emperor during the Thirty Years' War

Making Religion the Enemy

Ten days before the earthshaking events around the New York World Trade towers and the Pentagon of September 11, 2001, Prince Turki al-Faisal, the head of the Saudi Arabian General Intelligence Directorate, *Al Mukhabarat Al A'amah*, abruptly resigned the post he had held for some 23 years. He had run the Kingdom's intelligence agency since 1979, when the CIA, Saudi Intelligence, and Pakistan's ISI intelligence services joined to create the Jihadists of the Mujahideen in Afghanistan to fight the Soviet Army.[1]

The resignation was abrupt and surprised many. He had just been named to serve another four-year term in May of 2001 and gave no hint of wanting to step down. Prince Turki had also mentored Osama bin Laden from the very start of the Afghan Jihad in 1979.

Ten days after the prince's resignation, three giant towers of the New York World Trade Center fell to the earth in a heap of rubble and powder. The Pentagon, the world's most important military building, incurred an attack that left a gaping hole in one side.

Within hours of those September 11 attacks, presenting no firm evidence or proof, the US Government named Osama bin Laden and his Jihadist Al Qaeda organization as the terrorists behind the deed. US President George W. Bush declared at a White House press conference, "This is a new kind of—a new kind of evil. . . . And the American people are beginning to understand. This Crusade, this war on terrorism is going to take a while. . . . It is time for us to win the first war of the 21st century, decisively."[2]

The so-called War on Terror was, in reality, a War using Religion, or the intensity of religious feelings of populations. Despite their vehement denials, it was being shaped by the CIA, the Pentagon and the Bush Administration as a war against the entire Islamic world using the attacks of September 11, 2001, as justification. Predictably, in the ensuing decade and a half, radicalized elements in the Islamic world responded with their own forms of Holy Crusade, namely with Jihad, or Islamic Holy Wars, against all "Infidels," whether Christian or other rival religious groups—Sunni against Shi'ite and Alawite, against Coptic Christians, and against Buddhists. Israel's right-wing Likud and the Ehud Barak government seized on the Washington war on terror to justify its brutal treatment of Palestinian and Arab Muslims.

The world may never know the full truth of who and what was really behind the traumatic events of September 11, 2001. The official US Government's claim that it was Osama bin Laden who allegedly masterminded the extremely sophisticated attack from a remote cave in Tora Bora in Afghanistan—using 19 loyal, fanatical Mujahideen followers with minimal flight pilot training, 14 of them alleged Saudi nationals, armed only with box-cutting small knives—became less and less credible the more that serious people investigated.

Another theory that Vice President Dick Cheney and a cabal of war hawks called neoconservatives masterminded the event to create a "new Pearl Harbor" that would revive America's military and give her a new "enemy" after the collapse of the Soviet Union was also not convincing. The risk of discovery was far too great.

Nor was the argument by some that elements inside the Israeli political establishment had orchestrated the deed very convincing, for similar reasons.

What *was* clear was that each of those groups appeared to have had forewarning of the coming attack. And each—the Bush-Cheney militarist war hawks, the Israeli conservative government of Likud leader Ariel Sharon, the Saudi monarchy—was clearly prepared to use the deed to advance its own ends.

Israel used the attacks to tell the world she was justified in establishing Jewish settlements in Palestinian lands and in building a gigantic wall to separate Israeli Jews from their neighbors.

The Bush Administration used the event—"Mr President, the Nation is under attack"—to rally the nation to patriotic new wars in Afghanistan, Iraq, and far beyond. Severe curtailment of the Constitution's Bill of Rights was justified in a new Patriot Act passed by Congress amid the climate of fear and panic. A repressive Department of Homeland Security was formed to intrude into the most intimate corners of everyday life of Americans. All was justified on the argument of "national security" and the new War on Terror. The US military–industrial complex and NATO finally had a new reason to exist, even to expand, as far away as Poland, Bulgaria, the Czech Republic, and Afghanistan.

The different strains of political Islam, whether Salafist or Wahhabi, whether Muslim Brotherhood or its derivative organizations, taking various names under the nebulous umbrella of al Qaeda, used the American declaration of a War on Terror as their justification for a renewed Jihad, or war, against the "infidels" of the Christian West, as well as within Islam.

A "Thirty Years' War" on Religion

In the weeks after President George W. Bush proclaimed his War on Terror, a number of backers of the new war, including former CIA Director James Woolsey and other neoconservative hawks, spoke of a global war lasting perhaps thirty years. For them, it was clearly a new global war, and, like the European Thirty Years' War from 1618 through to the Peace of Westphalia in 1648, it was a war of religions, of each against the other.[3] The comparison of Washington's War on Terror to the 17th century European great war of religion was more than fitting.

Increasingly across Christian Europe during the 1500s, some three centuries after the last blood from the Holy Crusades had been spilled, the Roman Catholic Church faced an existential crisis. The power of the Pope was being challenged fundamentally by various reformers led by a rebel German Catholic priest, Martin Luther, and later by the French theologian Jean Calvin and others. The Catholic Church's Council of Trent, lasting eighteen years to 1563, had defeated the notion that general councils of the Roman Church collectively were God's representative on Earth rather than the Pope. It established the Pope as an absolute ruler. That was to portend ominous developments.

The corruption permeating the highest levels of the Vatican and Church had become notorious, with open papal polygamy to homosexuality to financial corruption. The corruption and decadence spread from such Popes as Innocent VI and Pope Leo X—the Medici pope who sold indulgences to wealthy Catholics to build St. Peter's Basilica in Rome—to Pope Clement VII. It was creating severe strains and widespread abandonment of the Church among believers far from Rome.

The new Protestant Reformation threatened Papal power from within and without as never before. Luther had committed heresy in the eyes of the Vatican by making knowledge accessible to ordinary citizens. He did that through translating the Bible into German in 1534 from the Hebrew and ancient Greek version done earlier by Erasmus of Rotterdam. That simple act was a threat so great the very power of the Vatican was threatened as never before.

Luther had made the contents of the Bible directly accessible to ordinary Germans. It was no longer the elite domain of the educated priests of the Roman Catholic Church to interpret. It in fact, Luther, in doing so, created the German language as a written language.

Five years later, in 1539, Thomas Cranmer, the Archbishop of Canterbury, at the bequest of King Henry VIII, published the "Great Bible" in English—the first English Bible authorized for public use and distributed to every church, where it was chained to the pulpit and a reader was even provided so that the illiterate could hear the Word of God in plain English. The Roman Catholic Church responded with no soft persuasion attempts. They threatened anyone possessing a non-Latin Bible with execution. For the first time, millions of professing Christians could find out the truth that the Roman Catholic official Latin Vulgate Bible bore little relation to the earlier Greek and Hebrew texts that were now in German.[4]

Johan Guttenberg's invention of the printing press some seven decades earlier made it possible for the Bible translations to spread knowledge as never before. The Roman Church's monopoly on knowledge was under deadly attack from all sides. Having God's Word available to the public in the language of the common man meant disaster for the Church. No longer could they control access to the scriptures to specially educated priests taught in Latin.

As people began to read the Bible in their own tongue, the church's income and power began to crumble. Their lucrative selling of indulgences (the forgiveness of sins) or selling the release of loved ones from a church-manufactured "Purgatory" was under severe attack. People began, all across the Christian world, to challenge the Roman Church's authority as the Church was exposed as being led by frauds and thieves.

To reverse the dangerous tide, in the 1540s, Pope Paul III gave official Vatican recognition to a powerful new Military Order within the Church: the Society of Jesus, or the Jesuits, founded by two Spanish noblemen, Ignatius of Loyola and Francis Xavier, namesake of the Pope Francis today. [5]

The Jesuits, much like the Muslim Brotherhood and Fethullah Gülen's *Cemaat*, concentrated their main effort on shaping the education of Europe's future nobility and monarchs in the strict obedience of the Society and a fanatical militancy against Protestant reformers, as well as against heretics within the Church. Their pledge to the Pope in Rome was to roll-back the Protestant threat and put knowledge back where it belonged—in the monopoly of the Roman Catholic Church and its select priests. They would lead a Counter-Reformation. Knowledge, reason, and Christian love were to be replaced by fear, darkness, and destruction as the Jesuit influence grew across Europe, especially the German lands and principalities.

By 1618, the Jesuit Order was the crucial string-puller of the Jesuit-educated Catholic Holy Roman Emperor Ferdinand II (1619–1637) through his Jesuit confessor-advisor, Father Martin Becan, and later his Father-confessor, Jesuit Father Wilhelm Lamormaini. As Emperor Ferdinand unleashed one of the most destructive and bloody wars in history, later known as the Thirty Years' War, "there now began a regular system of Protestant persecution—more mean, cruel, and horrible bloody things happened, indeed than can well be conceived—and according to the evidence furnished by the Jesuits themselves, the originator of all this was their distinguished brother, William Lamormaini."[6]

The Jesuit Father-Confessor Lamormaini used his influence on the Holy Roman Emperor Ferdinand II to drive one of the bloodiest wars in history.

Indicating how deep the scars of the war and killings in the name of religion went, one of the greatest military atrocities during that Thirty Years War was committed by Roman Catholic Croats, much in the manner of the Croatian fascist Ustaši three hundred years later. Croat soldiers of the Habsburg Catholic forces were employed, with drawn swords, in hunting down the people, forcing them to the Mass with dogs and whips, and throwing the refractory ones into the cages in which they could neither sit, lie down, nor even stand, while they were compelled to witness, at the same time, the most horrible violence [forcible rape] applied to their poor wives and daughters, until the husbands and fathers swore upon their knees to renounce heresy.[7]

The three decades of war were prosecuted by the Catholic Habsburg Emperor Ferdinand II with a cruelty and ferocious fanaticism that can only be described as Satanic in nature.

Catholic Bishops across German states initiated witch trials and tortured and burned at the stake hundreds of Protestants accused of witchcraft. The population in the German states was reduced by between 25 percent and 40 percent. Württemberg lost three-quarters of its population during the war. In Brandenburg, the losses had amounted to half. Overall, the male population of the German states was reduced by almost half. The population of Bohemia and Moravia fell by a third due to war, disease, famine, and the expulsion of Protestants. Much of the destruction of civilian lives and property was caused by the cruelty and greed of mercenary soldiers.[8]

The Jesuits used Emperor Ferdinand II and the Catholic League in opposing the Protestant Union, a process that resulted in the deaths of what was estimated as over ten million people. One historian states, "It has been estimated that this benign [Catholic] sovereign went into the world of spirits with the blood of ten millions of people on his soul. . . . In the whole history of the German race no other sovereign ever contributed so largely to the woes of the people."[9]

That war against religion ultimately drew in Muscovy, Sweden, Denmark, England, Holland, and France on the one side against a Catholic League and the Holy Roman Empire of the Habsburg alliance that also included Spain and the princes of Poland and Lithuania. The soil of what became Germany was the battlefield where most of the blood was shed over a span of three decades, until the Peace of Westphalia in 1648 ended the war and divided Europe into religious enclaves that remained down to the 21st century. The German poet and historian Friedrich Schiller, in his history of the war, described it as

Habsburg Emperor Ferdinand II was guided to wage war against Protestant "heresy" by the Jesuits.

> a desolating war of thirty years, which, from the interior of Bohemia to the mouth of Scheldt, and from the banks of the Po to the coasts of the Baltic, devastated whole countries, destroying harvests, and reduced towns and villages to ashes; which opened a grave for many thousand combatants, and for half a century smothered the glimmering sparks of civilization in Germany, and threw back the improving manners of the country into their pristine barbarity and wildness.[10]

It was one of the bloodiest wars in history, a war of nominal Christian against Christian. One historian described its consequences for generations of Europeans afterward: "The deep misery which followed the war of religion, the powerless politics, the intellectual decadence, the moral corruption, a frightful decrease in the population and impoverishment of the whole of Germany—these were the results of the [Jesuit] Order's actions."[11]

At the end of the religious war, its toll on civilization was staggering, so horrible that it had not only destroyed the very social and economic fabric of Europe, but it had severely damaged the spiritual and intellectual framework as well by destroying faith in a divine God and in a renaissance man, opening the door to a new nihilism—a belief in nothing.

War on Terror. War on Religion.
War on Intelligent Beings.

The Unites States' War on Terror, begun in September 2001, was to become tragically similar: a covert and often overt war on religion. Little more than a decade into the new war of religion against religion, the ancient cradle of civilization, Iraq, had been destroyed in the name of "democracy," which was, in effect, the new "Pope."

The War in Afghanistan began only days after September 11. The nominal excuse used by the Bush Administration was that the fundamentalist Sunni Jihadist Taliban regime refused to extradite Osama bin Laden to the USA without proof of his complicity in the terror attacks in the USA.

Bin Laden had been brought to Afghanistan in 1996 by Prince Turki, head of Saudi Intelligence and mentor of Bin Laden. Washington decided to "negotiate" with saturation bombing of the Afghan landscape and toppling of the Taliban, a regime its own CIA, along with old Mujahideen ally Pakistan's ISI and the Saudi Intelligence of Prince Turki al-Faisal, had brought to power.[12]

The United States refused to speak with the Taliban, instead launching Operation Enduring Freedom on October 7, 2001, in violation of the UN Charter and all precepts of international law. Washington's only ally at the time was Britain's Tony Blair. Curiously or not, all the top leadership of Taliban, as well as Osama bin Laden and his entourage, miraculously managed to escape capture. Washington installed a long-time CIA collaborator, who had spent years in exile in the US, Hamid Karzai, as President.

The US military built bases in Afghanistan in the wake of its blitzkrieg war long after it had given up the charade of searching for Osama bin Laden in the caves of Tora Bora. Notably, along with the US occupation of Afghanistan, the cultivation of opium for heroin reached record high levels under the new US military presence. Karzai's brother, Ahmed Wali Karzai, had been in the pay of the CIA at the same time he became warlord over Afghanistan's largest opium fields in Kandahar Province.[13]

Strong evidence emerged from Interpol and US surveys and reports that US forces in Afghanistan had more than a passing interest in the explosion of opium cultivation in Afghanistan after 2001. Along with the opium cultivation came an explosion in permanent US military bases as well. [14] It seemed that—much as during the Vietnam War in the 1970s, when the CIA worked with Hmong tribesmen from Laos to push heroin onto the world market to finance their black operations—the CIA was doing the same in Afghanistan, only on a larger scale.

Under US occupation, after 2001, Afghanistan emerged as the world's premier opium and heroin source. According to UN statistics, by 2007, 92 percent of the non-pharmaceutical-grade opium products on the world market originated in Afghanistan. Afghanistan was also the largest producer of cannabis, mostly as hashish, in the world. The Afghani warlords were "high" on Washington's peculiar version of democracy.[15]

One million have died from Afghan heroin since the 2001 US Occupation. US Marine Corps Sgt. Noel Rodriguez, Regimental Combat Team 6, on patrol in Sangin, Helmand province, Afghanistan, May 1, 2012. Marines patrolled to provide security in the opium-producing area under strict orders not to eradicate the poppy fields.

In December 2004, during a visit to Kabul, US Defense Secretary Donald Rumsfeld announced plans to build nine new bases in Afghanistan in the provinces of Helmand, Herat, Nimruz, Balkh, Khost, and Paktia. They were, in addition to the three major US military bases already installed in the wake of its occupation of Afghanistan in winter of 2001–2002, ostensibly to isolate and eliminate the terror threat of Osama bin Laden. The Pentagon had built its first three bases at Bagram Air Field north of Kabul, the US' main military logistics center, Kandahar Air Field in southern Afghanistan, and Shindand Air Field in the western province of Herat. Shindand, the largest US base in Afghanistan, was constructed a scant 100 kilometers from the border of Iran and within striking distance of Russia, as well as China.[16]

Afghan President Hamid Karzai, longtime CIA-asset, stands in the center of a crowd of soldiers from the US Special Forces Team during Operation Enduring Freedom in October 2001.

The massive US-UK military presence in Afghanistan, later widened to German and other NATO countries, went parallel with thousands of civilian deaths and casualties of Afghanis at the hands of NATO. That, in turn, provided the incubator for a new generation of Jihadist Islamist terrorists in Afghanistan and Pakistan, some genuine and some CIA "false flag" terrorists that served to justify the permanent US military bases.

Writing just after the September 11 attacks, Rahul Bedi, in *Jane's Defense Weekly* of the UK, described the cauldron of rage and hate that the earlier US Mujahideen war in the 1980s had planted the seeds for. Those seeds were about to blossom into cadres of a Global Jihad against the West:

> Afghanistan has been steadily devastated by internecine battles
> in which the Pakistan-backed Taliban militia has emerged

partially victorious. Nearly two million Afghans of the country's population of some four million became refugees in Pakistan, Iran and Central Asia. The majority of those who were part of the jihad became unemployed, lacking food and shelter and, most importantly, patrons. This, in turn, made them ideal recruits for exploitation by the ISI and Pakistan's increasingly fundamentalist army. According to intelligence estimates over 10,000 Islamic mercenaries, trained in guerrilla warfare and armed with sophisticated weapons, are unemployed in Pakistan today, waiting to be transported to the next jihad.[17]

For Pentagon planners, it was less about Holy War and more about an excuse to build permanent bases in Central Asia for the first time since the Cold War, bases that could threaten both China and Russia. Afghanistan was in an extremely vital location, straddling South Asia, Central Asia, and the Middle East. Afghanistan also lay along a proposed oil pipeline route from the Caspian Sea oil fields to the Indian Ocean, where the US oil company, Unocal, along with Enron and Cheney's Halliburton Inc., had been in negotiations for exclusive pipeline rights to bring natural gas from Turkmenistan across Afghanistan and Pakistan to Enron's huge natural gas power plant at Dabhol near Mumbai.

At that time, the Pentagon also signed an agreement with the government of Kyrgyzstan in Central Asia to build a strategically important base there: Manas Air Base at Bishkek's international airport. Manas was not only close to Afghanistan, but it was also within easy striking distance of Caspian Sea oil and gas, as well as the borders of both China and Russia. As part of the price of accepting Pakistan's military dictator General Pervez Musharraf as a US ally rather than a foe in the "War on Terror," Washington extracted an agreement from him—to allow the airport at Jacobabad, about 400km north of Karachi, to be used by the US Air Force and NATO to support their campaign in Afghanistan. Two additional US bases were built at Dalbandin and Pasni.[18] In the 1980s, Musharraf had been engaged in training the Jihadist Mujahideen.

To feed the rage and hatred against the West, in 2004, the Central Intelligence Agency's Special Activities Division began ongoing attacks on targets in northwest Pakistan using drones. These attacks, allegedly, were to defeat the Taliban and Al-Qaeda militants who were thought to have found a safe haven in Pakistan. The ongoing killing of countless innocent civilians served as a recruitment vehicle for radical Jihad volunteers seeking revenge.

Once Afghanistan had been largely destroyed and occupied by US forces—this time, unlike in 1989, with permanent US air and other military bases—the Bush Administration turned its guns on someone with no ties or relationship to Osama bin Laden, Saddam Hussein, the Baath Party Arab socialist dictator of Iraq, as part of what was termed an "Axis of Evil," a term chosen clearly to keep the religious zeal high among gullible Americans. With what is now well established were fabricated "proofs" of Saddam's arsenal of Weapons of Mass Destruction—nuclear, chemical, and biological weapons aimed directly at America and its allies— Washington went to war again, in March 2003, against a hapless Saddam amid worldwide protest.

Iraq was no match for the full "Shock and Awe" assault of the world's military colossus. By 2006, the US had constructed no fewer than 14 permanent bases in Iraq—a country only twice the size of the state of Idaho. The freedom seemed mainly to be freedom for Washington to build its military garrisons along Iraqi oil fields and on the Iraqi border with Iran.[19]

The US military moved into Iraq and facilitated the looting of the National Museum with its treasures going back some 5,000 years. US military jets bombed the Imam Ali Shrine in Najaf, one of the holiest sites in Shi'ite Islam, despite promises from US forces that they would not harm the Mosque. Over the course of the war and occupation, an estimated 1,033,000 deaths resulted from the conflict which went on until 2007. The wars in Afghanistan and Iraq and related veterans' health costs were estimated to cost, over the next four decades, up to $6 trillion.[20]

Hired Assassins

The US Pentagon "privatized" the dirtiest operations in the War on Terror. One of the prime beneficiaries was a private "security" firm named Blackwater, which hired former senior CIA and Pentagon officials. Robert Richer, Blackwater Vice President of Intelligence in 2005, came from the CIA, where he was Associate Deputy Director of Operations and head of the CIA's Near East Division. Blackwater's first major contracts were in Iraq, and it was hired by the CIA to carry out assassinations of "Islamic terrorists" to avoid Congressional restrictions on direct CIA assassinations.

Cofer Black, Blackwater vice chairman, was the Bush administration's top counter terrorism official when September 11 occurred. In 2002, he stated, "There was before 9/11 and after 9/11. After 9/11, the gloves come off." [21]

In Iraq, Blackwater ex-CIA and Special Forces mercenaries, here with automatic guns guarding US Proconsul Paul Bremer III, were finally forced to leave after many incidents of killing innocent civilians, as the US Government had made them immune from Iraqi legal actions.

It wouldn't take long before it became clear what he meant. In Iraq, Blackwater mercenaries soon became notorious for random killings and shooting of civilians. Blackwater killed a security guard working for the Iraqi Vice President. In late May 2007, Blackwater contractors "opened fire on the streets of Baghdad twice in two days . . . and one of the incidents provoked a standoff between the security contractors and Iraqi Interior Ministry commandos." [22]

In another incident, Blackwater shot an Iraqi civilian deemed to have been "driving too close" to a State Department convoy being escorted by Blackwater. On September 17, 2007, a Blackwater team escorting a convoy of US State Department vehicles drew close to Nisour Square. A car driving very slowly on the wrong side of the road ignored a police officer's whistle to clear a path for the convoy.

Shortly after this, Blackwater fired lethal shots at the car. Iraqi Army soldiers, mistaking the sound bombs for explosions, opened fire at the Blackwater team, to which the Blackwater team responded, killing many innocent civilians in downtown Baghdad with dozens of witnesses. "We see the security firms . . . doing whatever they want in the streets. They beat citizens and scorn them," Baghdad resident Halim Mashkoor told AP Television News. Hasan Jaber Salman, one of the wounded and an Iraqi lawyer, charged that "no one did anything to provoke Blackwater. As we turned back they opened fire at all cars from behind."[23]

As news of the Blackwater killings was broadcast across the Muslim world, rage grew and the recruits to Jihad along with it. Washington's War on Terror was creating a Frankenstein's Monster. Before the US invasion to "wage war on Osama bin Laden and Saddam's WMD threat," al Qaeda did not exist in Iraq. That changed dramatically over the ensuing several years of senseless looting and killing by Western occupation forces.

The CIA as well hired mercenary firms like Blackwater to carry out illegal torture of "suspected terrorists" captured from around the world, including waterboarding. Terror suspects were kidnapped and brought, in many cases without charges or right to attorney, to a US base on Guantanamo Bay in Cuba to avoid US law.

Global War on Terror—Global Jihad

The ambiguous War on Terror, which was clearly understood in the Muslim world as a War on Islam, could expand to any place where a significant Muslim population lived and where various assets of the CIA or US Special Forces could incite Jihad terror and suicide bombing reactions to the brazen US or NATO war incursions.

Military analyst Zoltan Grossman noted, "The most direct US intervention after the Afghan invasion had been in the southern Philippines, against the Moro (Muslim) guerrilla militia Abu Sayyaf. The US claimed the tiny Abu Sayyaf group was inspired by Bin Laden, rather than a thuggish outgrowth of decades of Moro insurgency in Mindanao and the Sulu Archipelago."[24]

That Abu Sayyaf presence gave US Special Forces the excuse to enter the Philippines and train forces there, which, in turn, further fanned the flames of more Moro attacks. US Special Forces trainers were soon carrying out joint exercises with Philippine troops in an active combat zone. Their goal was, allegedly, to achieve an easy victory over the 200 rebels for the global propaganda effect against Bin Laden. Once in place, the counter-insurgency campaign was used to achieve the other major US goal in the Philippines: to fully reestablish US military basing rights, which had ended when the Philippine Senate terminated US control of Clark Air Base and Subic Naval Base after the Cold War ended.[25]

In February 2002, US Special Forces went to the Republic of Georgia to begin an "anti-terror" training program to combat al-Qaeda-linked Jihadists. That October, in the Horn of Africa, the Pentagon began the local version of Operation Enduring Freedom. That brought US military "advisors" to Sudan, Somalia, Djibouti, Ethiopia, Eritrea, Seychelles, and Kenya. In addition, the US command had operations in Mauritius, Comoros, Liberia, Rwanda, Uganda, and Tanzania.[26]

By 2008, the Bush Administration had created a unified Africa Command, AFRICOM, to make a focused intervention into the resource-rich continent. The motivation was triggered by massive Chinese investment that began, in earnest, in 2006 to secure raw materials and oil from some forty African nations.[27]

What Washington's War on Terror—deploying terror to fight terror—accomplished with its torture, wanton murders of civilians with drone and other attacks, and use of chemical weapons and depleted uranium shells (that caused horrendous birth deformities and cancer among the populations of Iraq and elsewhere) was the dramatic global spread of Islamist Jihad terror as revenge.

In 2006, the US Government's official National Intelligence Estimate (NIE) report declared that the war in Iraq had become a primary recruitment vehicle for violent Islamic extremists, motivating a new generation of potential terrorists around the world "whose numbers may be increasing faster than the United States and its allies can reduce the threat." The estimate, a consensus of all US intelligence agencies, concluded that the US invasion of Iraq, and the insurgency that followed, was "the leading inspiration for new Islamic extremist networks and cells that are united by little more than an anti-Western agenda. Rather than contributing to eventual victory in the global counterterrorism struggle, the situation in Iraq has worsened the US position."[28]

By little more than a decade into the new war of religion against religion, terror against terror, already the ancient cradle of civilization in Iraq had been destroyed, Afghanistan bombed back to the Stone Age as its own thirty years' war against foreign occupation raged on. Americans had been terrorized into yielding their basic liberties in exchange for a "security" that never came.

Power to Destroy Intelligence

The new War on Terror, like those before it, would be used to terrorize all of mankind. However, for those orchestrating the events at the highest levels, it was not about religion. It was about who had the power—the power, ultimately, to destroy the entire world and to destroy intelligent, moral, thinking beings and their civilized culture. As the French Emperor Napoleon Bonaparte was quoted to have said some two centuries earlier as his armies marched across Continental Europe, "Religion is excellent stuff for keeping common people quiet. Religion is what keeps the poor from murdering the rich."[29]

In essence, those behind the new religious wars at the beginning of the 21st century—the new Crusades, the new Jihad—were a global power elite who saw their power threatened as never before. Their arch "enemy" was the growing population of intelligent, thinking human beings, whose numbers began to increase dramatically after the American Revolution and, especially, across Continental Europe after the Revolutions of 1848.

Those revolutions, or attempts, terrified the oligarchical elites of the day as groups of ordinary citizens, the "masses" as the elites saw them, were unified in putting forward demands for more participation in government, more democracy, demands of the working classes for better education for their children, higher wages, and better conditions. Pitted against this was a regrouping of the reactionary forces based on European royalty, the aristocracy, the army, and a largely illiterate peasantry as "cannon fodder" controlled by those elites.

Intelligent, thinking human beings in dramatically increasing numbers, as these decadent elites saw it, were the mortal enemies of their continued power, a power based on maintaining the vast majority of the population in a state of superstition, fear, and ignorance.

As a totality, mankind at the onset of the 21st century, most recently the populations of the developing world in Africa, South America, the Arab world, and Asia, had become vastly more intelligent. That meant—as the printing of the Bible by Luther in the common language of German or English more than four hundred years before had meant—that ordinary people would be less vulnerable to their tricks, their magic, their manipulations, and, above all, their control. In the centuries from the Great Crusades to the Industrial Revolution, those tricks, illusions, and manipulations of superstitions had enabled a tiny power elite to subjugate the majority of mankind, to keep them in darkness, ignorance—basically, in a state of stupidity.

For those malevolent power elites, whether Christian or Muslim, their goal was now, in the first decades of the 21st century, to reintroduce a new age of darkness, superstition, fear, hate, death, and destruction. Religion was to be twisted to serve that goal. It was an old script based on the era of darkness and wars going back to the Great Crusades of Western Christian Rome against Eastern Islam and Byzantine Christianity and to the Thirty Years' War of the 17th century.

No other interpretation after September 11, 2001, of the wanton violence, terror, and cruelty of both sides, whether Christian or Islam, made sense. The death and destruction were not owing to the stupidity of Washington planners. It was a central part of a strategy of wars of religion against religion. And as history had demonstrated time and again, religious wars were the most devastating form of war since time immemorial. Through the War on Terror and its Islamic reflex, Global Jihad, these circles aimed to destroy the intelligent civilization and bring mankind back into the dark ages of the past or worse, a new kind of "Planet of the Apes."

By 2010, that global war was to explode with a new ferocity as a project originally named The Greater Middle East Project, later renamed by the mainstream media as Arab Spring, was unleashed by Western intelligence agencies, beginning with a remote event in Tunisia.

Endnotes

1   Talib Mahfoudh, *Prince Turki: Resistance to Soviet occupation was jihad*, Saudi Gazette, December 21, 2010, acceded in http://www.saudigazette.com.sa/index.cfm?method=home.regcon&contentID=2010122189717.

2   George W. Bush, *Remarks by the President Upon Arrival*, Washington, DC, 16 September, 2001, accessed in http://georgewbush-whitehouse.archives.gov/news/releases/2001/09/20010916-2.html.

3   Paul Rogers, *A thirty-year war?*, OpenDemocracy.net, 3 April 2003, accessed in http://www.opendemocracy.net/conflict/article_1127.jsp; also see Charles Feldman and Stan Wilson, *Ex CIA director US faces' World War IV*, CNN, April 3, 2003, accessed in http://edition.cnn.com/2003/US/04/03/sprj.irq.woolsey.world.war/.

4   The Bible Museum, Inc., *English Bible History*, accessed in http://www.greatsite.com/timeline-english-bible-history/index.html.

5   Leo Lyon Zagami, Pope Francis: The Last Pope? Money, Masons and Occultism in the Decline of the Catholic Church, 2015, San Francisco, p.37ff.

6   G. B. Nicolini, *History of the Jesuits: Their Origin, Progress, Doctrines, and Designs*, London, Henry G. Bohn, 1854, pp. 45, 92, 93, 34.

7   Arthur R. Pennington, *The Counter-Reformation in Europe*, London, Elliot Stock, 1899, pp. 57, 58.

8   US Library of Congress, *Germany: Historical Setting—The Peace of Westphalia*, accessed in http://historymedren.about.com/library/text/bltxtgermany16.htm.

9   Jim Arrabito, *The History of the Jesuits*, Angwen, California: LLT Productions, 1988; quoting from *The Fiery Jesuits*; originally published in 1667.

10 Frederich Schiller, *History of the Thirty Years' War*.

11 J. Huber, *Les Jesuites*, 1875, Paris, cited in Edmond Paris, *The Secret History of the Jesuits*, Chick Publications, Ontario, 1975, p. 37.

12 Deep Politics Forum, *Prince Turki Al Faisal*, April 2, 2009, accessed in https://deeppoliticsforum.com/forums/showthread.php?1200-Prince-Turki-Al-Faisal#.Ux2gwYUtqZQ.

13 Dexter Filkins, et al., *Brother of Afghan Leader Said to Be Paid by CIA*, October 28, 2009, New York Times, accessed in http://www.nytimes.com/2009/10/28/world/asia/28intel.html?pagewanted=all&_r=0.

14 F. William Engdahl, *Full Spectrum Dominance: Totalitarian Democracy in the New World Order*, edition.engdahl, Wiesbaden, 2009, p. 132.

15 UNITED NATIONS Office on Drugs and Crime. Afghanistan Opium Survey 2007. Also, *UN: Afghanistan is leading hashish producer*, Fox News. March 31, 2010.

16 Ibid.

17 Rahul Bedi, *Why? An attempt to explain the unexplainable*, Jane's Defense Weekly, 14 September 2001.

18 F. William Engdahl, op. cit., pp. 133–34.

19 Ibid., p. 134.

20 Ernesto Londono, *Iraq Afghan wars will cost to 4 trillion to 6 trillion dollars Harvard study says*, Washington Post, March 29, 2013, accessed in http://www.washingtonpost.com/world/national-security/study-iraq-afghan-war-costs-to-top-4-trillion/2013/03/28/b82a5dce-97ed-11e2-814b-063623d80a60_story.html.

21 Pratap Chatterjee, *Blackwater USA*, CorpWatch, accessed in http://www.corpwatch.org/article.php?list=type&type=210.

22 Ibid.

23 Inid.

24 Ibid.

25 Ibid., p. 135.

26 Larry Foos, Petty Officer 1st Class, *Joint Force Core Staff Taking Reins in Horn of Africa*, CJTF-HOA Public Affairs, February 5, 2010, accessed in http://www.africom.mil/NEWSROOM/Article/7170/joint-force-core-staff-taking-reins-in-horn-of-afr.

27 AP, *Africans Fear Hidden U.S. Agenda in New Approach to Africom*, September 30, 2008, Associated Press, accessed in http://www.foxnews.com/story/2008/09/30/africans-fear-hidden-us-agenda-in-new-approach-to-africom/.

28 Karen De Young, *Spy Agencies Say Iraq War Hurting US Terror Fight*, Washington Post, September 24, 2006, accessed in http://www.washingtonpost.com/wp-dyn/content/article/2006/09/23/AR2006092301130.html; and Washington's Blog, *US War On Terror Has Increased Terrorism*, Global Research, October 22, 2013, accessed in http://www.globalresearch.ca/u-s-war-on-terror-has-increased-terrorism/5355073.

29 Quotes of Napoleon Bonaparte, accessed in http://www.goodreads.com/author/quotes/210910.Napoleon.

CHAPTER FOURTEEN

NATO's Arab Spring and Unintended Consequences

"Potentially the most dangerous scenario would be a grand coalition of China, Russia and perhaps Iran, an 'anti-hegemonic' coalition, united not by ideology but by complementary grievances. . . . Averting this contingency . . . will require a display of US geostrategic skill on the western, eastern and southern perimeters of Eurasia simultaneously."

—Zbigniew Brzezinski, former foreign policy adviser to Barack Obama

Drastic Measures

The Bush-Cheney wars against Iraq and Afghanistan after September 11, 2001, were a failure in every dimension. The staggering costs of the wars, counted over ensuing decades in trillions of dollars, were dumped onto American taxpayers and indirectly to those trade surplus countries, like China and Russia, or Japan, who bought hundreds of billions of dollars of US Government debt as the only "secure" haven for their massive trade dollar surpluses.

Then in March 2007, the American Sole Superpower faced a profound, terrifying new challenge. This time it was from within.

The US financial system began a domino-style collapse as the market for fraudulent real estate loans, especially so-called "sub-prime" home loans, collapsed. It had been a speculation bubble unlike every other bubble in US history, including the 1920s Wall Street stock market bubble. Unlimited military spending for the expansion of the global domination of the USA was threatened by the financial crisis and with it, American hegemony.

By September 2008, it was clear to powerful circles in Washington and Wall Street that if drastic measures were not undertaken, the role of the USA as the sole superpower would soon end in collapse.

To shift the global power calculus again to their favor, they needed drastic and bold measures. The response was a policy that was meant primarily to block an emerging Eurasian economic challenge coming from Russia and China.

The strategy involved inciting revolutions, later called "Arab Spring," across the Islamic world to directly challenge the oil and energy flows of China and Russia, each in different ways. It was also intended, finally, to open the staggering sovereign wealth of absolutist Arab oil monarchies—such as Saudi Arabia, Egypt, Libya, Tunisia, and beyond—to Western financial domination, using the IMF as they had done so successfully in Latin America and Yugoslavia in the 1980s.

Using their "free market" mantra that had seemed to work so well, they believed they could force open the vast wealth of Arab oil monarchies to looting by Wall Street and the City of London financial institutions. The people who dreamed it up clearly thought they were very intelligent. They weren't.

New Thirty Years' War

In 2008, the Pentagon released a document titled *2008: Army Modernization Strategy*. That document stated that the objective of US Army strategy was to span and dominate the entire universe, not just the planet.

It called for "an expeditionary, campaign-quality Army capable of dominating across the full spectrum of conflict, at any time, in any environment and against any adversary—for extended periods of time . . . achieving Full Spectrum Dominance."[1]

No other army in world history had had such ambitious goals, not even that of Alexander of Macedonia. The Pentagon aimed for control, essentially, of everything and everyone, everywhere.

Most relevant, the policy paper stated that Army modernization envisioned that the United States, for at least the next "thirty to forty years," would be engaged in continuous wars to control raw materials and to ensure that potential challengers, such as China and Russia, would be kept in their place.[2]

In a clear reference to China and Russia, the Pentagon's strategic plan declared, "We face a potential return to traditional security threats posed by emerging near-peers as we compete globally for depleting natural resources and overseas markets." [3] In terms of economic growth, the only "emerging near peer" on the planet in 2008 was China, which was looking everywhere for secure sources of oil, metals, and other raw materials to sustain its dramatic growth projections.

In terms of military power, the only potential "emerging near peer" was Russia. Russia was the only power with a nuclear strike force capable of challenging NATO. US military bases in Afghanistan and Iraq, following the onset of the 2001 War on Terror, posed a certain conventional military challenge to China and Russia.

But short of a highly risky all-out nuclear war, something more diabolical was deemed necessary by the Pentagon, CIA and State Department planners. It was to be called the Arab Spring.

Consequences of Stupidity

What unfolded after the launching of the Arab Spring regime destabilizations in 2010, a massive chain of simultaneous US-backed Color Revolutions, were the unintended consequences of policies not thought through in their complexity.

Real intelligence in politics, as in science, is the ability to recognize connections that are not necessarily obvious, to see relationships—seeing the interconnectedness of all life, all peoples, and all wars. Real intelligence is the ability to understand that when you unleash a destructive force in one place, it affects all mankind destructively, including those who unleash it.

The strategists at the CIA, the State Department, the Pentagon, and White House were only capable of thinking in a one-dimensional way. They simply blacked out anything that showed how their actions and strategies were interconnected, viewing the complexities, instead, with narrow blinders, reduced to isolated atoms or singularities.

That inability to appreciate the connectedness of all would ultimately "blowback" on the perpetrators themselves and on their succeeding generations. The consequences of their stupidity led the world to animal results, to bestiality, on a scale that would resonate for decades, if not centuries. They called that stupidity Arab Spring.

There was no real intelligence beyond the idea of unleashing a proxy army of killers. There was no real intelligence behind the CIA's strategy to use the Muslim Brotherhood, to pit Islamic warriors against Christians, fanatical Jihadists against other Islamic forces—Sunni against Shi'ite, Alawite, or Sufi, Sunni Turks against Alawite Syrians, Muslim Brotherhood Sunnis against Wahhabite Sunnis or other "infidels." It was a stupidity that led to disaster, human and material, on an unimaginable scale.

Instead, the policy of the United States might have encouraged real, peaceful development of nations in a climate of peace and cooperation, creating the conditions of economic growth that could have served as the natural cauldron to create a democratic process in nations with no exposure to such. That cooperation could have included China and Russia instead of encirclement, confrontation, chaos, and war.

That would have been something different. That could have even lessened the hatred for America in the world. Tragically, Washington in 2010 was deaf and blind to such ideas.

The CIA and other Western intelligence services believed that they could simply use the same template of Jihad they had used in the 1980s against the Soviets in Afghanistan with the Saudi-financed Osama bin Laden, scale it up, and detonate the entire Middle East in "democratic revolutions" that would merely replace one group of old tyrants with Washington's newly favored choice, the Muslim Brotherhood.

The Obama White House and Hillary Clinton's State Department engaged members or backers of the Muslim Brotherhood at the highest levels, including key Brotherhood members in top policy posts at the State Department, Department of Homeland Security, and White House. Leading Muslim Brotherhood members were granted a VIP treatment reserved for diplomats by Homeland Security when they passed through US airports.[4]

Israel and Saudi Arabia were deeply alarmed by that US shift to back the political Islam of the Muslim Brothers, to put it mildly. The self-confident Israelis of the 1990s seemed now confused, lacking a clear strategy, fearful, and aggressive in an increasingly futile manner.

The peace faction of Israel's traditional Labor Party had been decimated after September 11, 2001, with the onset of Washington's War on Terror. Peace was replaced by a permanent state of war—war against

Palestinians, against Libya, against Syria, and an increasingly covert war against Washington. It was run by a militant Likud in its domination of internal Israeli politics from Ariel Sharon to Benjamin Netanyahu.

The internal toll of thirteen years of constant war, fear of war, and threats of war by the Netanyahu government had been severe, as countless Israeli mass protests demonstrated. The result of the war policies was an internal rotting of the Israeli economy, an exodus of its brightest youth, and a polarization of her society.

For their part, the US military industry and their neoconservative agents in government and in Washington think tanks, like RAND Corporation or Georgetown CSIS, thought they could again weaponize political Islam, this time to gain control of the entire world by encircling, active Islamist revolts, and weakening China and Russia, the only potential contenders for global hegemony.

The Saudi Royal House and its Wahhabite allies in the monarchies of Kuwait and the Emirates, alarmed at the threat that the Muslim Brotherhood could be turned against their own rule, thought they could use their vast oil billions to dominate.

Their strategy seemed to be to build new "Las Vegas" skyscrapers and glittering, extravagant mosques around the world, whether in Erdoğan's Turkey or Syria or Central Asia, and, thereby, buy control of the world and claw back gains made by Shi'ite Iranians in Iraq and Syria since the disastrous, unintended consequences of the earlier US military occupation after 2003. Kind of a "Petrodollar Caliphate." It was a silly, in fact a ridiculous, strategy.

The secretive Muslim Brotherhood—with operations across the entire Islamic world, Western Europe, and even the United States, Central Asia, Russia, and China, saw the chance finally to realize their Global Jihad. They began in Tunisia, then Egypt, and on across the entire Arab Middle East, all with the full backing of the Obama White House and Hillary Clinton's State Department. The report of one Egyptian citizen on the impact of the Muslim Brotherhood rule there was emblematic:

> They burn churches (80 to date). They kill Christians and steal their businesses. They kill policemen and army officers and mutilate the officers and soldiers and then cut their bodies and drag them in the streets. They lynch cadets on vacation. They

lie them on the ground, tie their hands behind their backs and then shoot them in the back of their heads at 20 centimeters distance. They throw children from the top of buildings. They use orphan children, five and six year old, as human shields. They rob banks and commercial centers, killing the employees. They bomb government buildings all over Egypt. They stop fire trucks from reaching fires that are started by them. They invade universities trying to disrupt studies and exams. They beat up professors and teachers. . . .[5]

As the violence, done in the name of Allah, spread like a brushfire, children of the "wrong faith," even other Muslims, deemed infidels, were decapitated. Women were brutally gang raped, then murdered, all in the name of Jihad. The Jihadists were serious believers, at least in killing other humans.

There were combined but, at the same time, conflicting goals of a universal Sharia, of the attempt at geopolitical containment of Russia and China, and of Washington's Full-Spectrum Dominance.

All the major players in that cynical great game of religious wars were soon to realize that their dreams of empire and power were turning into catastrophic nightmares as the deadly unintended consequences of the "Arab Spring" began to become manifest.

The brilliant CIA strategists, in truth, were not so brilliant; they were shallow, arrogant, and, ultimately, blind to the complex consequences of igniting fires of religious hatred.

Unleashing Global Jihad

The Western intelligence services that had used political Islam as a weapon since the Afghanistan war in the 1980s decided during the earliest days of the Obama Presidency, from Hillary Clinton's State Department and the CIA, that they were ready to massively scale up their use of Islamic terrorism. They would set the entire Islamic world afire in an Arc of Crisis, from Afghanistan to Egypt to Libya to Morocco.

The aim would be to use Washington-organized Color Revolutions across the Arab world from Libya to Syria to Egypt and beyond in order to create chaos and ungovernability across the entirety of Eurasia, from the Caucasus to Syria to Xinjiang in China, thereby to destabilize the emerging economic and political bonds between Russia, China, Iran, and the countries of Central Asia—Brzezinski's much-feared "anti-hegemon" coalition that was becoming all too real. Andrew Marshall of the Pentagon Office of Net Assessments called it deliberate unleashing of chaos. [6]

The Pentagon plan was first set off in the North African land of Tunisia. The CIA and State Department spent millions of dollars beforehand training Tunisian student activists in protest techniques using the Belgrade-based Otpor, now renamed, CANVAS organization.[7] On December 17, 2010, mass protests across Tunisia against the government of President Zine El Abidine Ben Ali exploded. In the Western media it was called the Jasmine Revolution after the country's national flower. [8] Every image was prepared with Madison Avenue sophistication.

In a January 13, 2011, speech in Doha, Qatar, US Secretary of State Hillary Clinton declared that Washington was on the side of the growing anti-regime protestors. Referring to the Arab Middle East, she said, "people have grown tired of corrupt institutions and a stagnant political order. They are demanding reform. . . the region's foundations are sinking into the sand." [9]

Hillary Clinton made another revealing reference in her speech. She stated, "People are. . . profoundly concerned about the trends in many parts of the broader Middle East, and what the future holds."[10]

The expression "broader Middle East" was a reformulation of a project proposed under the Bush-Cheney administration called The Greater Middle East Project. It was Washington's neoconservative blueprint for transformation of the political and religious balance of power of the entire Islamic world, from Afghanistan and Pakistan on to Morocco on Africa's West Coast.[11] The Greater Middle East Project was being implemented under the guise of the Arab Spring by the Obama Administration.

One day after Clinton's remarks, on January 14, 2011, mass protests in Tunisia forced President Ben Ali to flee into exile in Saudi Arabia.

Washington was backing a revolution across the Islamic world, where they planned to bring the Muslim Brotherhood into power across the spectrum, from Tunisia to Egypt, from Yemen to Libya and beyond. It was as grandiose in scale as it was lunatic in real consequences. On January 25, 2011, millions of Egyptians took to the streets to demand radical change in what came to be called the Lotus Revolution. The Arab Spring had been given the "green light" by the US Secretary of State, Hillary Clinton.

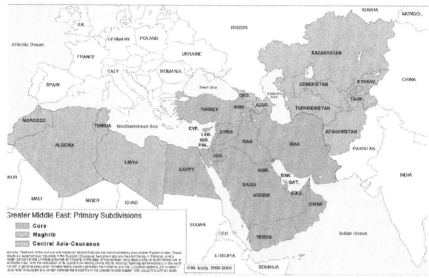

Washington's Greater Middle East Project, later called Arab Spring,
planned regime change across the Islamic world to install pro-free
market Muslim Brotherhood regimes and failed disastrously.

Revolution Template

The arsenal of regime change weapons that Washington used was the same in virtually every country. It consisted of the privatization and austerity demands of the International Monetary Fund in Washington that, predictably, led to mass protests and social unrest. US-trained cadre in every country were then activated who had been trained by the US State Department and the "democracy" NGOs it controlled, to call more mass protests using Facebook, Twitter, and new social media that caught local authorities totally by surprise. It used young students trained in CANVAS workshops, financed by the US.[12]

In every case, to disguise the key role of the United States government in a region where it was distrusted and even despised following the disastrous Iraq and Afghan wars, US-financed Non-Government Organizations—such as the National Endowment for Democracy, Freedom House, George Soros' Open Society Foundations, or the neoconservative Committee on the Present Danger—were used to identify opposing groups and factions, especially religious, and exacerbate tensions in the target country.[13]

Copycats or the Same "Mother"?

Logos of Georgian Kmara, Serbian Otpor!, and Egypt's April 6 Youth Movement.

Washington's Arab Spring protests then often used secret CIA and mercenary snipers to enflame the anger of the population against their government by creating innocent martyrs and blaming the killings on the regime. The US used Muslim Brotherhood-controlled *Al Jazeera* TV and other media to broadcast lies and distortions about the regimes under attack.[14] Crucially, it used the secret and open networks of the Muslim Brotherhood, who were given the green light by Washington to consolidate a new power in the aftermath of the "democratic revolution."

After the uprising in Tunisia, similar protests took place in almost all Islamic countries, from Morocco to Iraq, from Gabon to Albania, Iran, Kazakhstan, India, and others. Following weeks of protests, Egyptian president Hosni Mubarak resigned on February 11, 2011. Protests against Libyan leader Muammar Gaddafi broke out on February 17 and deteriorated into civil war, NATO bombings, and the destructive downfall of the Gaddafi regime. Syria, by 2014, was in the third year of terror and chaos financed by the US, Saudi Arabia, France, and Qatar, all calling for the removal of President Bashar al-Assad, but hopelessly divided on who or what should replace his rule. Yemen, Bahrain, and Algeria saw major protests.

By December 2013, entrenched rulers had been forced from power in Tunisia, Egypt (twice), Libya, and Yemen. Civil uprisings had erupted in Bahrain and a full-blown Islamic war in Syria. Major protests had broken out in Algeria, Iraq, Jordan, Kuwait, Morocco, and Sudan; minor protests had occurred in Mauritania, Oman, Saudi Arabia, Djibouti, Western Sahara, and the Palestinian territories. Tuareg fighters returning from the Libyan war against Ghaddafi ignited Jihad in Mali, and clashes in Lebanon had erupted. The entire Islamic world was in flames.

Washington's Arab Spring didn't work at all the way it had been intended. Chaos spread widely, but it was not a chaos the US could control. It was a disastrous failure in every country from Libya to Egypt to Tunisia to Syria.

By the early months of 2014, Libya was a state in anarchy and lawlessness and in the grip of armed roaming bands. Its oil economy, once the model for Africa, was a shambles. Egypt's military was in a deadly battle to destroy the Muslim Brotherhood after Saudi Arabia financed a de facto military coup to oust Muslim Brotherhood President Mohammed Morsi. Washington was surprised and outraged by the coup. Turkey's Recep Erdoğan was battling for his political life against his once ally Fethullah Gülen, who orchestrated Turkish events from his CIA-sponsored safe house in Saylorsburg, Pennsylvania. Syria was a war-ravaged battlefield. Washington was reviled and laughed at around the world. The EU was impotent and increasingly irrelevant.

ISIS and a New Resurrection Fable

After the failure of their initial Arab Spring "democracy" projects became clear, and after the failure of three years of US-backed war in Syria to topple Alawite President Bashar al-Assad, Washington and its allies tried a new phase of Jihad terrorism. In early 2014 a bizarre and savage organization calling itself Islamic State of Iraq and Syria (ISIS) and later simply, Islamic State(IS), launched a suspiciously successful attack capturing the rich city of Mosul in the midst of Iraqi oilfields. They claimed to have seized hundreds of millions of dollars from the Bank of Mosul and gold bullion. The western media dramatized their victories as if the entire Islamic world were soon to join the Islamic Caliphate.

The self-proclaimed leader of IS, Abu Bakr al-Baghdadi, claimed to have traced his own lineage back to Prophet Muhammad. In June 2014 the group proclaimed a new Caliphate with al-Baghdadi as its Caliph. According to strict Saudi Wahhabite tradition the legitimate Caliph can demand allegiance of all Muslims worldwide. It mattered little that IS could produce no proof of al-Baghdadi's claim to be Caliph.

IS soon issued a proclamation that stated: "The legality of all emirates, groups, states and organisations becomes null by the expansion of the Caliphate's authority and arrival of its troops to their areas." This was a rejection of the political divisions in the Middle East established by the Western powers during World War I in the Sykes–Picot Agreement. [15]

Middle East sources reported that IS had been trained in the months before their dramatic emergence in Iraq and Syria at secret military bases in Turkey, Jordan and Libya, by US intelligence special forces, CIA and by Israeli Mossad. A "trusted source" close to Saudi multi-billionaire and former Lebanese Prime Minister Saad Hariri said, on condition of anonymity, that the final green light for the war on Iraq and Syria with ISIS was given behind closed doors at the Atlantic Council's Energy Summit in Istanbul, Turkey, November 22–23, 2013. The Atlantic Council was one of the most influential US think tanks with regard to US and NATO foreign policy and geopolitics. [16]

The same source stated that the key coordinator of ISIS, or Da'ash, military actions was US Ambassador to Turkey Francis Riccardione. "As far as I know, nothing moves without Ambassador Riccardione," the Hariri intimate declared.[17]

In May, 2015 Judicial Watch, a US legal watchdog group, obtained classified Pentagon documents in a court case that revealed that the US and other select Western governments deliberately allied with al-Qaeda in Iraq and Syria, in their effort to topple Syria's Bashir al-Assad. In late 2013 al-Qaeda in Iraq and Syria made a formal split with Abu Musab al-Zarqawi, head of the Osama bin Laden-affiliated al Qaeda in Iraq since 2004 after the US invasion. The new organization under al-Baghdadi was called ISIS or Islamic State in Iraq and Syria. [18]

The formerly classified Pentagon document further revealed that in coordination with the Gulf states and Turkey, the West intentionally sponsored violent Islamist groups to destabilize Assad, despite anticipating that doing so could lead to the emergence of an 'Islamic State' in Iraq and Syria (ISIS). [19]

According to the US document, the Pentagon foresaw the rise of the 'Islamic State' as a direct consequence of the strategy, describing that outcome as a strategic opportunity to "isolate the Syrian regime." [20] The USA trained and armed IS terrorists who then advanced the Washington agenda of deliberate chaos by carrying out ethnic cleansing on a mass scale, gang rapes of captured non-Sunni girls and women, beheadings of soldiers, civilians, journalists and aid workers, and the deliberate destruction of cultural heritage sites.

Excuse for US to bomb Iraq, Syria

Conveniently for Pentagon war planners, on August 3, 2014, IS captured the cities of Zumar, Sinjar, and Wana in northern Iraq. The IS proceeded to cut off food and water for thousands of Kurdish Yazidis, members of an ancient monotheistic religion linked to Persian Zoroastrianism.

The Yazidis fled up a mountain out of fear of approaching hostile IS militants. Threat of genocide to Yazidis as proclaimed by IS, in addition to protecting Americans in Iraq and supporting Iraq in its fight against IS, gave the Obama Administration the pretext for the US to launch a "humanitarian" mission on 7 August 2014, to aid the Yazidis stranded on Mount Sinjar. Washington used that to start an aerial bombing campaign in Iraq on 8 August and later Syria. By May 2015 little military success against IS was evident amid reports that instead of hitting IS terrorists, US planes were dropping military supplies and food to the IS zones to reinforce their efforts to topple Assad.[21]

By 2015 IS was claiming allied organizations or terrorist "Jihad" groups in Egypt, Afghanistan, Libya, Boko Harem in Nigeria, rebels in Yemen and even in the European Union, where they disguised themselves as innocent war refugees seeking humanitarian asylum.[22] Virtually all the assorted CIA terror groups masquerading as Islamic Jihadists were being put under the one IS umbrella. It was simply a crass attempt to reincarnate the CIA's Al Qaeda.

The Lost Hegemon

By 2014, the only thing that was clear from the US effort to weaponize Islam through the Arab Spring and their later creation of the IS was the unintended consequences of that effort. The US-backed regime of Muslim Brotherhood President Mohamed Morsi in Egypt was ousted in a military coup backed and financed by Saudi Arabia and other conservative Gulf monarchies. Egypt, a traditional military partner of Washington, turned to Russia's Putin instead—with Saudi mediation—to purchase needed arms.

Saudi Arabia, Kuwait, and the United Arab Emirates united to blacklist neighboring Qatar for the latter's continuing support of the Muslim Brotherhood in Syria and elsewhere. Saudi Arabia itself was undergoing a royal succession as King Abdullah died and the new King apparently felt he needed to prove himself by bombing Yemen. Washington was becoming a laughing stock across the Islamic world—a symbol of imperial decline—as President Obama's policies swerved from one hapless option to another with no clear direction. Obama himself had to be saved from a war he did not want over Syria in 2013 by Vladimir Putin.

In terms of its security, Israel found itself surrounded by unstable regimes and hostile Jihadists on every side. Prime Minister Benjamin Netanyahu formed an unlikely and unholy alliance with Saudi Arabia against Syria, Iran, and, most remarkably, against her traditional ally, the United States.

The neo-conservative war faction in the Washington government, think tanks, and the CIA—the architects of weaponizing Islam in new Holy Wars—then created a violent coup d'état in Ukraine beginning with yet another Color Revolution protest in Kiev's Maidan Square in November, 2013. This time Muslims played no role. Ukraine was a part of the American Oligarchs' larger war against any possible challenge to US sole hegemony. China, Russia, Iran and other Eurasian states, along with Brazil in the BRICS group and other states in South America were moving clearly away from the destructive effects of the dollar and from US dictates. The American Century proclaimed by Henry Luce so grandiosely in 1941 was rotting at its very foundations, a mere 73 years into that century.

The Washington coup in Ukraine threatened to restart a new Cold War and possibly a hot war as Russia acted to defend its strategic survival. The foreign policy of the sole Superpower, the United States, was a disastrous shambles in the early months of 2014. European powers struggling with their own financial and economic crisis were unable to implement constructive, peaceful alternatives.

The deadly, unintended consequences of not very intelligent people—in Washington, Tel Aviv, Riyadh, Damascus, Ankara, Brussels, and beyond—had brought the world to the brink of a global conflagration by the spring of 2015. It was because of their inability to see the deeper significance of relationships that they had destroyed and the consequences of that destruction, by their schemes to use political Islam as a weapon.

The West, especially the CIA and those in the USA military industrial and political complex believed they could weaponize currents within Islam as their killing machine without any unintended consequences. For their part, Jihadists of all currents believed that in the name of Allah their hate and killings of any and all "infidels" would give them innocence in an afterlife. Truly, whom the gods wish to destroy they first make mad.

Sane voices around the world were beginning to ask whether there was another better way of creating true democracy—constructive diplomacy, development of common and beneficial economic initiatives to lift mankind out of poverty and hunger, respecting national borders, peacefully negotiating changes when necessary, respecting fellow human beings regardless their faith, building bridges of cooperation between nations and between peoples. They began to grasp that there might possibly be a more intelligent and a more human alternative to the current agenda of those oligarchs, one where people could feel again, "I'm good and I want to be good to me, to my family and friends, to others, to my country. After all, in the end, we are, every one, human beings."

Endnotes

1   Stephen M. Speakes, Lt. General, 2008 *ARMY MODERNIZATION STRATEGY*, 25 July 2008, Department of the Army, Washington D.C., cited in F. William Engdahl, *Full Spectrum Dominance: Totalitarian Democracy in the New World Order*, Wiesbaden, 2009, edition.engdahl, pp. 75–76.

2   Ibid.

3   Ibid.

4   Raven Clabough, *Muslim Brotherhood Linked to Malik Obama and Obama Admin*, 24 September 2013, accessed in http://www.thenewamerican.com/usnews/foreign-policy/item/16606-muslim-brotherhood-linked-to-malik-obama-and-obama-admin.

5   Shadi Hamid, *Letter from Egypt about how "great" life could be under the Obama-supported Muslim Brotherhood*, January 12, 2014, accessed in http://www.barenakedislam.com/2014/01/12/letter-from-egypt-about-how-great-life-could-be-under-the-obama-supported-muslim-brotherhood/.

6   John Gore, Chaos, Complexity and the Military, National defense University/National War College, 1996, ADA446991-1.pdf.

7   ORF, *World: The Revolution Business,* Vienna, ORF TV, 27 May, 2011, accessed in http://www.journeyman.tv/?lid=62012&tmpl=transcript. The role of Gene Sharp and the Soros Fund for the Reform and Opening of China in and around the student nonviolent protests in Tiananmen Square in 1989 have been discretely buried and are scarcely known. Both Sharp's people and

Soros' Fund people had apparently been present in Beijing at the time of the student protests. Gene Sharp actually admitted to being in Beijing just prior to the outbreak of the nonviolent student protests at Tiananmen Square. The Chinese Government, at the time, openly accused the Soros' foundation of having ties to the CIA, forcing it to leave the country. Sharp, in indirect email correspondence with the author some years ago, vehemently denied any ties between his Albert Einstein Institute in Cambridge, Massachusetts, and the US military. Facts spoke otherwise. Among the advisors to Sharp's institute at the time of the Serbia Otpor! Operation, in addition to Colonel Helvey, was a high-ranking US intelligence specialist, Major General Edward B. Atkeson, US Army (Ret.), former Deputy Chief of Staff Intelligence, US Army Europe, and member of the National Intelligence Council under the Director of the CIA. General Atkeson also served with the Bureau of Political-Military Affairs, Department of State. Another advisor to Sharp's Albert Einstein Institution was former US Admiral Gene R. La Rocque, head of the Center for Defense Information. Sharp's handbook was used in every major Color Revolution up to and including the Egyptian Tahrir Square one. No doubt the US Ambassador in Beijing at the time, James Lilley, an old CIA crony of then President G.H.W. Bush, could shed more light on the covert US role. See F. William Engdahl, *Full Spectrum Dominance: Totalitarian Democracy in the New World Order*, Wiesbaden, edition.engdahl, 2009, pp. 42–43.

8   Sputnik News, How Color Revolutions Are Made, February 15, 2015, http://in.sputniknews.com/infographics/20150215/1013440294.html.

9   Hillary Clinton, US Secretary of State, *Remarks: Forum for the Future: Partnership Dialogue Panel Session*, Ritz Carlton, Doha, Qatar, January 13, 2011, accessed in http://www.state.gov/secretary/20092013clinton/rm/2011/01/154595.htm.

10   Ibid.

11   Gilbert Achcar, *Greater Middle East—the US plan: Fantasy of a Region that Doesn't Exist*, Le Monde Diplomatique, April 2004, accessed in http://mondediplo.com/2004/04/04world.

12   Jijo Jacob, *What is Egypt's April 6 Movement?*, February 1, 2011, accessed in http://www.ibtimes.com/articles/107387/20110201/what-is-egypt-s-april-6-movement.htm. The key group on April 6 in Egypt was Kefaya. The word Kefaya! is translated to "enough!" In the US-backed Color Revolution in the Republic of Georgia in 2003, in the Rose Revolution that brought in US-trained President Saakashvili, the US-financed NGO there had chosen the motto for their movement Kmara! Kmara in Georgian means "enough!" Notably, Georgia's Kmara! student cadre were trained by the Serbian NGO

Otpor! and financed by the US government's NED and the Open Society Institute (OSI), connected with billionaire hedge fund speculator George Soros according to an article by Roger Cohen, *Who Really Brought Down Milosevic?*, New York Times, November 26, 2000. The Pentagon-linked neoconservative Washington think tank the RAND Corporation had conducted a detailed study of Kefaya already in 2008. The Kefaya study, as RAND themselves noted, was "sponsored by the Office of the Secretary of Defense, the Joint Staff, the Unified Combatant Commands, the Department of the Navy, the Marine Corps, the defense agencies, and the defense Intelligence Community." (cf. Nadia Oweidat, et al., The Kefaya Movement: A Case Study of a Grassroots Reform Initiative, Prepared for the Office of the Secretary of Defense, Santa Monica, Ca., RAND_778.pdf, 2008, p. iv.). In May 2009, US Secretary of State Hillary Clinton hosted a group of young Egyptian activists in Washington under the auspices of Freedom House, another "human rights" Washington-based NGO with a history of involvement in US-sponsored regime change from Serbia to Georgia to Ukraine and other Color Revolutions. Clinton and Acting Assistant Secretary of State for Near Eastern Affairs Jeffrey Feltman met the sixteen activists at the end of a two-month "fellowship" organized by Freedom House's New Generation program. Washington networks were deeply engaged in preparing the Arab Spring "spontaneous" protests.

13   Policy Perspectives, *The Muslim World—The US Greater Middle East Initiative*, Policy Perspectives, Volume 4, No.2, August 26, 2013, http://www.wikileaks-forum.com/middle-east/350/the-muslim-world-the-us-greater-middle-east-initiative/22120/.

14   Daily Mail Reporter, *Libya uses mercenaries to keep order on streets as 200 die in violent clashes*, 20 February 2011, accessed in http://www.dailymail.co.uk/news/article-1358761/Libya-protests-Mercenaries-order-200-die-violence.html; as well, *Video Reporting Possible CIA Saudi Snipers in Syria*, April 25, 2011, accessed in http://landdestroyer.blogspot.de/2011/04/video-reporting-possible-ciasaudi.html.

15   Mark Tran, Matthew Weaver, Isis announces Islamic caliphate in area straddling Iraq and Syria, 30 June, 2014, The Guardian.

16   Christof Lehmann, US Embassy in Ankara Headquarter for ISIS War on Iraq Hariri Insider, nsnbc, June 22, 2014, http://nsnbc.me/2014/06/22/u-s-embassy-in-ankara-headquarter-for-isis-war-on-iraq-hariri-insider/.

17   Ibid.

18 Nafeez Ahmed, Secret Pentagon report reveals West saw ISIS as strategic asset, https://medium.com/insurge-intelligence/secret-pentagon-report-reveals-west-saw-isis-as-strategic-asset-b99ad7a29092.

19 Ibid.

20 Ibid.

21 Barack Obama, President, Statement of the President, White House, August 7, 2014, https://www.whitehouse.gov/the-press-office/2014/08/07/statement-president

22 Mike Giglio, ISIS Operative: This Is How We Send Jihadis To Europe, BuzzFeed News, http://www.buzzfeed.com/mikegiglio/isis-operative-this-is-how-we-send-jihadis-to-europe#.mnELldden

GLOSSARY

Holy Crusades—The first of nine Holy Crusades was declared by the Roman Catholic Church in 1096. It presaged, in many respects, the Jihad for a Global Caliphate today in its brutality. Pope Urban II apparently sought to regain the Holy Lands taken in the Muslim conquests of the Levant (632–661), taking Jerusalem in 1099 and massacring many of the city's Muslim, Christian, and Jewish inhabitants. One of the unstated goals of the Pope's Crusade was the reconquest of the Orthodox Christian East of Europe, divided from the Pope's authority in 1054 by the Great Schism.

Jihad—also called *Jihad of the Sword,* or Holy War against non-believers, or Infidels, including Muslims who do not follow certain strict Islamic sects.

Sharia—Sharia is religious Islamic law generally not accepted by civil governments. It has laws governing hygiene and purification; economic laws, including prohibition on interest; and dietary laws, including for ritual slaughter. It includes laws on "Stoning of the Devil," marriage, including divorce, and dress code, including hijab. Other topics include customs and behavior, slavery, and the status of non-Muslims.

Shi'ite—Shia Muslims are the second largest group of the Muslim world with between 10 to 20 percent and almost 40 in the Middle East, mainly in Iran, Iraq, Syria, Lebanon, Bahrain, and parts of Saudi Arabia. They believe that Muhammad's son-in-law and cousin, Ali, was meant to be Muhammad's successor in the Caliphate.

Sunni—Sunni Muslims are the largest group within the Muslim world; they differ, sometimes violently, with Shi'ite Muslims in that they say that not his cousin Ali but the companions of the Prophet Muhammad were the true believers, since they were given the task of compiling the Quran.

Sunnis dominate in Saudi Arabia, the Gulf Arab states, Turkey, Pakistan, Afghanistan, and Indonesia.

Salafists—a militant group of extremist Sunnis who believe themselves the only correct interpreters of the Quran and consider moderate Muslims to be infidels; they seek to convert all Muslims to their extreme views and beyond.

Wahhabism—an extreme, ultraconservative branch of Sunni Islam named after Sheikh Muhammad ibn Abd al-Wahhab (1703–1792) of Saudi Arabia, a Bedouin who created a severe Islamic revival movement that tried to purge Islam of "decadent" influences. It is concentrated in Saudi Arabia, Qatar, the UAE, and Kuwait.

Koran—the main religious text of Islam, which Muslims believe to be a revelation from God. Muslims believe that the Quran was verbally revealed from God to Muhammad through the angel Gabriel. Muslims consider the Quran to be the only book protected by God from distortion or corruption.

Cemaat—a specific Islamic religious community today in Turkey associated with the Fethullah Gülen Movement, or Cemaat.

Muslim Brotherhood—an Islamic secret society founded in Egypt in 1928 by Hasan al-Banna. They believe that death in the service of Allah or in killing "infidels" is the highest form of life.

Mujahideen—A person engaged in **Jihad** is called a *mujahid*; the plural is *mujahideen*.

Madrassa—Muslim schools or colleges, often part of a mosque.

Imam—in Sunni Islam, an Islamic leadership position, usually a worship leader of a mosque and Muslim community.

Caliphate—an Islamic state led by a supreme religious and political leader known as a caliph, or "successor," to Muhammad and other prophets of Islam. The Muslim empires that have existed in the Muslim world are described as "caliphates," theocratic sovereign states.

Neoconservatives—a small group of extreme right ideologues who advocate war to advance American "democracy." They control a number of Washington private think tanks, many financed by the US military industry, and dominated the foreign policy of President George W. Bush. They were behind the invasion of Afghanistan and Iraq and creation of the Bush "War on Terror" as a war on Islam.

Al-Qaeda—radical umbrella for assorted followers of Saudi Osama bin Laden who formed paramilitary jihad cells during the 1980s Mujahideen war against the Soviets in Afghanistan. They are historically linked with the Muslim Brotherhood. Many of their cells were trained by the CIA and NATO intelligence agencies.

ETIM—East Turkestan Islamic Movement, also known as the Turkistan Islamic Party (TIP) or the Turkistan Islamic Movement (TIM), made up of Uyghur Muslims; a Waziri-based group demanding independence of China's Xinjiang province, which they call East Turkestan. According to the Chinese government, it is a violent separatist movement often responsible for terror incidents in Xinjiang. ETIM has strong ties to the Turkey-based Fethullah Gülen Movement of the CIA.

IMU—Islamic Movement of Uzbekistan, a militant Islamist Jihadist group formed in 1991 by ethnic Uzbeks from the Fergana Valley to overthrow President Islam Karimov of Uzbekistan and to create an Islamic state under Sharia.

Hizmat—another name for the Turkish-based Fethullah Gülen Movement.

Hizb ut-Tahrir—A militant Sunni fundamentalist political organization from the Muslim Brotherhood created in Palestine in 1953 to work for a global Caliphate. They are reported to have infiltrated the Pakistani military and there are reportedly strong links between Hizb ut-Tahrir and the Islamic Movement of Uzbekistan.

IMU—Islamic Movement of Uzbekistan, a militant Islamist Jihadist group formed in 1991 by ethnic Uzbeks from the Fergana Valley to overthrow

President Islam Karimov of Uzbekistan, and to create an Islamic state under Sharia.

ISIS—Islamic State of Iraq and Syria, renamed simply Islamic State, whose origins are a product of the US-fostered Sunni vs. Shi'ite civil war in Iraq after 2003. They were trained by the CIA and US Special Forces Command at a secret camp in Jordan and in Turkey in 2012 and ordered back into Iraq and Syria. Their dramatic military victories in Iraq in 2014 gave the pretext for a US bombing campaign in Syria, as well as Iraq.

Taliban—The Taliban is an Islamic fundamentalist political movement in Afghanistan that founded the Islamic Emirate of Afghanistan from September 1996 until December 2001. They are financed and backed by Pakistan, Saudi Arabia, and the United Arab Emirates and were financed indirectly by the CIA until September 2001.

World Uyghur Congress—an organization of exiled Uyghur groups based in Washington, D.C., since its founding in 2004 and is financed by the US Congress via the National Endowment for Democracy NGO. Rebiya Kadeer, a wealthy Uyghur exile based in the US, is the current president. Their aim is to finance and foster unrest among Turkic Uyghur Muslims in Xinjiang Province in China and beyond.

Index

Symbols

Çeku, Agim 160

A

Abd Al-Rahman Al-Banna 70
Abdić, Fikret 136
Abedi, Agha Hasan 119
Abraham Vereide 90
Abramowitz, Morton 185–187, 192, 223, 228
Abrams, Elliott 173
Aburish, Said 47, 60, 63, 101
Abu Sayyaf (Philippines) 246
Adelman, Kenneth 173
Adham, Kamal 119
Adnan Thabit 39
Adolat (Justice) 227
Adolf Eichmann 81, 88
AFRICOM 44, 247
AKP (Turkey) 182, 193–195
Alfred Rosenberg 84
al-Hasanayn, Dr. Fatih 141–142
Allenby, General 54
Alptekin, Erkin 222
Al Qaeda 2, 5, 71, 114, 122, 126, 135, 146, 148–149, 152, 174, 177, 195–196, 212, 226, 229, 234, 264
Al-Turabi, Hasan 142
al-Zawahiri, Ayman 149, 157, 159
al-Zawahiri, Mohammed 149, 157, 159
Amanpour, Christiane 143, 153
Amin, Tabizullah 60, 76–80, 83–87, 108, 110–111, 137

Andropov, Yuri 111
Anglo-Persian Oil Company (BP) 57
Anglo-Saudi Friendship Treaty 52
Arab Spring 3, 42, 44, 65–66, 98, 110, 249, 253–256, 258–262, 264, 268
Arno Gruen 72–73
Asia Pivot 229
Azzam, Abdullah Yusuf 96, 114, 124
Azzam, Dr Abdullah 96, 114, 124

B

Baker, James III 6, 169, 176, 206
Baku–Tbilisi–Ceyhan (BTC) oil pipeline 169, 172, 206, 209, 213
Balfour, Arthur Lord 47, 54–58, 76
Balfour Declaration 47, 54–57, 76
Basayev, Shamir 170, 208–213, 217
BCCI 117–119, 125
Bilderberg Group 90, 107
Bin Laden, Osama 113–114, 122, 141, 170, 186, 208, 211, 240, 246–247
Bissett, James 155, 159, 163, 174–175
Black, Cofer 167, 170, 204, 206, 245
Bosnia-Herzegovina 2, 85, 128–129, 134–136, 139, 142–143, 146, 148–149, 151, 155, 161, 164
BP 57, 168, 173, 208, 213, 216
Brynjar Lia 79
Bryza, Matt 169–170
Brzezinski, Zbigniew 2, 33–35, 45, 103–107, 110–114, 122, 134, 169, 186, 201–202, 206, 214–215, 219–220, 229–230, 253, 259

Z

CPSIA information can be obtained
at www.ICGtesting.com
Printed in the USA
LVOW13s0819221216

518406LV00008B/511/P